Promoting Justice Across Borders

Promoting Justice Across Borders

The Ethics of Reform Intervention

LUCIA M. RAFANELLI

OXFORD
UNIVERSITY PRESS

Oxford University Press is a department of the University of Oxford. It furthers
the University's objective of excellence in research, scholarship, and education
by publishing worldwide. Oxford is a registered trade mark of Oxford University
Press in the UK and certain other countries.

Published in the United States of America by Oxford University Press
198 Madison Avenue, New York, NY 10016, United States of America.

© Oxford University Press 2021

First issued as an Oxford University Press paperback, 2024

All rights reserved. No part of this publication may be reproduced, stored in
a retrieval system, or transmitted, in any form or by any means, without the
prior permission in writing of Oxford University Press, or as expressly permitted
by law, by license, or under terms agreed with the appropriate reproduction
rights organization. Inquiries concerning reproduction outside the scope of the
above should be sent to the Rights Department, Oxford University Press, at the
address above.

You must not circulate this work in any other form
and you must impose this same condition on any acquirer.

Library of Congress Cataloging-in-Publication Data
Names: Rafanelli, Lucia M., author.
Title: Promoting justice across borders : the ethics of reform intervention / Lucia M. Rafanelli.
Description: New York, NY : Oxford University Press, [2021] |
Based on author's thesis (doctoral - Princeton University, Department of Politics, 2019). |
Includes bibliographical references and index.
Identifiers: LCCN 2021011905 (print) | LCCN 2021011906 (ebook) |
ISBN 9780197568842 (hardback) | ISBN 9780197770566 (paperback) |
ISBN 9780197568866 (epub)
Subjects: LCSH: Intervention (International law)—Moral and ethical aspects. | Social justice.
Classification: LCC JZ6368 . R33 2021 (print) | LCC JZ6368 (ebook) | DDC 172/.4—dc23
LC record available at https://lccn.loc.gov/2021011905
LC ebook record available at https://lccn.loc.gov/2021011906

DOI: 10.1093/oso/9780197568842.001.0001

Paperback printed by Marquis Book Printing, Canada

For my mom, Mary Rafanelli, a true inspiration and the strongest woman I've ever known

Contents

Acknowledgments	ix
Introduction	1
1 Beyond the State, beyond War: Re-conceptualizing Reform Intervention	11
2 Toleration as Engagement	59
3 Degrees of Legitimacy	113
4 Collective Self-Determination without Isolation	163
5 Chaos and Consequences: Promoting Justice in a Nonideal World	203
6 Conclusion	243
References	247
Index	257

Acknowledgments

This book is based on my doctoral dissertation, which I completed at Princeton University. I benefited immensely from being part of Princeton's vibrant intellectual community. My dissertation committee members—Chuck Beitz, Annie Stilz, and Steve Macedo—deserve special thanks. To Chuck, I am grateful for countless hours spent turning over ideas together and an earnest engagement with my work that both challenged me to improve it and renewed my enthusiasm whenever it was flagging. To Annie, I am grateful for perennially insightful comments, incisive criticisms, and encouragement in the face of both personal and professional challenges, which helped me believe I might have a chance to make something meaningful of this work after all. To Steve, I am grateful for spirited disagreement, engaging with which surely made my scholarship stronger, for pushing me to bring the real-world stakes of my writing to the fore, and for always bringing joy to our work.

I am also grateful to Alan Patten, the fourth reader at my dissertation defense, whose detailed and insightful comments were a great help as I began to transform the dissertation into a book manuscript.

For cherished friendship and camaraderie, as well as intellectual partnership, I would like to thank Paul Baumgardner, Ying Chan, Emilee Booth Chapman, Fiona Cunningham, John DiIulio, Cassie Emmons, Ben Hofmann, Amy Hondo, Jennie Ikuta, Des Jagmohan, Dongxian Jiang, Nicole Kliewer, Trevor Latimer, Isi Litke, Ted Lechterman, Minh Ly, Jade Ngo, Tom Pavone, Ian Walling, and Jake Zuehl.

After I left Princeton, I spent a year as a research associate at Chapman University's Smith Institute for Political Economy and Philosophy. While there, I hosted a workshop on an earlier version of this manuscript. I am grateful to the Smith Institute, its staff and faculty, and its director, Bart Wilson, for their support—financial and otherwise—of the workshop. I was also extraordinarily lucky to have had five outstanding discussants at the workshop. Michael Blake, Simone Chambers, Aaron James, Inés Valdez, and Bas van der Vossen were all diligent and careful readers and commenters, generous and critical in exactly the right measure.

X ACKNOWLEDGMENTS

Ingrid Creppell very kindly read a full draft of this manuscript just before I submitted it to Oxford University Press and read a revised draft of the chapter on toleration at a very late stage in the writing process. Her comments were most attentive, and I am very grateful for her insight and enthusiastic support.

There are many others who, over the years, have engaged with my ideas in ways that enriched and influenced my thinking, and I'd like to thank them as well: Jordan Adamson, Brandon Bartels, Susan Brison, Daniel Brunstetter, Josh Cherniss, Charles de la Cruz, Stefan Eich, Paulina Ochoa Espejo, Mark Fisher, Jason Frank, Johann Frick, Michael Goodhart, Eric Grynaviski, Anna Jurkevics, Bob Keohane, Adam Kern, Erik Kimbrough, Melissa Lane, Christian List, Jamie Mayerfeld, Alison McQueen, Dick Miller, Erin Miller, Jan-Werner Müller, Shmulik Nili, Philip Pettit, Eric Schliesser, Joel Alden Schlosser, Melissa Schwartzberg, Quentin Skinner, Anna Marie Smith, Shannon Stimson, Johan Trovik, Virginia Warren, and Fabian Wendt.

My work on the research underlying this book has been financially supported by the Princeton University Center for Human Values (UCHV), including the UCHV's Political Philosophy Graduate Student Research and Travel Fund and the UCHV Graduate Prize Fellowship. I have presented related work at Chapman University, George Washington University, Western University, the American Political Science Association annual meeting, the Western Political Science Association annual meeting, the 2016 LSE-Princeton Political Theory Conference, the University of Pennsylvania Graduate Conference in Political Science, the University of California: Irvine Political Theory Working Group, the Georgetown University Political Theory Speaker Series, and the Laurance S. Rockefeller Graduate Prize Fellows' Seminar, as well as multiple workshops internal to the Princeton Politics Department. I am grateful to audiences and commenters in all these venues—especially to my Graduate Prize Fellows cohort (Merrick Anderson, Emad Atiq, Jessica Cooper, Emily Kern, David Zuluaga Martínez, Anna Offit, Mercedes Valmisa, and Paula Vedoveli, along with John DiIulio, whom I've already mentioned).

Some material in this book was published previously in Lucia M. Rafanelli, "Promoting Justice across Borders," *Political Studies* (2019), doi:10.1177/0032321719875402.

Finally, I'd like to thank my family. My husband, Greg Stein, has believed in and supported me through many years—years that included the kind of extended long-distance relationship an academic life too often necessitates, personal turmoil, and philosophical upheaval. I could not have asked for a better partner to share in and cultivate life's joys, or with whom to weather its sorrows. My parents, Mary and Gerry Rafanelli, taught me to care about both people and ideas—commitments that, I hope it is safe to say, have shaped the trajectory of my life so far and without which I would not have written this book.

Introduction

The global political arena is diverse and dynamic, alive with multitudes of state and nonstate actors striving to influence each other with every tool at their disposal. We need a political theory of global politics to help us navigate this arena in all its complexity. And this requires moving beyond the field's traditional focus on states engaging in global politics by waging wars or employing other conventional tools of coercive foreign policy. In this book, I begin to develop a new political theory of global politics better suited to an increasingly interconnected world, in which nonstate actors play an ever more important role and in which global political actors of all sorts influence each other using many tactics besides force and coercion.

Transcending the usual focus on state action in global politics also allows me to highlight precisely those modes of political contestation—such as boycotts, divestment campaigns, and transnational activism—most accessible to historically and currently marginalized people. The most disadvantaged and oppressed among us are often excluded from the exercise of state power, and the traditional means of conducting foreign policy—such as waging wars and imposing state sanctions—are often closed to them.[1] However, they often *are* able to exert power in less formal and less conventional ways. Thus, these currently under-theorized means of cross-border political contestation deserve our attention as promising instruments of emancipatory global politics. Moreover, an ethical theory that centers these alternative forms of contestation can give us the conceptual resources to recognize the political agency of those excluded from other avenues of exerting political power—those whose agency is too often denied or ignored.

With this in mind, I develop an ethics of foreign political influence that recognizes the wide variety of means (ranging all the way from persuasion to military force) that an equally wide variety of political actors (including

---

[1] James Pattison makes a similar point about "smaller and middle powers" lacking the capacity to "undertake large-scale military interventions" in *The Alternatives to War: From Sanctions to Nonviolence* (Oxford: Oxford University Press, 2018), 10.

Promoting Justice Across Borders. Lucia M. Rafanelli, Oxford University Press. © Oxford University Press 2021.
DOI: 10.1093/oso/9780197568842.003.0001

2 PROMOTING JUSTICE ACROSS BORDERS

individuals, activist networks, NGOs, corporations, and states) can and do use to exert influence outside their own societies. I construct a more complete, nuanced ethics of foreign political influence than any currently on offer by recognizing the ways in which these varied modes of influence raise correspondingly varied moral issues. Ultimately, this yields a set of ethical standards better able to give us guidance in the current geopolitical landscape. Though I will argue that foreign political influence is sometimes, all things considered, morally permissible, even those not convinced of this conclusion should at least be convinced that *if* a political actor engages in the sorts of foreign influence I discuss, it would be better that they followed the ethical standards I propose than not.

More specifically, I develop ethical standards for foreign political influence aimed at promoting justice in recipient[2] societies—which I call *reform intervention*.[3] I mean *reform intervention* to be a broad category, encompassing *any deliberate attempt to promote justice in a foreign society.*

Reform intervention so understood has the potential to be a real force for good in the world, but it has often, understandably, been subject to significant moral criticism. There are three objections, which I'll call the *standard*

---

[2] I call intervened-upon parties "recipients" because this term avoids a number of pitfalls that plague alternative terms. One might instead call them the "targets," "subjects," or "intended beneficiaries" of an intervention, or might refer to interveners and those they intervene upon as "partners," but each of these options has serious problems. The word "target" presumes an adversarial relationship between interveners and the intervened-upon people, which there's no reason to presume ex ante. The word "subjects" implies that intervention *necessarily* involves power asymmetry, such that interveners are always much more powerful than those whose affairs they intervene in. As we'll see later, this isn't always the case. Conversely, the word "partners" obscures even the possibility of such a power asymmetry, which is equally misleading. The term "intended beneficiaries" obscures the fact that reform interventions are not always meant to "benefit" everyone in the society in which they are conducted (at least not on standard definitions of the term "benefit"). For example, an intervention aiming to reduce the power of a tyrannical minority and defend the rights of the majority does not, by standard definitions, seek to benefit the minority. But members of the minority are still intervened upon. The moral issues that intervention raises still apply in their case, even though they are not the "intended beneficiaries" of the intervention. In addition to avoiding the other problems outlined above, the term "recipients" includes all people whose behavior (or laws or social institutions) an intervention is meant to change, regardless of whether they are "intended beneficiaries." While some may object that the term "recipients" presents the intervened-upon people as passive patients, rather than as agents, I'm not convinced this is so. After all, members of an equal partnership can also be recipients, as when allies "receive" help and support from one another. Moreover, that a person is on the "receiving" end of an exercise of power, even when they are not an equal partner with the other party, does not imply that they aren't also an agent or that they may not react to being a recipient in any number of active ways, including by objecting or resisting.

[3] I borrow this term (but not this definition of it) from Lefever and Beitz. See Charles R. Beitz, "Nonintervention and Communal Integrity," *Philosophy and Public Affairs* 9, no. 4 (1980): 385–91, 391; Charles R. Beitz, *Political Theory and International Relations* (Princeton, NJ: Princeton University Press, 1979), 82; Ernest W. Lefever, "The Perils of Reform Intervention," *Worldview* 13, no. 2 (1970): 7–10.

objections, frequently leveled against reform intervention: first, that it treats recipients with intolerance; second, that it objectionably denies or disregards the legitimacy of their political institutions; and third, that it undermines their collective self-determination. We must take these objections seriously, but the impression that they apply to all instances of reform intervention is mistaken. The error results from two things: (1) a failure to recognize the full range of forms reform intervention can take (some of which are more, and some less, vulnerable to the standard objections), and (2) a widespread misunderstanding of how appropriate commitments to the values underlying the standard objections (toleration, legitimacy, and collective self-determination) would require global political actors to behave.

In what follows, I address both these problems, correcting the misconception that reform intervention is generally impermissible because it's vulnerable to the standard objections and providing a philosophically grounded, principled account of when it is and isn't. In Chapter 1, I construct a typology of reform intervention, identifying the different forms it can take and their morally significant distinguishing features. Chapters 2–4 examine whether, or under what conditions, the different types of reform intervention are impermissible because they fall prey to the standard objections. Consider the case of Tostan, an international NGO that runs classes about human rights and democracy in western Africa.[4] The classes are geared toward achieving goals like ending female genital cutting (FGC) and child marriage and promoting grassroots democracy and public health.[5] Importantly, Tostan enters a community only after having been invited;[6] its course curriculum was revised early on in response to participants' feedback and emphasizes interactive learning;[7] and its classes are taught in local languages and use traditional

---

[4] See Tostan, "Where We Work," *Tostan: Dignity for All,* accessed 13 July 2016, http://tostan.org/where-we-work; Tostan, "About Us," *Tostan: Dignity for All,* accessed 9 June 2017, https://www.tostan.org/about-us/mission-history/; Tostan, "Areas of Impact," *Tostan: Dignity for All,* accessed 13 July 2016, http://tostan.org/impact_areas; Tostan, "Community Empowerment Program: Program Structure," *Tostan: Dignity for All,* accessed 9 June 2017, https://www.tostan.org/programs/community-empowerment-program/program-structure/; Tostan, "Today. Tomorrow. Together: Tostan Annual Report 2014," https://tostan.org/wp-content/uploads/2014_annual_report_final.pdf, 6–7.

[5] See Tostan, "Areas of Impact."

[6] Tostan, "Community Empowerment Program: Program Structure."

[7] See Beniamino Cislaghi, Diane Gillespie, and Gerry Mackie, "Expanding the Aspirational Map: Interactive Learning and Human Rights in Tostan's Community Empowerment Program," in *Human Rights Education: Theory, Research, Praxis,* ed. Monisha Bajaj (Philadelphia: University of Pennsylvania Press, 2017): 198–209; Diane Gillespie and Molly Melching, "The Transformative Power of Democracy and Human Rights in Nonformal Education: The Case of Tostan," *Adult Education Quarterly* 60, no. 5 (2010): 477–98.

4 PROMOTING JUSTICE ACROSS BORDERS

African teaching techniques.[8] Tostan also oversees the establishment of community governance committees meant to lead local development and social change campaigns once the Tostan program is over.[9]

Thus, though Tostan attempts to change deeply entrenched practices in recipient communities—such as FGC, child marriage, and other forms of gender-based subordination—its activities don't obviously raise the moral concerns we would normally associate with such an attempt if it were made by a state using force or coercion. We might be tempted to think, for example, that trying to change another society in this way would reflect a judgment that its members were inferior, incapable of deciding on their own how to live their lives, and in need of foreign supervision. However, Tostan's model of activism doesn't treat the recipients of its influence as incapable, irrational, or in need of supervision, but rather as partners in a dialogue about what justice requires and as potential leaders of social change within their own communities.

Though scholars have explored these sorts of interventions using a sociological or otherwise descriptive lens,[10] many prominent *prescriptive* treatments of the *ethics* of intervention focus on the most invasive forms of intervention (state-led violence and coercion), creating the impression that reform intervention is justified only in extraordinary circumstances, when the injustice to be remedied is so grave as to make the serious moral concerns raised by such invasive interventions comparatively unimportant. But the case of Tostan—and the many others like it that fall outside the existing literature's primary focus—cast doubt on this impression because they don't raise the same moral concerns as more invasive interventions would. The ethical standards I develop here will allow us to better understand the moral stakes of interventions, like Tostan's, that prominent literature neglects and to generate a more accurate account of when they are and aren't permissible.

---

[8] Tostan, "Community Empowerment Program: Program Structure."

[9] See Tostan, "Community Empowerment Program: Program Structure"; Tostan, "Today. Tomorrow. Together," 6; Tostan, "Community Empowerment Program: Ensuring Sustainability," *Tostan: Dignity for All*, Tostan, accessed 2 May 2018, https://www.tostan.org/programs/community-empowerment-program/ensuring-sustainability/.

[10] See, e.g., Cristina Bicchieri, *Norms in the Wild: How to Diagnose, Measure, and Change Social Norms* (Oxford: Oxford University Press, 2017); Cristina Bicchieri and Peter McNally, "Shrieking Sirens: Schemata, Script, and Social Norms. How Change Occurs," *Social Philosophy and Policy* 35, no. 1 (2018): 23–53; Margaret E. Keck and Kathryn Sikkink, *Activists beyond Borders: Advocacy Networks in International Politics* (Ithaca, NY: Cornell University Press, 1998); Gerry Mackie, "Social Norms Change: Believing Makes It So," *Social Research: An International Quarterly* 85, no. 1 (2018): 141–66; Sally Engle Merry, *Human Rights and Gender Violence: Translating International Law into Local Justice* (Chicago: University of Chicago Press, 2006).

INTRODUCTION 5

Similarly, consider consumer boycotts, like that associated with the Palestinian Boycott, Divest, Sanction campaign. These movements are distinctive because they aim to produce political change in recipient societies but operate largely outside recipients' formal political institutions. Prominent thinking on the ethics of intervention, which focuses on interventions that interfere adversarially with recipients' institutions, is ill-suited to guide our judgments about such cases. Again, the literature's overly narrow focus creates the impression that reform intervention is permissible only in the extraordinary circumstances when adversarial conflict is called for. I will argue this is mistaken, and the ethical standards I develop help us understand why.

Not only does the existing literature's focus on the most invasive and adversarial forms of intervention produce unreliable answers about when reform intervention is permissible, but it also encourages us to ask the wrong questions. This distortion is reflected in the literature's preoccupation with identifying "thresholds" of justice or legitimacy below which a society must fall before it becomes liable to intervention. Once we recognize the wealth of different forms reform intervention can take, the salient question is not "Below what threshold is intervention justified?" Rather, it's the much more complicated confluence of questions, "What types of intervention are justified (or not) under what circumstances, and who is justified (or not) in intervening where?" This book seeks to answer these questions.

In Chapters 2–4, I also offer important correctives to the ways prominent political theory scholarship treats the foundational political-moral values of toleration, legitimacy, and collective self-determination. For example, toleration is often thought to require people in different societies to leave each other alone and stay out of each other's politics. However, I develop a novel account of international toleration according to which a commitment to toleration sometimes generates reason *in favor* of reform intervention. I argue that we treat people in other societies tolerantly when we treat them as presumptively entitled to live by their own values and choices, and that doing so doesn't require simply leaving them alone. In reality, there are ways to engage with people in other societies—even while trying to change their behavior—that treat them as independent agents with weighty claims of their own about what values should animate their politics and how they should organize their public life.

Similarly, I argue, against conventional wisdom, that there are ways to engage in reform intervention without denying or disregarding the legitimacy of recipients' political institutions. In fact, some types of reform

6 PROMOTING JUSTICE ACROSS BORDERS

intervention—such as consumer boycotts, civil-society-led divestment campaigns, and state-led boycott or divestment campaigns that challenge status quo geopolitical hierarchies—are justifiable even when recipient states are fully legitimate. Other types of reform intervention—such as those meant to obstruct a particular government agency or stop the enforcement of a particular law, but that stop short of seeking regime change—don't show recipient states the respect owed *fully* legitimate states. But since they stop short of seeking regime change, they do show recipient states *some* degree of respect. Thus, these kinds of interventions aren't justified in fully legitimate recipient states, but they may be justified in recipient states that are neither fully legitimate nor fully illegitimate. Indeed, I argue that to better understand the ethics of reform intervention, we must acknowledge that legitimacy comes in degrees. Most political theorists writing on legitimacy are reticent to acknowledge this, and even when they do, they do little to flesh out its normative significance for global political actors. Thus, my treatment corrects a common mischaracterization of political legitimacy as a binary quality that states either have (in full) or don't (at all), and improves upon existing work by providing the resources to understand the normative implications of this conceptual shift.

Further, I argue that reform intervention doesn't always undermine—and in fact sometimes bolsters—recipients' collective self-determination. Paying attention to the full range of forms reform intervention can take allows us to see how it can challenge the colonial and other geopolitical hierarchies that rob societies on their bottom rungs of self-determination. Reform interveners can also lend much-needed support to marginalized people within recipient societies, helping to bring them into the mainstream political fold in their own communities or representing their interests to governments that would otherwise ignore them—or worse. Reform intervention can thereby make recipient governments more, rather than less, responsive to their own citizens' needs. This analysis reveals that shoring up collective self-determination doesn't require (as is often assumed) fortifying the boundaries between societies, ensuring that each is as isolated from the political influence of others as possible. Rather, collective self-determination is best protected when political actors around the world work together to dismantle the power relationships—both domestic and international—that threaten it.

Taken together, Chapters 2–4 present a vision of conscientious global political contestation through reform intervention. They articulate a new way of thinking about what it means to treat people in other societies well—not by leaving them to tend to their own affairs but by engaging with them in political contestation to advance the cause of justice.

Chapter 5 then argues that this vision isn't simply a high-minded ideal but is one we can put into practice in the real world. There are serious pragmatic obstacles to implementing the ethical standards this book develops, such as the lack of global institutions capable of effectively coordinating compliance and the risk that even well-intentioned reform intervention will produce negative side effects. But we are not powerless to surmount these obstacles.

For example, sometimes interveners are morally required to consult with global political actors unlikely to share their predictable biases—to ensure their judgments about the moral importance and likely effects of an intervention are reliable. Without global institutions able to coordinate such consultation, would-be interveners should turn to global civil society in search of more informal modes of consultation. They should look, for instance, to the publicly taken positions of citizens, officials, or political groups unlikely to share their own biases. Granted, would-be interveners may not be eager to consult diverse global publics about their interventions. But when such consultation is a precondition of an intervention's permissibility, we should refuse to support the intervention if interveners refuse to consult. As citizens, this is a standard to which we should hold our governments; as donors, it's a standard to which we should hold NGOs; as potential participants, it's a standard to which we should hold transnational movements, and so on.

To avoid unacceptable negative side effects, would-be interveners should of course evaluate the likely consequences of each proposed intervention on a case-by-case basis. However, in the absence of a case-specific analysis, I argue they should adopt two presumptions—one in favor of less-controlling types of intervention (those that leave recipients with more freedom to decide for themselves whether or not to adopt interveners' desired reforms) and one in favor of counter-hegemonic interventions (those that defy existing and historical geopolitical hierarchies). Again, these are not only presumptions interveners should adopt but presumptions we—as participants in global politics—should pressure them to adopt.

Ultimately, I argue that some identifiable types of reform intervention (and some actual reform interventions) are, all things considered, morally permissible. They are compatible with appropriate commitments to toleration, legitimacy, and collective self-determination (they aren't rendered impermissible by any of the standard objections) *and* they successfully

8 PROMOTING JUSTICE ACROSS BORDERS

surmount the main pragmatic obstacles to responsible reform intervention in a nonideal world.

Moreover, at least some of these morally permissible ways to engage in reform intervention are generally open to some global political actors at any given time. Thus, just as there are generally permissible ways to engage in political contestation for justice in the domestic sphere, there are generally permissible ways to engage in political contestation for justice in the global sphere. This is not true only in extraordinary circumstances, as prominent literature on the ethics of intervention tends to suggest. Rather, reform intervention is a morally open option in the quotidian circumstances of global politics.

Further, if there is—as I'll argue in Chapter 1—a globally applicable natural duty of justice requiring us to help support and establish just institutions everywhere (at least when we can do so without bearing unreasonable costs), then some of these morally permissible reform interventions are in fact morally required. This is especially true in an increasingly globalized world where engaging in political contestation across borders without substantial cost to oneself is arguably easier than ever. Over the course of the book, I'll argue that, if there is a global natural duty of justice, we are each morally required to adopt a set of life-projects that involves promoting justice (including in foreign societies) whenever we can do so without significantly disrupting the pursuit of whatever other projects we see as central to our lives. The exact actions any given person is required to take in the pursuit of justice will depend on what projects they see as central to their own life, as well as on their capacities, and perhaps on other things as well (such as whether they have contributed to or benefited from certain injustices in particular). But the bottom line is that the natural duty of justice requires us to make justice promotion a significant part of our lives. As individuals, this might mean donating to NGOs, joining transnational social movements, changing which corporations we patronize, and voting certain politicians in and others out of office. Further, not only does the natural duty of justice sometimes require us to *engage* in reform intervention; it also requires us to *open up our own political institutions* to certain kinds of potentially justice-promoting intervention from abroad.

Thus, while this book mostly focuses on determining what kinds of reform intervention are morally permissible under what circumstances, it also addresses the related but distinct question of when reform intervention is morally required by the natural duty of justice. Those not convinced there is a natural duty of justice, or that reform intervention is ever required by it, should still be able to endorse my conclusions about reform intervention's permissibility. But for those convinced there is a natural duty of justice that could in principle require us to promote justice outside our own societies, I will clarify this duty's precise scope by examining which particular ways of discharging it are both morally permissible and potentially feasible.

The ethical standards I develop in the following chapters call on us to rethink received notions about the ordinary bounds of politics, and particularly to abandon the thought that politics does or should take place primarily within the confines of the state. The ethical standards I develop give us a model for how to engage in political struggles for justice on a global scale—not only in conditions of supreme emergency but in the ordinary circumstances of everyday global politics. They therefore form the basis of a cosmopolitanism that is neither premised upon nor aimed at bringing about the end of politics. They show how the promotion of justice everywhere can be the legitimate (political) concern of people anywhere.

1

Beyond the State, beyond War

Re-conceptualizing Reform Intervention

Introduction

We need a new political theory of global politics better suited to our increasingly complex and interconnected world, and this book begins to develop one. More specifically, it develops an ethics of *reform intervention*,[1] by which I mean *any deliberate attempt to promote justice in a foreign society*. The "reform" in "reform intervention" is not meant to suggest the category is limited to interventions that promote only modest changes in recipient societies. As we'll see, reform interventions may involve radical—even revolutionary—action. Rather, the term "reform" is meant to signal that the interventions this book examines all seek to promote justice. This is important because it means they raise a distinct set of moral questions—questions that arise whether they promote justice in piecemeal or revolutionary fashion.

Reform intervention, you'll notice, is an expansive category. It includes actions existing scholarship typically characterizes as "interventions"—states using coercion or force to interfere in foreign societies' domestic politics. But it also includes much more—for instance, actions taken by nonstate actors and that involve the use of means besides coercion or force.

Some may worry this is too broad a topic to be treated usefully in a single book and argue that I should limit my focus to the ethics of interventions undertaken by a certain kind of political actor or using certain tactics (as, e.g., Jennifer Rubenstein focuses on humanitarian international NGOs [INGOs][2] and Cécile Fabre focuses on states using economic leverage to

---

[1] I borrow this term from Lefever and Beitz, though neither of them defines it as I do here. See Charles R. Beitz, "Nonintervention and Communal Integrity," *Philosophy and Public Affairs* 9, no. 4 (1980): 385–91, 391; Charles R. Beitz, *Political Theory and International Relations* (Princeton, NJ: Princeton University Press, 1979), 82; Ernest W. Lefever, "The Perils of Reform Intervention," *Worldview* 13, no. 2 (1970): 7–10.

[2] Jennifer C. Rubenstein, *Between Samaritans and States: The Political Ethics of Humanitarian INGOs* (Oxford: Oxford University Press, 2015).

Promoting Justice Across Borders. Lucia M. Rafanelli, Oxford University Press. © Oxford University Press 2021.
DOI: 10.1093/oso/9780197568842.003.0002

12 PROMOTING JUSTICE ACROSS BORDERS

intervene in other states[3]). More narrowly focused work like this is certainly valuable. Its narrower focus allows it to explore the moral challenges faced by certain actors or associated with certain tactics in great detail. But this narrow focus is also limiting. For example, Rubenstein's analysis of the ethics of INGO activity is so specifically tailored to the distinctive features unique to these organizations that her findings can't be generalized to other kinds of actors exerting influence on the global stage. Rubenstein herself suggests this when she writes that the ethical challenges INGOs face are "built into their very structure as organizations" and when she presents her conclusions as designed particularly for a "distinctive type of political actor": "large-scale, Western-based, donor-funded humanitarian INGOs."[4]

On the other hand, by developing ethical standards meant to govern all different types of reform intervention, undertaken by different actors, I can provide insight and guidance regarding how to evaluate alternative types *compared to each other*. The ethical standards I develop will not only help us decide (for example) whether a given NGO's influence in a specific case was morally justified but also whether similar influence exercised by a different actor or using different means might have been justified when the NGO's action wasn't (or vice versa).

So I'll proceed with the broad focus specified above: on the ethics of reform intervention, meaning any deliberate attempt to promote justice in a foreign society. This chapter develops a typology of reform intervention that identifies several morally significant dimensions along which reform interventions can vary: the degree of control interveners exercise over recipients, the urgency of an intervention's objectives, the costs an intervention is likely to impose on recipients, and the degree to which an intervention interferes with the operation of recipients' political institutions. This typology—elaborated and put to use through persistent engagement with several real-world cases of reform intervention—will form the basis of a more complete, nuanced ethics of reform intervention than any currently on offer.

Before developing the typology, though, it's worth specifying in more detail what exactly the category "reform intervention" encompasses. Some important questions include these: Does whether or not an action counts as reform intervention depend on its executors' intentions and motivations

---

[3] Cécile Fabre, *Economic Statecraft: Human Rights, Sanctions, and Conditionality* (Cambridge, MA: Harvard University Press, 2018).
[4] Rubenstein, *Between Samaritans and States*, 3.

(i.e., their mental states)? What sorts of goals must an action seek to accomplish in order to count as an "attempt to promote justice"? To count as a reform intervention, must an action be undertaken solely by foreigners, or may foreign actors collaborate with local ones?

Defining "Reform Intervention"

Regarding the first question, the answer is no. For the purposes of deciding whether real-world cases count as reform interventions, I'll look to how they are publicly presented. If an intervention is publicly described as promoting justice or attempting to promote justice, I will count it as a reform intervention. Of course, interveners might describe their actions as attempts to promote justice when they in fact intend to accomplish other goals (either in addition to or instead of promoting justice). Similarly, interveners might describe their actions as attempts to promote justice when they are motivated to act (partly or fully, consciously or subconsciously) by something other than a concern to promote justice. Nonetheless, I will treat any intervention presented as an attempt to promote justice as a reform intervention, for a number of reasons.

First, it is often difficult—if not impossible—to surmise interveners' unstated intentions and secret motivations. Certainly, it would be prohibitively difficult for the bulk of ordinary participants in global politics to do in real time, as interventions are being proposed and carried out (as opposed to, say, historians and biographers, who could spend years analyzing interveners' past actions with the benefit of access to once private information). And one main aim of the present work (if you'll take my word for it) is to provide standards ordinary participants in global politics can use to make judgments about real interventions in real time. After all, we—as individuals, members of political parties and social movements, patrons and employees of multinational corporations, potential contributors to NGOs, citizens, and so on—should be able to decide, in a principled way, whether to support or oppose interventions undertaken by these myriad actors. And we should be able to decide in time to do something about our support or opposition—to vote politicians in or out of office, donate to or withdraw from NGOs, join or protest a boycott, keep working or strike, and so on. We shouldn't have to suspend judgment—or action—until we're able to discern the inner workings of interveners' minds.

14 PROMOTING JUSTICE ACROSS BORDERS

Second, I take it that the truth about interveners' *real* motives or intentions won't make any direct difference to whether or not an intervention is justified. It will make an enormous difference to whether the interveners themselves are morally good, but this is not the issue I'm interested in here. My main purpose is to provide standards by which to judge whether an actual or proposed intervention is impermissible, permissible, or obligatory. Interveners' true motives and intentions are generally unimportant for making this determination, though they are important for determining the moral character of the interveners. Polemically, the right action done for the wrong reason is still the right action, even if the actor is condemnable for doing it.

That said, there is one way in which interveners' true motives and intentions can affect an intervention's justifiability: they can do so indirectly, by rendering interveners less effective pursuers of their *stated* ends. Interveners claiming to care about justice may be unlikely to actually promote justice if they're in fact motivated by a concern for their own political or economic advantage. And, in (at least) some cases, we will have to evaluate the likelihood of an intervention achieving its stated aims without producing unacceptable side effects in order to decide whether it's justifiable. I don't mean to downplay the importance of these assessments. However, I take it they are better left for the stage of normative analysis rather than that of conceptual construction. That is, we should make these assessments once we're at the point of actually deciding whether an intervention is justified, rather than invoking the possibility of mal-intentioned interveners to rule certain cases out of the category "reform intervention" altogether.

Third, we'll be better off if we're able to evaluate political actors' claims on their own terms and in terms of publicly shared standards of political morality—to hold them accountable to the values they profess and that their audiences affirm. Thus, when public figures claim an intervention is an attempt to promote justice, and when they invoke this claim in its support, it's important that other political actors (again, we, as individuals, members of political parties and social movements, patrons and employees of multinational corporations, potential contributors to NGOs, citizens, and so on) be able to judge whether the intervention is justified, even taking what the public figures have said about its purpose at face value. Of course, an intervention's opponents can always accuse its architects of concealing the intervention's true aims. But these accusations will often be hard to make credibly, since interveners' true intentions won't be readily observable. An intervention's principled opponents would be much better off if they had the resources to claim it didn't meet the appropriate moral standards, even conceding its noble aims. In other words, it may often be useful to treat interventions *presented as* aiming at justice promotion as if they're *actually* aimed at justice promotion, even if we suspect otherwise.

Moreover, the world is made up of many publics, all of which should value justice promotion, and many of which in fact do. Assuming you and I belong to at least one of these justice-valuing publics, we'll inevitably want to evaluate proposed and actual interventions in terms of this value that we ourselves share—regardless of whether would-be or actual interveners also share it. Given that these are some of the uses to which I hope people will put the standards I develop, I see no reason to limit the cases this book considers to those in which we can be sure interveners' intentions are pure.

Fourth, this book won't defend a particular explanatory or causal theory of how or why different participants in global politics act. (To accomplish that it would surely be necessary to identify their true intentions and motivations.) Rather, it will attempt to answer the normative questions of when and what kinds of reform interventions are permissible or obligatory. Examining actual cases of intervention that *could* be justified (or not) *as attempts to promote justice* will further this purpose. Thus, it will be useful to treat interventions presented as justice-promoting interventions, *arguendo*, as if they actually aim at justice promotion. In this way, we'll be able to discover whether they, or interventions like them, would be justified if they aimed at justice promotion. This, after all, is a question worth answering even if the actual interveners in a given case don't *really* intend to promote justice.

For all these reasons, I'll treat any intervention whose aim is *presented* as justice promotion as a *reform intervention*. This brings us to our next question: What sorts of goals must an intervention (really or ostensibly) seek to accomplish in order for its (real or ostensible) aim to count as "justice promotion"—and in order for it, in turn, to count as a reform intervention? I'll count any intervention that seeks to bring the recipient society into closer alignment with the requirements of justice as aiming at "justice promotion"—and therefore as a reform intervention. This means reform interveners may adopt many different ends. They may seek to remedy very grave injustices or comparatively minor ones. Possible ends for a reform intervention include—but are not limited to—protecting human rights; promoting distributive justice, political equality, and racial and gender equality; and protecting individual liberty and due process rights. This is by no means an exhaustive list. I include it only to illustrate the wide range of objectives reform interveners may have.

16 PROMOTING JUSTICE ACROSS BORDERS

That this book develops ethical standards we can use to evaluate interventions aimed at remedying *all kinds* of injustices sets it apart from other work that addresses only the ethics of interventions meant to remedy extraordinarily grave injustices.[5] This book's broader scope is an advantage in two respects. First, it allows me to offer insight into how the ethical considerations surrounding attempts to alleviate very grave injustice could fit into a more general theory of the ethics of promoting justice across borders. Just as we would improve our understanding of how to resist particularly grave domestic injustice by incorporating it into a complete and coherent theory of how we ought to pursue domestic justice generally, we can improve our understanding of how to resist particularly grave global injustice by incorporating it into a complete and coherent theory of how we ought to pursue justice on the global stage. Here, I develop the conceptual and normative tools to accomplish this.

Second, work focusing on interventions responding to very grave injustice can give guidance about which specific tactics interveners should use, but only in those cases in which international involvement is comparatively uncontroversial in the first place (such as when it's meant to avert gross human rights violations). This book goes further, arguing that political involvement in foreign societies is often morally permissible even in those cases in which it is highly controversial (when it's meant to alleviate injustice that doesn't rise to the level of gross human rights violations). Ultimately, I'll argue there are generally morally permissible—and sometimes morally required—ways to engage in justice promotion across borders *not only* in emergency conditions *but also* in the quotidian conditions of global politics. And I can make this argument only because I develop ethical standards that tell us when reform intervention aimed at remedying relatively minor injustices—those that occur in the quotidian conditions of global politics—is justified.

Also worth noting, I will assume throughout the book that all the requirements of justice can be articulated in terms of people's rights. (People have rights to be treated in certain ways and to be subject to institutions of a certain kind.) I'll therefore describe all the possible goals of reform intervention as rights protection of some kind. I don't deny there may be other valid ways of expressing justice claims that don't rely on rights discourse, nor do

---

[5] E.g., Cécile Fabre, "The Case for Foreign Electoral Subversion," *Ethics and International Affairs* 32, no. 3 (2018): 283–92; James Pattison, *The Alternatives to War: From Sanctions to Nonviolence* (Oxford: Oxford University Press, 2018); James Pattison, "Covert Positive Incentives as an Alternative to War," *Ethics and International Affairs* 32, no. 3 (2018): 293–303.

I deny that rights discourse itself has been subject to moral criticism. My own account, though, must start somewhere, so I will put these criticisms aside. Assuming that it gives us *a* valid way to express justice claims, I will think and write within the conceptual framework of rights discourse.

My focus on justice promotion conceived of as rights protection means I won't discuss interventions aimed only at relieving suffering or otherwise improving recipients' welfare. Of course, justice may require that people enjoy a certain level of welfare. In such cases, we may say they have rights to that level of welfare or to the means necessary to attain it. Thus, if a reform intervention aims to secure the fulfillment of those rights, it may in fact aim to improve people's welfare. It will not *only* aim to improve people's welfare (regardless of what justice requires), though, because it will do so as part of an effort to ensure their rights are protected (i.e., to ensure they're treated justly).

I don't mean to suggest merely welfare-promoting interventions are unimportant or unworthy of theoretical scrutiny. They are simply not my topic here. As I stated in the Introduction, one of this book's goals is to elaborate the normative implications of our natural duty of justice for the conduct of global politics. This makes *justice-promoting* interventions especially relevant for present purposes. This book's concern to reconceive how appropriate commitments to toleration, legitimacy, and collective self-determination would require us to conduct global politics, and to show that such commitments are compatible with a global politics in which cross-border political contestation plays a nontrivial role, also makes *justice-promoting* interventions especially relevant. After all, whereas there is broad agreement that avoidable suffering should be avoided, there is broad disagreement about what justice requires. Thus, justice-promoting interventions (as opposed to those meant merely to alleviate suffering) will more often be seen as promoting reasonably contested values in recipient societies. They will therefore more often be seen as intolerant or as objectionably interfering with political decisions recipient institutions have legitimate authority to decide on their own and the resolution of which is a critically important exercise of recipients' collective self-determination. That *justice-promoting* interventions specifically raise these issues makes them worthy of special focus.

Moreover, insofar as I must rely on an account of what justice requires— what people have rights *to*—I will rely on a broadly liberal account. For example, I assume that justice requires people to be treated such that they're

18 PROMOTING JUSTICE ACROSS BORDERS

reliably empowered to develop and pursue their own life projects, as long as their doing so is compatible with others doing the same. More specifically, I assume people have rights to life, to a minimal level of bodily security (e.g., to freedom from torture and persistent threats of assault or imprisonment), to the resources necessary to achieve some threshold level of functioning in their society, to freedom to choose from an adequate range of options for the course of their lives (e.g., with respect to education, employment, and family life), to freedom of conscience, and to democratic government. Though I won't endorse a particular theory of distributive justice in this book, I will assume people are entitled to equality of opportunity and that any socioeconomic inequalities should be justifiable to those they put at a relative disadvantage. That said, just as I can't offer a full-fledged defense of rights discourse here, I can't offer a full-fledged defense of liberalism. Rather, I'll offer an elaboration of what taking seriously certain basic liberal value commitments (articulated in the terms of rights discourse) would mean for the conduct of reform intervention.

Some may object that the liberal principles I've sketched above are still quite vague and that they leave unanswered many important questions about what justice requires. They do indeed. But this is not an oversight so much as an artifact of the limited role any particular conception of justice is meant to play in the ethics of reform intervention I develop here. One virtue of my view is that it generates principles we can use to morally evaluate reform interventions without necessarily passing judgment on whether the interventions in fact work to promote justice. Imagine, for example, interveners who seek to promote privatization and low taxation in a recipient society, ostensibly because justice requires those things. One way to morally evaluate their intervention would be to ask whether they were *right* about what justice required. But another way would be to ask, *putting aside the question of whether they are right*, if have they undertaken their intervention in a permissible way. The principles I develop here can help us answer the second question. Further, the legibility of this question shows that we need not settle all the details of what justice requires before morally evaluating a given reform intervention.

On the other hand, we can't afford to have all the details of what justice requires remain *unsettled* if we are to morally evaluate a reform intervention. This is because the ethical principles we should use to evaluate reform intervention do reflect *some* ideas about what justice requires. The range of conceptions of justice one could consistently endorse while also endorsing the principles for ethical reform intervention I defend here is not infinite. Imagine, for example, a conception of justice according to which justice required an enlightened dictatorship unencumbered by the constraints of collective self-determination. One's (subjective) reasons for endorsing such a view would likely contradict the presumption, which underlies my principles for ethical reform intervention, that collective self-determination is morally important. Moreover, in some cases, assessing the morality of a reform intervention requires weighing its good and bad consequences. This, in turn, requires assessing the ways in which it actually encourages or undermines the achievement of justice and therefore necessitates taking positions on what at least some of the requirements of justice are.

All this is to say that to proceed with developing an ethics of reform intervention, I must adopt *some* views about what justice requires but need not settle *all* the open questions about what that is: hence my presumption of some basic liberal principles and values, sketched above, and the absence of a fully fleshed-out theory of justice.

Finally, it's worth considering whether, to count as a reform intervention, an action must be undertaken solely by foreigners, or whether foreign actors may collaborate with locals. In reality, the line between "foreign" and "local" actors may not always be clear. Consider, for instance, a person who has lived and been educated almost entirely outside their country of origin returning to that country and engaging in its politics. I leave open the possibility that this could raise the same moral issues as an intervention undertaken by a clearly "foreign" actor claiming no membership in the country in question. But rather than posing a difficulty for the ethical principles I defend here, this reality only expands their potential scope of application.

Moreover, some of the cases I'll discuss here as examples of reform intervention do involve actions undertaken jointly by foreign actors (interveners) and domestic ones (members of the recipient societies). In fact, as we'll see, some level of collaboration—or at least cooperative interaction—between interveners and recipients is typically preferable to the alternative. Suffice it to say, though, that even when foreigners and domestic actors work together to promote justice, the foreigners' contributions will straightforwardly qualify as reform interventions—deliberate attempts to promote justice in a foreign society (with or without assistance). We'll want to know when foreigners' involvement (reform intervention) is justified and what (if any) forms it should take. This is exactly the kind of question this book seeks to answer, and it's

20 PROMOTING JUSTICE ACROSS BORDERS

made no less salient by the fact that foreign interveners sometimes collaborate with domestic actors.

Further, other foreigners not directly collaborating with the recipients of a given intervention will often have the opportunity to become involved in the intervention in some way, and they'll need a principled way to decide whether they should. Imagine, for example, an INGO tries to promote justice in some society. The INGO's work may involve close collaboration between foreign actors and members of the recipient society. But others on the world stage (perhaps unconnected to the recipient society's members) will also have to decide whether or not to donate to the INGO, whether to shop at its corporate partners, and so on. Am I, as a foreign individual, justified in contributing money to support the INGO's mission, though I don't (as the INGO's field workers do) have a direct connection to the local people where it works? Am I obligated to do so? In order to answer these questions, we'll need an account of when foreigners' involvement in justice promotion at the site of the INGO's work is permissible or obligatory, and what form it should take. Again, these are the questions this book seeks to answer. Thus, I will treat cases in which (some) foreign interveners collaborate with domestic actors as cases of reform intervention.

Changing Landscapes, Political and Moral

With the category of "reform intervention" clearly delineated, it's worth reviewing the reasons we have to rethink the ethics of intervention. This will help us understand why we must account for the full range of forms reform intervention can take in order to better understand its moral stakes and how the typology developed later in this chapter will help us do just that. There are two main reasons we should re-examine conventional ideas about the ethics of intervention. One has to do with the empirical conditions of global politics, and the other has to do with the need to better understand (and in turn better comply with) our moral duties.

The empirical conditions of global politics have changed as new political actors with new capabilities for exerting influence on the world stage have emerged as major players. Once, perhaps, global politics was simply a series of interactions among states employing the conventional tools of foreign policy. But this is true no longer. Nonstate actors have seen an upsurge in power in recent decades. Richard Falk, for example, writes of a "new geopolitics," which, although "still inchoate," is emerging out of what he calls "patterns of globalization-from-below" that are driven by members of global civil society.[6] Falk contrasts this "new geopolitics of peoples and soft power" with "the old geopolitics of states and hard power," continuing, "The new geopolitics is far more complex, as it introduces important non-territorial actors outside the state system and challenges ideas of sovereignty and territoriality."[7] Thus, we need an ethics of intervention that moves beyond the state-centrism of current thinking on the topic. If we hope to understand and evaluate the full range of global political activity, we'll need to account for the moral questions raised not only by the actions of states but also by those of NGOs, corporations, activist networks, social movements, and individuals.

In addition to bringing on this proliferation of new players, globalization has transformed global politics by making its participants more able to effect change outside their borders, using a variety of different means beyond those typical of a state's coercive foreign policy. In a globalized world, people in one society—whether individually, through civic organizations and social movements, or via their governments—have ever more opportunities to affect the political lives of people in other societies. This makes the moral questions surrounding intervention, broadly conceived, more salient than ever. These various political actors also have a wide range of means available to them which they can and do use to take advantage of their opportunities to affect foreign societies. Sometimes they use the means—such as military force and coercive sanctions—that prominent thinking on the ethics of intervention takes as its focus. But often they use other tools, such as persuasion, educational programs, boycotts, divestment campaigns, and conditional aid and trade agreements (which I take it are not always coercive). Once again, to understand and evaluate what goes on in a global politics that looks like this, we need an ethics of intervention more sensitive to the many different ways influence is actually peddled.

In sum, recent history has witnessed a proliferation of new political actors with new capabilities for exerting influence on the global stage. These changes have made received notions about the ethics of intervention less relevant for real-world global politics. To remedy this mismatch—and ensure we have the theoretical tools to understand and evaluate the bulk of global politics—we must acknowledge the many forms intervention can take, besides states' use

---

[6] Richard Falk, *Power Shift: On the New Global Order* (London: Zed Books, 2016), 6–7.
[7] Ibid., 7.

22 PROMOTING JUSTICE ACROSS BORDERS

of coercive foreign policy, and work to understand the morally significant differences among them. The typology of reform intervention this chapter develops will help us do just that. My ultimate conclusions will draw on this typology, allowing us to see when different types of reform intervention are and aren't justified and thereby providing an ethics of reform intervention appropriate to the current geopolitical landscape.

The second reason for reconsidering conventional ideas about the ethics of intervention is that doing so will allow us to better understand what the natural duty of justice really requires of us—and so will put us in a better position to carry it out. Below, I'll argue that we have a natural duty of justice like the one Rawls specifies, requiring us "to support and to comply with just institutions that exist and apply to us" and "to further just arrangements not yet established, at least when this can be done without too much cost to ourselves."[8] It's really the second requirement (to further just arrangements not yet established) that's of special importance for the ethics of reform intervention. (If just arrangements were already established, reform intervention would be unnecessary.) That said, the conjunction of both requirements can be summarized as a duty to do our part to ensure that just institutions become and remain operational—to ensure that people live, and continue to live, in just conditions. When just institutions already exist, doing our part to ensure people live in just conditions means supporting and aiding those institutions' smooth operation (the first requirement of the natural duty of justice). When just institutions don't exist, doing our part to ensure people live in just conditions means helping to bring them about, when this isn't too costly for us (the second requirement of the natural duty of justice). So, from here on, I'll take the natural duty of justice to be synonymous with the natural duty to do our part to ensure people live in just conditions.

Though an entire book could probably be written on the natural duty of justice alone, and though I can't give it such a lengthy treatment here, I will offer some considerations in favor of the view that there is a natural duty of justice and that it is global in scope—that it requires us to do our part to ensure people *everywhere* live in just conditions. Later on, I'll take as given that we have a global duty of justice and argue that there are feasible and morally permissible ways to fulfill it in everyday global politics—showing that it's not merely a formal requirement but that it requires us to take action (including

---

[8] John Rawls, *A Theory of Justice*, revised edition (Cambridge, MA: Belknap Press of Harvard University Press, 1999), 99.

engaging in reform intervention) here and now, in the real world. This argument will take the entirety of the book to unfold.

Though I will, later on, take it for granted that there's a global natural duty of justice, readers who aren't persuaded by this claim need not accept the conclusion that engaging in reform intervention is sometimes morally required. (My arguments for this conclusion depend on there being a global natural duty of justice.) However, these readers should still accept the ethical standards I develop throughout the book as identifying the kinds of reform interventions that are morally permissible. (None of my arguments for these standards considered as standards of permissibility relies upon the existence of a global natural duty of justice.) All readers should therefore accept that anyone who does in fact engage in reform intervention should adhere to these standards. Given the frequency with which global political actors intervene in foreign societies in the name of justice promotion, this is no small matter. All readers, regardless of their views on the natural duty of justice, should also accept the novel understandings of toleration, legitimacy, and collective self-determination I develop in Chapters 2–4 and the evaluation of how we ought to implement the ethical standards I develop, which I undertake in Chapter 5. Thus, nearly all of the book's conclusions stand whether or not one accepts that there is a global natural duty of justice. It is only the conclusion that reform intervention is sometimes morally required that depends on there being such a duty.[9]

With that said, here are some considerations in favor of the existence of a natural duty of justice that is global in scope: I'll start from the premise that persons, even in the state of nature, have a duty to treat other persons as equals, with equal moral worth. Treating others as equals in this way requires taking their interests into account when we act, assuming we're in a position to affect them. (I assume throughout my argument that there may be an exception to this requirement if accounting for others' interests is prohibitively costly.) If I were in a position to affect you but didn't take your interests into account when I acted—if they didn't enter into my practical reasoning—I would fail to treat you as my equal. I would act as if my ability to pursue my own purposes (which I exercised through my action) was more important than yours. (I assume you have an interest in being able to pursue your own purposes, which, *ex hypothesi*, I refused to grant consideration.) This is a basic failure of equality. So, in order to treat you as an equal, I must take your

---

[9] Thank you to Ingrid Creppell and Michael Goodhart for helpful discussion on this point.

24   PROMOTING JUSTICE ACROSS BORDERS

interests into account whenever I act and am in a position to affect you. This doesn't mean that I must always act in your interest; there's no natural duty of pure altruism. But your interests must play a role in my practical reasoning. I may not simply ignore or disregard them.

Given this, when I'm in a position to affect you, not only must I decide whether and how to affect you, but I must do so while taking your interests into account. If I do this, whatever decision I make reflects (or, if you prefer, performs or instantiates) a judgment about your current condition and the relative importance of various ends I might pursue with my action. Even a decision *not* to act so as to affect you reflects a judgment of this kind—that your current condition is tolerable, at least compared to the alternatives I might generate with my action, and that my resources are better spent doing other things besides trying to change your condition.

This will sometimes be a reasonable judgment. Sometimes, but not always. Treating you as an equal, after all, doesn't *merely* require I take your interests into account when I'm in a position to affect you. It also requires I take them sufficiently seriously. (Again, I assume an exception may be made if this is prohibitively costly.) I could take your interests into account but still treat you as a subordinate if, for example, I heavily discounted the importance of your interests. In extremis, I could act as if my fulfilling some trivial interest (like enjoying a modicum more pleasure) was more important than your fulfilling even your most important interests (like staying alive). In such a case, though I might take your interests into account when deciding how to act, I would count them for almost nothing. This, too, is a basic failure of equality.

What, then, does it mean to take someone's interests "sufficiently seriously" so as to treat them as an equal? There's a longer argument to be made than I can give now about precisely how much weight I must assign another's interests in order to treat them as an equal. It's not obvious, for example, that I always must treat every person's comparable interests as equally weighty (that I may *never* prioritize satisfying my own interests or those of people I'm close to). Of course, some philosophers do argue for this position, but it's controversial. In any case, we need not resolve this question here.

After all, there are some circumstances under which it should be clear— on a wide range of views about what the precise resolution is—that one person has failed to take another person's interests sufficiently seriously so as to treat them as an equal. I propose that a case in which I could help eliminate an injustice someone else suffered without significantly disrupting the projects I took to be central to my own life, but I nonetheless refused to do so, would be one such circumstance. Why is this so? First of all, I assume that justice requires people to be treated such that they're reliably empowered to develop and pursue their own life projects, as long as their doing so is compatible with others doing the same. This is, of course, a liberal assumption that I can't argue for here. Again, this book won't offer a defense of liberalism against its critics (except to the extent that its elaboration of liberal commitments might lend them plausibility). Rather, I hope to show that, taking certain liberal values and commitments for granted, we are generally permitted and sometimes required to pursue the achievement of justice beyond our own borders.

Assume, then, that anyone who suffers an injustice is by definition not reliably empowered to develop and pursue their own life projects. (They are disempowered to a greater or lesser extent, depending on the gravity of the injustice.) The victim of injustice is therefore deprived of a very important interest. It's not an interest in the possession of a particular good or the fulfillment of a particular purpose but a higher-order interest in being able to set and pursue their own purposes and adopt and pursue their own idea of what is good. On the sort of liberal view I take as a starting point, this is a tremendously important interest, so its deprivation is correspondingly significant. On such a view, the equality of persons' capacities to develop and pursue their own purposes is what grounds (or is one of the main things that grounds) their significant (and equal) moral worth. Ensuring people are reliably empowered to develop and pursue their own purposes is therefore the central (or a central) way to properly recognize their moral worth.

Now imagine that I can (help) empower someone to develop and pursue their own purposes (i.e., that I can help ensure they live in just conditions, or at least in conditions more closely approaching justice) and that I can do so *not only* without sacrificing anything comparable (i.e., without sacrificing my own power to develop and pursue my purposes) *but also* without even significantly disrupting the pursuit of any of the particular purposes I've actually adopted as central to my own life. In this scenario, if I refuse to help the other person (assuming I take their interests into account, as I ought to, when I decide not to help), this reflects a judgment that their not enjoying justice is tolerable compared to the alternatives I might generate by trying to help. It reflects a judgment that my resources are better spent pursuing other purposes besides their empowerment. Though I could use my resources to empower them to develop and pursue their own purposes—the very thing that's central to their enjoying the moral status they deserve—and I could do

26 PROMOTING JUSTICE ACROSS BORDERS

so without sacrificing anything that (by my own lights) is very important to my own central purposes, I opt not to.

This, too, strikes me as a basic failure of equality. It means the other person's interests count for so little to me that I'm unwilling to sacrifice even something I don't think is very important to help them secure a tremendously important interest of theirs (to be reliably empowered to develop and pursue their own purposes and therefore enjoy the moral status they deserve). If I refuse to help in this circumstance, I've failed to take the other person's interests sufficiently seriously and have therefore failed to treat them as a moral equal. So, in a case like this, I have a duty to help ensure the person in question lives in just conditions. In general terms, I have a duty requiring me to do my part to ensure others live in just conditions—that is, to help ensure others live in just conditions, when it's not too costly for me. This, you'll notice, is the duty of justice.

Moreover, I've argued that the duty of justice is a consequence of the duty to treat other persons as equals, with equal moral worth, which we would have even in the state of nature. The duty of justice is a natural duty.

The existence of this duty doesn't depend on our having any special relationship to people whose conditions we're positioned to improve, other than the simple fact that we're positioned to help them live in more just conditions. I've argued that, if I'm able to help ensure another person lives in just conditions, and I take their interests as seriously as I should when deciding (if and) how to act, I'll act so as to pursue justice for them when it's not too costly for me. Since this is true regardless of whether I share an association with them, it's true even if we belong to different societies. We all have the same natural duty to do our part to ensure others live in just conditions, and we owe this duty to all other persons, regardless of national membership. The natural duty of justice is a global duty.

One need not accept the existence of a global basic structure (roughly, a system of global economic, political, and legal institutions that profoundly affect people's life prospects and distribute the benefits and burdens resulting from global economic and political interaction among people around the world),[10] or that liberal principles of distributive justice apply to the globe as a whole, in order to accept that there's a global duty of justice like the one described here. Global interconnectedness does make the natural duty of justice more demanding, but not (necessarily) because it means there's

---

[10] See, e.g., Beitz, *Political Theory and International Relations*, 143–53.

a global basic structure to which principles of justice apply in the first instance. Rather, global interconnectedness makes the natural duty of justice more demanding because it means we have more opportunities to affect the lives of people outside our own societies. We're thus more often positioned to help ensure people elsewhere live in just conditions, so we're more often required to do our part to ensure they live in just conditions. Arguably, effecting change in foreign societies is also less costly the more interconnected we are. So, in a globalized world, we're more often positioned to help ensure people elsewhere live in just conditions without absorbing too much cost ourselves, which means we're more often required to help ensure they live in just conditions.

The reasoning articulated here, then, cuts across some of the central disagreements that divide theorists of global justice. Anyone who accepts the basic liberal values and commitments I've taken as starting premises, and who agrees that we ought, even in the state of nature, to treat other persons as equals, with equal moral worth, should also agree that there's a natural duty of justice and that it's in principle unbounded.

Of course, it may be tempting to think that, even if there is a global duty of justice, the reasons we have to promote justice in foreign societies are typically swamped by other concerns. One might think that virtually all attempts to promote justice in other societies involve mistreating the members of those societies in one way or another, such that the attempts are morally impermissible, all things considered. On this *skeptical view*, we have a duty to do our part to ensure all people live in just conditions, but "doing our part" oughtn't involve committing serious moral wrongs. And, so the argument goes, attempting to promote justice in other societies, as a rule, involves committing serious moral wrongs. Therefore, though we have a global duty of justice in some formal sense, the duty is not actionable for us in the real world: it isn't the case that we actually ought to pursue the achievement of justice in other societies.

Given the (at best) dubious record of reform intervention in world history, the skeptical view has significant intuitive pull. Indeed, there are several weighty moral objections frequently leveled against reform intervention that deserve our attention. It's often thought that reform intervention treats recipients with intolerance, objectionably denies or disregards the legitimacy of their political institutions, and/or undermines their collective self-determination. But I will argue that there are certain identifiable types of reform intervention that escape these standard objections—and in so doing

28 PROMOTING JUSTICE ACROSS BORDERS

will cast doubt on the skeptical view, suggesting instead that, if there's a global duty of justice, it requires us to actually pursue the achievement of justice in other societies in the world as we find it.

In order to show that certain kinds of reform intervention escape the standard objections, we'll have to appreciate the full range of forms reform intervention can take. In part, this is simply because if we leave some forms out of our analysis, we won't know whether or not they're vulnerable to the standard objections. Thus, even taking its conclusions at face value, existing literature that focuses narrowly on state-led interventions using force and coercion can't tell us whether other kinds of reform intervention are morally objectionable in the same ways. Moreover, the types of reform intervention the literature pays most attention to—state-led interventions using force and coercion—are arguably the most likely to fall prey to the standard objections. They are often the most invasive, adversarial, and dangerous kinds of foreign political influence. Our thinking, then, has been unduly biased toward a skeptical view of the global duty of justice. Only taking account of the many other ways in which global political actors can pursue justice beyond their borders will allow us to see that some of them escape the standard objections.

To do this, we'll need a typology like the one I develop below, which identifies the full range of forms reform intervention can take and their morally significant differences. And in order to know which types of reform intervention are vulnerable to the standard objections under what conditions, we'll need to consider these objections in light of the full typology—to evaluate how the different types of reform intervention implicate the values of toleration, legitimacy, and collective self-determination that underlie the standard objections. Ultimately, I'll argue that some types of reform intervention escape all three standard objections and are, all things considered, morally permissible. Thus, I'll contend that the skeptical view of the global duty of justice is mistaken. Since there are morally permissible ways to promote justice in foreign societies, the global duty of justice has significant normative implications for everyday world politics—we really ought, here and now, to help ensure people in other societies live under just conditions.

Reform Intervention: A Typology

This section identifies several dimensions along which particular cases of reform intervention can differ and uses them to develop a typology of reform intervention. Since the ultimate goal is to make normative recommendations, I focus on the differences most likely to be normatively significant: the degree of control interveners exercise over recipients, the urgency of an intervention's objectives, the costs to which an intervention exposes recipients, and the ways in which interveners treat and interact with recipients' existing political institutions.

Another approach would have been to distinguish reform interventions based on the specific measures with which they are carried out—for example, to treat interventions carried out via large-scale kinetic warfare as one "type," those carried out via aid conditionality as another, those carried out via preferential trade agreements as another, and so on. (This would resemble Pattison's approach in *The Alternatives to War*, where he devotes a chapter each to several different measures of intervention, including military assistance, economic sanctions, and positive incentives.)[11] However, on my view, we cannot say much that is meaningful about the ethics of a particular "measure" of intervention without assessing whether, in a given case, employing it treats recipients with toleration, respects the legitimacy of their institutions, and safeguards their collective self-determination. To make these judgments, we must assess a proposed intervention through the lenses of control, urgency, cost, and relationship to recipients' existing institutions—that is, in terms of the typology I develop below. I make no general pronouncements about whether, for example, interventions carried out using aid conditionality are ethical, because I don't think that question has a single answer, abstracted away from its place within the typology I develop here.

Later chapters draw heavily on this typology, examining under what conditions the different "types" of reform intervention are or aren't vulnerable to the standard objections sketched above, when they are permissible, and when they are obligatory. This typology forms the basis of a new ethics of reform intervention.

As I construct the typology, I'll also introduce several real-world cases of reform intervention that I'll return to again and again throughout the book. These cases will serve as touchstones of a sort. Thinking through the cases will help us appreciate the wide range of political actions taking place on the world stage—the many different forms that reform intervention can take— many of which are currently under-theorized. It will highlight the important moral issues state- and coercion-centric takes on the ethics of intervention

---

[11] Pattison, *The Alternatives to War*.

30 PROMOTING JUSTICE ACROSS BORDERS

overlook. And it will help us understand how the ideas developed here connect and apply to the real world of global politics.

Degrees of Control

Modes of reform intervention vary along several morally significant dimensions. One bound to be important is the degree to which interveners deprive recipients of the ability to freely adopt policies of their own choosing, as a result of their own freely formed judgments. Call this the degree of *control* interveners exercise. I will not develop a full account of what it means to adopt policies or make judgments "freely" here. This would be a project unto itself. Instead, I take as basic a few scenarios many prominent theories of free action and judgment would flag as problematic. Namely, I consider a person unfree in the relevant sense when they are induced to act—partially or fully—on something other than their own will, when acting on their own will is conditional upon its agreement with another's will, or when they are subject to conditions that make the content of their will dependent on others' judgments or preferences instead of their own independent judgments. Someone can be made unfree by coercion; depending on the particular conception of coercion in use, this may (for example) be accomplished by restricting the agent's options with respect to some relevant counterfactual,[12] by employing a threat to determine (or partially determine) their motivation to act,[13] or by making it impossible or unreasonably costly for them to act as they will. But they may also be made unfree by what is more commonly called manipulation—accomplished via indoctrination or deception, for example, in order to make them believe something they wouldn't under full information and given the unimpeded operation of their own rational faculties.

Note that, unlike some others, I don't assume an action that enlarges someone's option set compared to the status quo ante necessarily increases their freedom.[14] For example, Pattison considers a scenario in which a government offers aid to a desperately needy rebel in another country,

---

[12] See, e.g., Joseph Raz, *The Morality of Freedom* (Oxford: Oxford University Press, 1988), 377–8. For another sympathetic construction of a Razian view, see Michael Blake, *Justice and Foreign Policy* (Oxford: Oxford University Press, 2013), 20–4.

[13] See Robert Nozick, "Coercion," in *Philosophy, Science, and Method: Essays in Honor of Ernest Nagel*, ed. Sidney Morgenbesser et al. (New York: St. Martin's Press, 1969), 440–72.

[14] Pattison, *The Alternatives to War*, 141–2.

conditioned on the rebel's disarmament.[15] The rebel's situation is so dire that she "may have little reasonable option but to accept" the offer.[16] Nonetheless, Pattison insists, since the government's incentive "*increases* [the rebel's] potential options by offering an alternative that was not previously available to her," it also increases her freedom.[17] Pattison allows that the rebel may be to some extent unfree, but this is not because of the government's conditional offer; it is instead because of the background "situation in which she finds herself," in which she can't provide for her family's basic needs absent aid.[18] This view, though, underestimates the moral importance of the fact that the government has taken advantage of the rebel's situation, leveraging her material vulnerability to make her behave as the government wishes (to make her act on the government's will rather than her own independent will). Whether or not the government's actions are justified, it would be misleading to call them freedom enhancing, since their (deliberate) effect is to make the rebel's actions reflect someone else's (the government's) will rather than her own. Calling the government's offer freedom enhancing would obscure the distinct moral issues raised when interveners deliberately endanger (or refuse to secure) recipients' vital interests *in order to get recipients to do their bidding*. It is exactly this set of moral issues that my notion of "control" can help us address. And, as I'll argue later, this is crucial for understanding important cases of reform intervention via conditional offers (of aid, trade, or loans, for example). Thus, I will not assume interveners who give recipients new options always enhance, or never endanger, recipients' freedom.

Further, freedom and unfreedom as depicted above occur in degrees. An agent can be subject to more or less totalizing control; their action can be more free or less so. Thus, correspondingly, interveners can subject the members of recipient societies to more or less totalizing control; they can leave recipients more free to make their own judgments and decide on their own how to act, or can make them less so. On one end of the proverbial spectrum are cases of what I'll call *totally controlling* intervention. In such cases, an intervention makes it virtually impossible for recipients to act against interveners' wishes or to act on their own freely formed judgments. Interveners force recipients to acquiesce to their demands, and recipients have no choice but to go along.

---

[15] Ibid.
[16] Ibid., 142.
[17] Ibid.
[18] Ibid., 141–2.

Perhaps the clearest examples of reform intervention in this category are those involving military force. For instance, the Libyans who were violently subdued in NATO's 2011 intervention didn't freely decide to stand down or stop defending Qaddafi's government; they were forced to do so. Qaddafi didn't freely abdicate his position, nor was he induced to by the political pressure of a free citizenry; he was forced out.

However, interveners need not use *force* in order to exercise total control. Extreme manipulation, perhaps taking the form of totalizing indoctrination or misinformation campaigns, can also qualify as totally controlling. Take, for instance, the hypothetical nonviolent intervention Walzer imagines during which Sweden releases a chemical into Algeria's water supply to transform Algerians—who currently support a repressive military theocracy—into social democrats.[19] Releasing the chemical would prevent Algerians from acting on their freely formed judgments because it would prevent them from forming judgments freely. Thus, Sweden's intervention would be totally controlling, though not forceful. Admittedly, this hypothetical case is somewhat fantastical. Nonetheless, it shows that, in theory, one could exercise total control without using physical force. Moreover, there is some evidence that real political actors might develop the ability to exert total control in similar (if less dramatic) ways to Walzer's hypothetical Swedish state. For example, the US Army and CIA have both experimented with mind control via psychedelic drugs, and the CIA recently studied the use of "truth serum" as a potential interrogation tactic.[20]

Other interventions make recipients' acting against interveners' wishes possible only at the expense of their vital interests, or impair (without totally eviscerating) recipients' abilities to form judgments freely. These I call *highly controlling* interventions. I understand "vital interests" to include those interests the fulfillment of which is necessary for a minimally decent human life, a phrase I borrow from David Miller.[21] I use the phrase roughly as Miller does, to describe a life free from very serious and virtually universally

---

[19] Michael Walzer, "The Moral Standing of States: A Response to Four Critics," *Philosophy and Public Affairs* 9, no. 3 (1980): 209–29, 225–6.

[20] Eli Rosenberg, "The CIA Explored Using a 'Truth Serum' on Terrorism Detainees after 9/11, Newly Released Report Shows," *Washington Post*, 13 November 2018, https://www.washingtonpost.com/nation/2018/11/14/cia-explored-using-truth-serum-terror-detainees-after-newly-released-report-shows/; Harrison Smith, "James Ketchum, Who Conducted Mind-Altering Experiments on Soldiers, Dies at 87," *Washington Post*, 4 June 2019, https://www.washingtonpost.com/local/obituaries/james-ketchum-who-conducted-mind-altering-experiments-on-soldiers-dies-at-87/2019/06/04/7b5ad322-86cc-11e9-a491-25df61c78dc4_story.html.

[21] David Miller, *National Responsibility and Global Justice* (Oxford: Oxford University Press, 2007).

recognized physical and psychosocial harms.[22] Vital interests include, for example, interests in physical security, subsistence, basic education, and an *adequate* (though not a *maximal* or even necessarily a *fair*) range of choices of occupation, cultural and religious practice, and family life.[23]

Highly controlling interventions may involve, for example, imposing sanctions, altering trade or diplomatic relationships, organizing nonviolent resistance or other forms of political activism, and milder forms of manipulation (that don't rise to the level of the totalizing indoctrination described in Walzer's Sweden-Algeria hypothetical but that still interfere with recipients' abilities to form judgments freely). Arguably, the International Monetary Fund's (IMF's) and World Bank's imposition of "structural adjustment" programs on several developing countries in the 1980s constituted highly controlling intervention. At the insistence of US representatives, the IMF allowed political conditions to be attached to its loans even when they were desperately needed by a country undergoing economic crisis.[24] And in the 1980s, both the IMF and the World Bank exercised this prerogative, making badly needed loans available to the developing world only on the condition that local governments liberalize their trade policies and adopt other "free market" reforms.[25] Insofar as people in developing countries needed credit to alleviate economic crises that threatened their vital interests, they had no reasonable choice but to accept the IMF's and World Bank's terms, and their adopting the required policies primarily reflected the wills of IMF and World Bank members rather than their own.

Interveners may also impose sanctions, alter trade or diplomatic relationships, or organize nonviolent resistance or other forms of political activism as part of less controlling interventions—which I call *slightly controlling*—that make recipients' acting against interveners' wishes possible only at the expense of their *non*-vital interests. Take, for example, the preferential trade agreement the US signed with Oman in 2006. The agreement required that both countries follow their domestic laws protecting workers' human rights and discouraged weakening those protections.[26] It established

---

[22] Ibid., 178–85.

[23] Ibid., 178–85, 207–8.

[24] See Richard W. Miller, *Globalizing Justice: The Ethics of Poverty and Power* (Oxford: Oxford University Press, 2010), 137.

[25] Ibid. For a discussion of structural adjustment initiatives as (largely) assertions of American power in the developing world, often against vocal local opposition, see ibid., 136–41.

[26] Emilie Hafner-Burton, *Forced to Be Good: Why Trade Agreements Boost Human Rights* (Ithaca, NY: Cornell University Press, 2009), 146.

34 PROMOTING JUSTICE ACROSS BORDERS

that a tribunal would enforce compliance if there were any violations and that both the US and Oman were guaranteed the ability to seek remedies if they suffered abuses.[27]

The US certainly leveraged its disproportionate political and economic power to get Oman to agree to its terms and to adopt several progressive labor reforms during the negotiations leading up to the trade agreement's finalization.[28] During this time, Oman's government extended existing workers' rights to foreigners working in the country and entered into talks with the International Labour Organization (ILO) about ways to better meet their core standards.[29] In response to objections from the US Congress, Oman's labor minister committed to curtailing forced and child labor.[30] Shortly after the US signed the trade agreement, Oman adopted reforms in line with the ILO's standards, giving workers rights to unionization, collective bargaining, and freedom from forced labor.[31] Emilie Hafner-Burton argues that Oman wouldn't have taken these steps so soon—if at all—if they weren't necessary to win a trade deal with the US.[32]

Indeed, Oman had strong reason to want a trade agreement with the US. Namely, Oman's economy was at the time heavily dependent on its oil reserves, which were projected to potentially run out in the coming decades; thus, the country wanted to diversify its economy, and a trade deal with the US would help it do so.[33]

Oman was put in the position of having to choose between adopting the US's desired labor reforms or absorbing a significant cost (losing the trade deal with the US and the prospect of a diversified economy along with it). However, the trade deal wasn't so central to the achievement of Omanis' basic interests that they essentially had no choice but to agree to whatever terms the US proposed. It wasn't as if they were facing imminent economic collapse and the only way to escape it was to start a preferential trading relationship with the US. Oman was not in the same position with respect to the

---

[27] Ibid. The US also conditioned the deal on Oman leaving the Arab League's boycott of Israel. Here, I'll focus on the conditions related to workers' rights, because their imposition is more plausibly described as an attempt to promote justice (and therefore as part of a reform intervention); see Abigail B. Bakan and Yasmeen Abu-Laban, "Palestinian Resistance and International Solidarity: The BDS Campaign," *Race and Class* 51, no. 1 (2009): 29–54, 36.

[28] Hafner-Burton, *Forced to Be Good,* 147–9.

[29] Ibid., 148.

[30] Ibid.

[31] Ibid., 149.

[32] Ibid.

[33] Ibid., 147.

US as those subject to structural adjustment programs were in with respect to the IMF and World Bank.

The American intervention in Oman occupies a gray area of sorts. The US obviously exercised *some* control over Oman, leveraging its disproportionate market power to significantly incentivize Oman to reform its labor laws. However, the US didn't obviously coerce or exploit Oman as it would have if it made an offer Omanis couldn't reasonably refuse. Many reform interventions fit this model—with interveners exercising power in ways that take advantage of and may reinforce various geopolitical hierarchies but that don't clearly coerce or exploit recipients. But prominent literature on the ethics of intervention, with its central focus on coercive and forceful intervention, is ill-equipped to guide our judgments about these middling yet consequential exercises of power.

Finally, moving along the spectrum of control, some interveners—those who use persuasion (but not deception) to encourage certain behavior—exercise no control (though they exercise influence) over recipients. They engage in what I will call *persuasive* or *non-controlling* intervention. For instance, a state may publicly criticize another state. An NGO or international organization may contribute to or organize a political campaign, or otherwise participate in advocacy within a foreign community in an attempt to persuade its public or leaders to adopt a certain policy. My discussion of real-world persuasive interventions will center on two in particular: Tostan's work in western Africa and several Latin American countries' submission of amicus briefs opposing an Arizona immigration law.

Tostan is an international nonprofit organization that has worked in Guinea, Guinea-Bissau, Mali, Mauritania, Senegal, and the Gambia.[34] Its representatives enter a community (after being invited) and establish what the organization calls a "Community Empowerment Program." This consists of a series of classes, taught in local languages by people who live in the community for their duration and employ (among others) traditional African teaching techniques.[35] Topically, the classes are human-rights focused, typically geared toward promoting specific ends within the host community.

---

[34] See Tostan, "Where We Work," *Tostan: Dignity for All*, accessed 10 September 2019, http://tostan.org/where-we-work.

[35] See Tostan, "About Us," *Tostan: Dignity for All*, accessed 10 September 2019, https://www.tostan.org/about-us/mission-history/; Tostan, "Community Empowerment Program: Program Structure," *Tostan: Dignity for All,* accessed 10 September 2019, https://www.tostan.org/programs/community-empowerment-program/program-structure/; Tostan, "Today. Tomorrow. Together: Tostan Annual Report 2014," 6–7.

36 PROMOTING JUSTICE ACROSS BORDERS

(Commonly adopted goals include ending female genital cutting and child marriage, and promoting grassroots democracy and public health.)[36] Importantly, Tostan's curriculum was collaboratively designed—having been revised early on in response to participants' feedback—and is centered around interactive learning.[37] Tostan also oversees the establishment of community governance committees whose purpose is to lead local development campaigns once the Tostan program is over.[38]

Rather than imposing its desired policies on the communities with which it interacts, Tostan seeks to educate them in the hope that they will adopt those policies on their own.[39] In the case of FGC, for example, Tostan's goal (achieved in many instances) has been to encourage host communities to declare an end to the practice, not to forcibly end it regardless of host community sentiment.[40]

Many elements of Tostan's program reflect a commitment to treating the people with whom it works as moral agents in their own right, who are capable of making and carrying out judgments of their own about how to live their lives. Tostan's collaboratively designed and interactive classroom curriculum ensures participants are taken seriously as contributors to and authors of the influences to which they are subject rather than treated as passive recipients. Similarly, Tostan's reliance on persuasion to accomplish its policy objectives indicates it recognizes that recipients are capable of reason (they *can* be persuaded) and are entitled to decide for themselves how to act (they *should* be persuaded rather than forced). Tostan's model of "organized diffusion," whereby participants in Tostan classes are encouraged to "adopt" another person in their community to whom they'll pass on what they

---

[36] See Tostan, "Areas of Impact," *Tostan: Dignity for All*, accessed 13 July 2016, http://tostan.org/impact_areas.

[37] See Beniamino Cislaghi, Diane Gillespie, and Gerry Mackie, "Expanding the Aspirational Map: Interactive Learning and Human Rights in Tostan's Community Empowerment Program," in *Human Rights Education: Theory, Research, Praxis*, ed. Monisha Bajaj (Philadelphia: University of Pennsylvania Press, 2017), 198–209; Diane Gillespie and Molly Melching, "The Transformative Power of Democracy and Human Rights in Nonformal Education: The Case of Tostan," *Adult Education Quarterly* 60, no. 5 (2010): 477–98.

[38] See Tostan, "Community Empowerment Program: Program Structure"; Tostan, "Today. Tomorrow. Together," 6; Tostan, "Community Empowerment Program: Ensuring Sustainability," *Tostan: Dignity for All*, accessed 10 September 2019, https://www.tostan.org/programs/community-empowerment-program/ensuring-sustainability/.

[39] For a statement of Tostan's general commitment to empowerment and host communities' agency, see "Today. Tomorrow. Together."

[40] See Tostan, "Cross-Cutting Issues: Female Genital Cutting," *Tostan: Dignity for All,* accessed 13 July 2016, http://tostan.org/female-genital-cutting; Nafissatou J. Diop et al., "The TOSTAN Program: Evaluation of a Community Based Education Program in Senegal" (Washington, DC: US Agency for International Development, 2004).

BEYOND THE STATE, BEYOND WAR   37

learn,[41] and its support for community governance bodies meant to outlast the Tostan program also communicate Tostan's commitment to facilitating recipients' active involvement in shaping their own communities.

Thus, though Tostan seeks to change some long-established and deeply entrenched practices in recipient communities—such as FGC, child marriage, and other forms of gender-based subordination—its activities don't obviously raise the moral concerns we would normally associate with such an attempt. We might be tempted to think, for example, that trying to change another society in this way would reflect a judgment that its members were inferior, incapable of deciding on their own how to live, and in need of foreign supervision. It's not clear, though, that engaging in the kind of work Tostan does reflects any such judgment. As the analysis above suggests, Tostan's model of activism doesn't treat the recipients of its influence as incapable, irrational, or in need of supervision—but rather as partners in a dialogue about what justice requires and as potential leaders of social change within their own communities.

Given its focus on coercive and forceful interventions, existing literature on the ethics of intervention doesn't often account for cases like Tostan's. It therefore can't explain the difference (I expect) we intuitively see between what Tostan does, on the one hand, and interventions meant to change a society's long-established and deeply entrenched practices with force or coercion, on the other. The ethical standards I develop here will give us a principled way to account for this difference and help us understand the true moral stakes of interventions like Tostan's.

Our second case of persuasive intervention comes from Latin America. When Arizona passed its now-infamous immigration bill, SB 1070, it faced significant opposition, some from outside the US. The bill's most controversial provisions included a requirement that law enforcement officials check the immigration status of those they had "reasonable suspicion" to believe were undocumented, a requirement that all immigrants acquire immigration registration records, a provision criminalizing undocumented immigrants seeking or taking jobs, and one allowing warrantless arrests of those police believed to be undocumented.[42]

---

[41] Nafissatou J. Diop, Amadou Moreau, and Helene Benga, "Evaluation of the Long-Term Impact of the TOSTAN Programme on the Abandonment of FGM/C and Early Marriage: Results from a Qualitative Study in Senegal" (Washington, DC: US Agency for International Development, 2008), 27; Tostan, "Today. Tomorrow. Together," 7.
[42] State of Arizona, Senate Bill 1070, unofficial version, 2010, https://apps.azleg.gov/BillStatus/GetDocumentPdf/192028; Mark Sherman, "Supreme Court Issues Ruling on S.B. 1070," *Huffington*

38 PROMOTING JUSTICE ACROSS BORDERS

When SB 1070 made its way to the US Supreme Court, several Latin American countries submitted amicus briefs opposing the law. Mexico issued a brief, which Argentina, Bolivia, Brazil, Chile, Colombia, Costa Rica, Dominican Republic, Ecuador, El Salvador, Guatemala, Honduras, Nicaragua, Panama, Paraguay, Peru, Uruguay, and Haiti joined.[43] Thus, they attempted to bring about a policy change in the US (the nullification of SB 1070) by persuading US judges to decide a certain case in a certain way.

Moreover, in its brief, Mexico invoked the rights of its citizens and those of other Latin Americans in the US.[44] It wrote that SB 1070 "creates an imminent threat to the human and civil rights of its nationals."[45] The brief continued, "SB 1070 adversely impacts Mexico-U.S. bilateral relations, as well as the rights and lives of Mexican citizens *and other persons of Latin American descent in Arizona*."[46] Like Tostan, the briefs' signatories tried to promote change and improve rights protections (i.e., promote justice) in the recipient society (the US) using only persuasion, clearly recognizing the recipients of their influence (US judges and the people they represent) as worthy interlocutors.

Contrary to Tesón's startling assertion that "intervention is governed by the same principles throughout the spectrum of coercion,"[47] whether a proposed intervention falls in one or another of the categories of control laid out above will have significant normative implications. In this chapter, I can only hint at what these might be. Fully working them out is one goal of the book as a whole. Thus, here, I hope only to highlight some possible normative consequences by discussing the ways in which using more or less controlling tactics differentially implicates the moral questions (regarding toleration, legitimacy, and collective self-determination) surrounding reform intervention.

Post, 25 June 2012, http://www.huffingtonpost.com/2012/06/25/supreme-court-sb1070_n_1614121.html.

[43] Amicus Curiae Brief of the United Mexican States in Support of Respondent, Arizona v. US, 567 US 387 (2012); Motion of the Republic of Haiti for Leave to join the United Mexican States as Amicus Curiae in Support of Respondent, Arizona v. US, 567 US 387 (2012); Motion of Argentina, Bolivia, Brazil, Chile, Colombia, Costa Rica, Dominican Republic, Ecuador, El Salvador, Guatemala, Honduras, Nicaragua, Panama, Paraguay, Peru, and Uruguay for Leave to Join the United Mexican States as Amici Curiae in Support of Respondent, Arizona v. US, 567 US 387 (2012).

[44] See, e.g., Amicus Curiae Brief of the United Mexican States in Support of Respondent, Arizona v. US, 567 US 387 (2012), at 1–4.

[45] Ibid., at 2.

[46] Ibid., at 4, emphasis added.

[47] Fernando R. Tesón, *A Philosophy of International Law* (Boulder, CO: Westview Press, 1998), 60.

One standard objection to intervention says it treats recipients with intolerance. And interventions may be more intolerant when they are more controlling. It is, I take it, generally agreed that we risk being intolerant of others when we coerce or manipulate them into abandoning their existing ways of life for our own ways of life; it is less clear that we risk being intolerant when we merely try to persuade them to do so. Intolerance typically manifests itself as one person or group attempting to change the behavior of others without regard for the others' values or preferences. Arguably, this would aptly describe an intervention in which interveners coerced or manipulated recipients to get them to change their behavior. However, if interveners bring about the desired change by *convincing* the recipients they should act differently, we may no longer be entitled to say the interveners have treated recipients with intolerance. Far from disregarding recipients' preferences, the interveners seem committed to changing recipient behavior *on the condition* that the change can be made in line with those preferences.

Of course, in order to determine if a given intervention runs afoul of toleration, we need an account of what toleration requires in the global sphere. And determining whether a given intervention is, all things considered, justified further requires a set of principles that tells us how we ought to weigh toleration against other values. The next chapter—which develops a novel account of international toleration—addresses both these issues.

The degree of control interveners exercise may also affect the degree to which they threaten recipients' collective self-determination. Understanding collective self-determination as a society's ability to determine the content of its own laws and how its institutions are organized, it isn't obviously undermined when that society is subject to merely persuasive intervention. In such cases, the society still has the ultimate authority to decide what policies to adopt and what institutions to establish. In other words, the recipient society can choose whether to take the course of action interveners recommend. If it chooses to do so when it could have done otherwise, it is far from obvious that we should think of the choice as externally imposed in a way that threatens collective self-determination.

We could say something similar about cases where recipient societies adopt reforms in response to slightly controlling interventions. In these cases, though interveners incentivize recipients' adopting some reform, recipients can reasonably refuse. Thus, if recipients choose to adopt interveners' desired reforms, they do so to some degree (insofar as they are responding to interveners' incentives) because the interveners will that they

40 PROMOTING JUSTICE ACROSS BORDERS

do so. But recipients' choice also reflects their own will, to a degree (insofar as they can reasonably act otherwise but do not).

Thus, it seems, all else equal, more controlling interventions pose more of a potential threat to collective self-determination. Again, though, we would need a closer examination of exactly how reform intervention might undermine collective self-determination in order to decide which interventions were genuine threats to it. This analysis comes in Chapter 4.

Finally, less controlling interventions may be justified in the face of greater uncertainty than their more controlling counterparts. I propose there are three major types of uncertainty with which any potential intervener must contend, and therefore with which any credible ethics of intervention must contend. The first is *moral uncertainty*—uncertainty about what justice requires. The second is *factual uncertainty*—uncertainty about the conditions on the ground in a recipient society. The third is *political uncertainty*—uncertainty about the effects of a proposed intervention, including about whether it would actually achieve its stated ends. Clearly, any judgments we make about the merits of an intervention must ultimately be subject to evaluation based on the level of certainty we are justified in assigning to them.

Moral and political uncertainty are particularly important to our present discussion. All else equal, higher moral and political uncertainty means that a given intervention is riskier than it would otherwise be. It imposes upon the recipients whatever costs it involves without a corresponding guarantee of achieving the benefits it promises if successful. (It may seem odd to say moral uncertainty has this effect. Note, however, that in the case of a *reform* intervention, the promotion of justice must be among its supposed benefits. Thus, uncertainty about whether an intervention will help achieve justice—which surely increases when uncertainty about what justice requires increases—makes it "riskier" in the sense described here.)[48] Exposure to such risk may be relatively easy to justify when it is taken on voluntarily, but less so otherwise. Hence the thought that less controlling interventions (in response to which recipients may adopt interveners' desired reforms voluntarily) may be acceptable even in the face of uncertainty that would preclude

---

[48] In the context of this discussion, factual uncertainty is primarily significant insofar as it increases political and moral uncertainty. Uncertainty about conditions on the ground in a recipient society can create uncertainty about whether justice requires implementing the specific reform an intervention aims to encourage (moral uncertainty) and about whether the intervention is likely to achieve its objectives (political uncertainty).

more controlling ones (which, if successful, would induce recipients to adopt reforms, but not entirely voluntarily).

Urgency of the Objectives

We can also distinguish reform interventions by the urgency of the objectives they seek to achieve. (I use the term "urgency" to denote *moral urgency*, not temporal urgency, though the two may sometimes be related.) I propose we divide the possible objectives into three categories: reform interventions may aim to secure basic rights, non-basic rights that nonetheless protect vital interests, or non-basic rights that protect non-vital interests.

Though I borrow the term *basic rights* from Henry Shue, I use it differently than he does.[49] I understand *basic rights* to include rights to life (including rights not to be killed and rights to subsistence) and to a minimal level of bodily security (including rights to freedom from torture and from persistent threats of assault or imprisonment). Basic rights protect very important material interests, but this isn't their (only) distinguishing feature. Their protection is also necessary to secure even a minimal level of individual autonomy. The violation of one's basic rights decimates their higher-order ability to set and pursue ends of their own—or, at least, makes it radically insecure. Even if they manage, heroically, to set and pursue ends at odds with those of their tormenters, the violation of their basic rights means they must bear extraordinary costs to even try such a thing. Someone subject to starvation, lethal force, torture, or the constant threat of assault or imprisonment is forced to do whatever is necessary to avoid or mitigate these grave harms, and their doing what's necessary can't really be described as the product of their own will. After all, in a very real sense, they have no choice.[50] Thus, when someone's basic rights are violated, the problem isn't only that they're prevented from taking specific actions or that their option set is very limited. The problem is also that they aren't in a position to decide for themselves

---

[49] Shue defines "basic rights" as those whose enjoyment is "essential to the enjoyment of all other rights"; see Henry Shue, *Basic Rights: Subsistence, Affluence, and U.S. Foreign Policy*, 2nd edition (Princeton, NJ: Princeton University Press, 1996), 19. I use the term "basic rights" to denote a set of rights that safeguard especially important interests and whose protection is necessary to secure even a modicum of individual autonomy—regardless of how their enjoyment relates to the enjoyment of other rights. Also unlike Shue (70–8), I don't identify rights to political participation as "basic rights."

[50] My view here parallels Joseph Raz's treatment of the "Hounded Woman" in *The Morality of Freedom*, 374–6. I thank Jade Ngo for pointing me toward this way of thinking about basic rights in a paper she presented to the Princeton Political Theory Research Seminar in 2018.

42 PROMOTING JUSTICE ACROSS BORDERS

what ends to pursue, even within a limited range. Their very ability to set and pursue ends of their own is significantly undermined. Again, they're simply forced to do what's necessary.

The next category of urgency picks out non-basic rights that nonetheless protect vital interests—those whose fulfillment is necessary for living what many in the literature call a "decent" human life.[51] In line with the definition of "vital interests" stipulated earlier, beyond freedom from killing, starvation, and ever-present physical danger, these include rights to whatever (presumably more than subsistence) resources are necessary to achieve some threshold level of functioning in one's society and freedom to choose from an adequate range of options for the course of one's life (with respect to education, employment, family life, etc.).[52] Taken together, the rights contained within these first two categories of urgency are commonly—though not universally—called human rights.[53]

The third and final category of urgency picks out all remaining rights not included in the first two but whose fulfillment is required by justice. On a liberal conception of justice, these may include, for example, rights to equality of opportunity, democratic government, full distributive justice, and full freedom of conscience.

There are, of course, innumerable possible ways in which we could delineate the categories of urgency. I have chosen these particular divisions because they track distinctions made in the existing literature on global justice and intervention reasonably closely. It has been accepted most widely and for the longest time that securing basic rights is an appropriate object of international concern and that their gravest violations may even justify military intervention.[54] Non-basic rights whose realization is still necessary for right-bearers to live decent human lives have more recently been accepted as

---

[51] See Miller, *National Responsibility and Global Justice*, p. 47, ch. 7; Andrew Altman and Christopher Heath Wellman, *A Liberal Theory of International Justice* (Oxford: Oxford University Press, 2009), 192; Cécile Fabre, *Cosmopolitan War* (Oxford: Oxford University Press, 2012), ch. 1, p. 181.

[52] For some accounts of what is necessary for living a decent human life, see Miller, *National Responsibility and Global Justice*, ch. 7; Fabre, *Cosmopolitan War*, 181; Altman and Wellman, *A Liberal Theory of International Justice*, 2–3.

[53] See Miller, *National Responsibility and Global Justice*, ch. 7; Altman and Wellman, *A Liberal Theory of International Justice*, 2–3, 192.

[54] We can take the global reception of the Genocide Convention, *jus cogens* norms, and the rise of the "Responsibility to Protect" doctrine as evidence of this. Note also Michael Walzer's account of when military intervention is justified in *Just and Unjust Wars: A Moral Argument with Historical Illustrations*, 5th edition (New York: Basic Books, 2015), ch. 6 and David Luban's discussion of the role of "socially basic human rights" in "Just War and Human Rights," *Philosophy and Public Affairs* 9, no. 2 (1980): 160–81.

objects of international concern, though the use of military force to secure them is perhaps more controversial.[55] And there is still much controversy about the proper status of non-basic rights that secure non-vital interests in the global sphere. Some deny that securing these rights (essentially, securing the full achievement of justice) is an acceptable goal of international political activity;[56] others are open to this being an acceptable goal one day, but they do little to articulate what (if anything) political actors here and now should do to further it;[57] and yet others think we already have expansive obligations to promote justice worldwide.[58]

With our categories of urgency set, we can now begin to examine the normative significance of a proposed intervention falling into one or another of them—and the difficulties associated with determining in which category it belongs. Commonly accepted principles of proportionality suggest that interventions meant to achieve more urgent objectives may permissibly employ riskier or more costly means than those meant to achieve less urgent objectives.[59] Additionally, those with more urgent aims may be less likely to problematically disregard recipient societies' legitimacy or undermine their collective self-determination. This is because, on many theories, a society must maintain a certain threshold level of justice in order to actually be legitimate or self-determining, and this typically requires protecting the rights picked out by the first and perhaps the second categories of urgency.[60]

---

[55] See, e.g., Altman and Wellman, *A Liberal Theory of International Justice*, ch. 5; Fabre, *Cosmopolitan War*, ch. 5; and David Miller's conception of human rights in *National Responsibility and Global Justice*, ch. 7.

[56] Michael Walzer sometimes takes a view like this; see, e.g., "Achieving Global and Local Justice," *Dissent* 58, no. 3 (2011): 42–8.

[57] Michael Walzer also sometimes takes a view like this; see "Beyond Humanitarian Intervention: Human Rights in Global Society," in *Thinking Politically: Essays in Political Theory*, ed. David Miller (New Haven, CT: Yale University Press, 2007), 251–63, 257–61. So does David Miller, for example, when he writes of a foreign community in *National Responsibility and Global Justice*, "we may be justified in encouraging its members to move, in due course, towards recognizing" what he calls "citizenship rights" (168). This echoes his earlier sentiment that foreigners can permissibly offer "advice and encouragement," but nothing more, to political communities attempting to decide for themselves what justice requires; see David Miller, "Defending Political Autonomy: A Discussion of Charles Beitz," *Review of International Studies* 31, no. 2 (2005): 381–8, 386.

[58] See, e.g., Simon Caney, *Justice beyond Borders: A Global Political Theory* (Oxford: Oxford University Press, 2005). Caney thinks it is incumbent on us to bring about the realization of the requirements of justice that are universal; on Caney's view, these requirements are quite expansive.

[59] For a discussion of what Walzer calls the "conventional" view of proportionality in war, see *Just and Unjust Wars*, 128–33. Note, though, that the present discussion of proportionality extends beyond the context of war to include all kinds of political activity that qualify as reform intervention.

[60] See, e.g., Altman and Wellman, *A Liberal Theory of International Justice*, esp. ch. 1 and Allen Buchanan, *Justice, Legitimacy, and Self-Determination: Moral Foundations for International Law* (Oxford: Oxford University Press, 2004), 43, 80–2. I discuss legitimacy in greater detail in Chapter 3 and collective self-determination in Chapter 4.

44   PROMOTING JUSTICE ACROSS BORDERS

Thus, if a society is in a position such that an intervention is needed to guarantee that, for example, its citizens' basic rights are secured, its government is probably not legitimate, and it is probably not genuinely self-determining. An intervention into its affairs is therefore relatively unlikely to disrespect legitimate institutions or to interfere with collective self-determination.

Intuitively, it may also seem that interventions aimed at achieving more urgent objectives pose less of a threat to toleration. Indeed, we may think that the more urgent the objective, the more widely accepted will be its importance. In other words, while interveners and recipients will often disagree (both with each other and among themselves) about what full-fledged justice requires, they will be relatively likely to agree that people ought not to be forced into a particular occupation, and even more likely to agree that they ought to be free from wanton killing (for example). On this view, then, interventions with more urgent ends will be less likely to impose political arrangements amenable to interveners' ideas about justice at the expense of recipients'—and therefore less likely to be objectionably intolerant.

This may be true as a general rule, but it is worth noting that there are still significant disagreements about the importance even of those objectives I take to be comparatively urgent. The continuing political debates within the US about whether torture is an acceptable interrogation technique are a case in point. Moreover, even if there is widespread agreement about the general contours of the categories of moral urgency—even if people agree, for example, that violations of basic rights are most urgent—they may disagree about the precise content of those categories; they may disagree about which rights are basic or what their realization requires. In Dworkin's language, people may agree about moral concepts but disagree about moral conceptions.[61]

I note these sources of disagreement because it seems classifying proposed reform interventions based on the urgency of their objectives can help us determine whether and what kinds of interventions are justified in different circumstances. However, to do this, we must assess the normative implications of disagreement regarding *how* to classify them—arising either from disagreement about what principles and values are morally most important or from disagreement about which specific rights must be guaranteed in order to adhere to those principles and values.

---

[61] See Ronald Dworkin, *Taking Rights Seriously* (Cambridge, MA: Harvard University Press, 1977).

BEYOND THE STATE, BEYOND WAR   45

Such disagreement has normative implications because of the potential we have to wrong people when we impose a course of action on them over their opposition. Part of treating people as independent agents equally worthy of moral concern is operating under the presumption that they should live lives that are the products of their own choices. And, as I argue in the next chapter, this is the core requirement of toleration. When people are subjected to laws they oppose or otherwise made to act against their wishes, there is one respect in which they are not allowed to live lives that are the products of their own choices. This is not always intolerant and is sometimes justified, but it is a condition in need of justification.

Consider, then, a case in which interveners forcefully subject the recipients of their intervention to a particular policy, operating under the assumption that it will solve an especially urgent problem, but some or all of the recipients think that problem minor and not at all urgent. It's tempting to say that the interveners' actions would be justified (and perhaps consistent with a principled commitment to toleration) if they *really did* address a very urgent issue, but that they would not be justified (and might constitute intolerance) otherwise. However, in order to decide whether this intervention treats recipients with toleration and whether it's justified, we need decide not only who (the interveners or the recipients) is correct about the urgency of the problem at issue. We must also decide whether the interveners are justified in overruling the recipients' judgments about its urgency, and therefore about the policies (if any) they should adopt to address it and the means by which those policies should be promoted.[62] Even if they turn out to be mistaken, recipients' judgments are judgments made by actual persons about how their lives should proceed (what laws and political conditions they should be subject to) and are therefore valuable and deserve consideration.[63] Moreover, unduly disregarding these judgments may qualify as objectionable intolerance—again, even if the judgments are mistaken.

The upshot is that we cannot simply conclude that interventions aimed at achieving more urgent objectives are easier to justify or less likely to be vulnerable to the standard objections against intervention. While the actual

---

[62] E.g., in "The Moral Standing of States," Walzer argues against intervention (except in very extreme cases) partially on the grounds that foreigners have no standing to override insiders' judgments about whether their government is legitimate, seemingly independently of their correctness.

[63] This is a version of Rawls' insight that persons are "self-authenticating sources of valid claims," though he means this to have the more specific normative implication that co-citizens should have equal standing to make claims on their shared institutions; see John Rawls, *Political Liberalism*, expanded edition (New York: Columbia University Press, 2005), 32–3.

46 PROMOTING JUSTICE ACROSS BORDERS

urgency of an intervention's objectives should certainly influence our determination as to whether it is justified, this determination must also be sensitive to the (inevitable) disagreement about what counts as a morally urgent matter—disagreement, in other words, about what justice requires.

Costs to the Recipients

We may say something similar about the cost an intervention is likely to impose on recipients. I divide these costs into three categories, which roughly parallel the categories of urgency discussed above. An intervention may threaten the interests protected by recipients' basic rights (call these basic interests), their other vital interests, or their non-vital interests.

Once again invoking the principle of proportionality, it makes sense to say an intervention ought not impose costs of greater urgency than its expected benefits. An intervention aimed at protecting non-basic rights, for example, shouldn't put recipients' basic interests at great risk. This doesn't mean an attempt to achieve some lesser goal ought never to involve *any* risk of bringing about a more serious harm. Arguably, people are always subject to *some* such risk—of being killed or starving, for example—even if these risks are typically minuscule. As it is generally understood in just war theory, proportionality doesn't require avoiding grave risk altogether but rather balancing its gravity and likelihood against the importance and likelihood of achieving the benefit sought.[64]

Altman and Wellman illustrate this type of reasoning in their analysis of the safe haven and no-fly zone erected in northern Iraq after the Gulf War.[65] According to Altman and Wellman, though this involved military activity, and therefore (arguably) *some* risk of seriously harming or even killing civilians in the region, the operation's task of protecting the Kurds was accomplished with very little actual exertion of force, and therefore very little risk of seriously harming civilians (and this outcome was predictable with reasonable certainty when the task was first undertaken).[66] Given all this,

---

[64] In just war theory, the potential "benefit" of a particular action is typically evaluated in terms of its centrality to successfully completing one's military mission (regardless of its moral merit, at least within certain limits); see Walzer, *Just and Unjust Wars*, 128–33. Here, I mean the importance of a particular benefit to be evaluated in moral terms (i.e., achieving a more morally urgent goal is a more important benefit).

[65] Altman and Wellman, *A Liberal Theory of International Justice*, 101–4.

[66] Ibid.

Altman and Wellman argue the mere fact that establishing the safe haven and no-fly zone constituted an *armed* intervention doesn't mean it put civilians at unjustifiable risk, even if it wasn't necessary to avert a "supreme humanitarian emergency."[67] Expanding upon Altman and Wellman's logic, we can conclude that, in certain similar cases, interveners might be justified in using forceful means (though they may technically involve a risk of death) to protect recipients from some less serious injury.

Put simply, the provisional lesson of this subsection is that more costly interventions should have a greater chance of doing more good. Evaluating an intervention based on its adherence to this principle, though, requires assessing the three kinds of uncertainty (moral, factual, and political) canvassed above. As a rule, costlier interventions may be permissible only when uncertainty is relatively low, whereas less costly interventions may be permissible even in the face of higher uncertainty. A full-scale military intervention, of the kind we saw in Libya in 2011, for instance, is likely to be extremely costly. Such interventions may therefore be justifiable only when the uncertainty about the moral importance of their objectives and about their actual consequences is quite low. Indeed, one prominent criticism of the Libya intervention is that it inflicted enormous costs on the Libyan population (by some accounts, dramatically increasing the civilian death toll) when its medium- and long-term effects were dubious at best (and have been, as of now, quite devastating).[68]

However, not every intervention imposes equally serious costs on its intended beneficiaries. Interventions that resemble peaceful political activism more closely than military force may be very low risk. Moreover, it may be acceptable to expose recipients to these very low levels of risk in the pursuit of a worthy objective, even if its worth or the effectiveness of the proposed intervention is comparatively uncertain. Take the international opposition to Arizona's SB 1070. When the states that submitted amicus briefs to the Supreme Court did so, they may not have been able to predict whether this would actually effect change in US or Arizona law. On its own, though, this

---

[67] Ibid., 102.

[68] See Christopher Hobson, "Responding to Failure: The Responsibility to Protect after Libya," *Millennium: Journal of International Studies* 44, no. 3 (2016): 433–54, 442, 445, 447–50, 453–4; Alan J. Kuperman, "A Model Humanitarian Intervention? Reassessing NATO's Libya Campaign," *International Security* 38, no. 1 (2013): 105–36; Alan J. Kuperman, "Obama's Libya Debacle: How a Well-Meaning Intervention Ended in Failure," *Foreign Affairs* 94, no. 2 (2015): 66–77; Alex de Waal, "African Roles in the Libyan Conflict of 2011," *International Affairs* 89, no. 2 (2013): 365–79, 379; Christopher Zambakari, "The Misguided and Mismanaged Intervention in Libya: Consequences for Peace," *African Security Review* 25, no. 1 (2016): 44–62.

48 PROMOTING JUSTICE ACROSS BORDERS

doesn't recommend we condemn their attempt, as even its total failure would apparently pose little or no risk to anyone.

This insight, that some forms of intervention may be permissible even when uncertainty surrounding their moral merit or effectiveness is high, is significant because such uncertainty is commonly cited as a reason to reject intervention as a mode of promoting political change—especially when it is (as reform intervention is) aimed at achieving (some element of) justice rather than merely reducing suffering or averting an impending humanitarian crisis. For example, Walzer argues, on the one hand, that outsiders to a political community can never know the conditions on the ground in that community sufficiently to be able to judge whether they reflect the community's values.[69] On the other hand, he holds, following Mill, that even without considering this difficulty, external intervention is an extremely and inescapably unreliable method for pursuing justice because it cannot produce the (political-cultural) conditions necessary for any community to uphold just institutions.[70]

Others argue that political uncertainty should rule out reform intervention for a different reason: it isn't merely that some technical difficulty (such as the impermeability of local cultures to liberal values) makes intervention an especially blunt instrument for promoting justice; instead (or also), interveners will reliably pursue their own interests, at the expense of the recipients', over the course of an intervention. Though the ostensible end of an intervention may be to promote justice, presumably at morally acceptable costs to the recipients, the likelihood that it will achieve this end is diminished (and therefore political uncertainty is augmented) to the extent that interveners prioritize their own interests, and they always will.

This argument is put forward, in different forms, by political realists as well as practitioners of Third World Approaches to International Law (TWAIL). While the former argue that interveners will inevitably co-opt humanitarian language and sentiment, using it to (mis)represent their self-interested ventures as noble crusades,[71] the latter argue that even ostensibly "humanitarian" intervention can be a tool of the powerful to entrench their power and

---

[69] See Walzer, "The Moral Standing of States."

[70] Walzer, *Just and Unjust Wars*, 87–91; see also John Stuart Mill, "A Few Words on Non-Intervention," in Michael Doyle, *The Question of Intervention: John Stuart Mill and the Responsibility to Protect* (New Haven, CT: Yale University Press, 2015), 205–26.

[71] See, e.g., E. H. Carr, *The Twenty Years' Crisis, 1919–1939: An Introduction to the Study of International Relations* (London: Macmillan, 1939).

exploit the global disadvantaged.[72] Under such circumstances, reform intervention can hardly be relied upon to accomplish its objective (enhancing justice in recipient societies), making the political uncertainty surrounding it especially high.[73]

One straightforward response to this kind of objection is that levels of uncertainty in fact vary from case to case. However, identifying different types of intervention based on the different costs they impose on recipients allows us to make a more nuanced reply, which says that the *morally acceptable level* of uncertainty will also vary from case to case, depending on the type of intervention proposed.

But it remains true that evaluating interventions according to the rule that the costlier ones should have a greater chance of doing more good requires making judgments about what qualifies as a high cost, what qualifies as a great good, and what qualifies as an acceptable trade-off between them— judgments, in other words, about what counts as more or less morally important. Thus, anyone attempting to judge the permissibility of an intervention on these grounds will have to grapple with the issues surrounding moral disagreement discussed in the previous subsection.

Relationship to Recipients' Existing Institutions

Finally, reform interventions may employ means that interfere more or less extensively (or not at all) with the operation of recipients' formal political institutions. And this too can have normative consequences. Some, like NATO's 2011 intervention in Libya, seek to achieve their ends (in this case, ostensibly, protecting Libyan civilians) by overthrowing recipients' institutions and replacing them entirely. Reform intervention need not rise to the level of *regime change*, however.

---

[72] For an explanation of the basic premises of TWAIL, see Makau Mutua, "What Is TWAIL?," *Proceedings of the Annual Meeting (American Society of International Law)* 94 (2000): 31–40.

[73] There is another aspect to the TWAIL criticism of intervention according to which "uncertainty" isn't the problem. On this view, it isn't (only) that interveners will take any opportunity to exploit the less powerful and will therefore be unreliable providers of justice. It is (also) that the act of intervention itself can constitute a wrong insofar as it reinforces or manifests existing unjust power structures. For one example of a view like this, see Antony Anghie, "The Evolution of International Law: Colonial and Postcolonial Realities," *Third World Quarterly* 27, no. 5 (2006): 739–53. I don't mean the present focus on uncertainty to deny the importance of this criticism, which I will address in more detail in later chapters.

50   PROMOTING JUSTICE ACROSS BORDERS

Interveners may instead work in opposition to *some* elements of recipients' existing institutions (by preventing the enforcement of a particular law or interfering with the normal operation of some government agency, for example), without attempting to bring about their total collapse. Arguably, the European Parliament, individual European states, and several European drug companies engaged in this kind of *oppositional intervention* when they stopped exporting lethal injection drugs to the US for the express purpose of getting the country to abolish the death penalty.

In 2005, the EU banned the export of products used for executions, explicitly citing its desire to play a leading role in abolishing the death penalty.[74] The EU said it aimed to be the "leading institutional actor and largest donor to the fight against the death penalty."[75] Barbara Lochbihler, chair of the European Parliament's human rights subcommittee, said, "Our political task is to push for an abolition of the death penalty, not facilitate its procedure."[76] And when Britain restricted the export of select lethal injection drugs in 2010, Business Secretary Vince Cable said, "This move underlines this government's . . . moral opposition to the death penalty in all circumstances."[77]

In the same year, the US began to feel the effects of the EU's ban, when an American company (Hospira), after having stopped manufacturing a drug used in lethal injections, considered restarting production in Italy, but Italian officials prohibited the drug's export for use in executions.[78] Recently, two European companies (the Danish Lundbeck and the German Fresenius Kabi) also stopped selling certain drugs to US correctional facilities after learning they were being used to carry out executions.[79]

That the refusal to export lethal injection drugs to the US was presented as an expression of moral opposition to the death penalty and as part of a campaign to abolish it means we can think of this refusal as a reform intervention.

---

[74] See Jeurgen Baetz, "EU's Stance Forces US Executioners to Improvise," *Seattle Times*, 18 February 2014, http://www.seattletimes.com/nation-world/eus-stance-forces-us-executioners-to-improvise/.
[75] Quoted in ibid.
[76] Ibid.
[77] Ibid.
[78] See Mark Berman, "The Recent History of States Scrambling to Keep Using Lethal Injections," *Washington Post*, 19 February 2014, https://www.washingtonpost.com/news/post-nation/wp/2014/02/19/the-recent-history-of-states-scrambling-to-keep-using-lethal-injections/?tid=a_inl&utm_term=.c8a028e78164; Baetz, "EU's Stance Forces US Executioners to Improvise."
[79] Holly Williams, "Meet the Woman behind a Shortage of Execution Drugs," *CBS News*, 30 April 2014, http://www.cbsnews.com/news/meet-the-woman-behind-a-shortage-of-execution-drugs/; Alan Scher Zagier, "Another Manufacturer Blocks Drug for Execution Use," *US News & World Report*, 27 September 2012, https://www.usnews.com/news/us/articles/2012/09/27/drug-maker-blocks-anesthetic-for-use-in-executions.

The Europeans involved, it seems, meant their actions to contribute to ending an injustice (execution) in a foreign society (the US).

We might interpret the Europeans' action as an attempt to prevent the enforcement of certain American laws (those calling for executions), though it doesn't obviously constitute a challenge to the general lawmaking authority of the US government. (I'll argue in more detail for this interpretation in Chapter 3.) Thus, European interveners in this case adopted the adversarial stance toward recipients' (Americans') institutions interveners are often assumed to have, to a degree—but only to a degree. Interventions like this therefore represent another gray area—a partial and targeted, as opposed to a full and general, challenge to recipients' lawmaking authority. This, too, is a gray area that existing literature is reticent to acknowledge, and one it certainly doesn't give us the requisite conceptual tools to analyze.

Alternatively, interveners might try to achieve their ends without directly interacting with recipients' formal political institutions: they may engage in what I'll call *extra-institutional intervention*. Boycott and divestment campaigns like the Palestinian Boycott, Divest, Sanction (BDS) movement exemplify this kind of intervention.

The BDS movement is a Palestinian civil society initiative whose leaders aim to bring about several specific changes to Israeli policy.[80] Their call to action clearly establishes the promotion of justice in Israel and Israeli-occupied territories as one of the movement's central goals and challenges conscientious people worldwide to join the campaign. It is worth quoting at length:

> We, representatives of Palestinian civil society, call upon international civil society organizations and people of conscience all over the world to impose broad boycotts and implement divestment initiatives against Israel similar to those applied to South Africa in the apartheid era. We appeal to you to pressure your respective states to impose embargoes and sanctions against Israel. We also invite conscientious Israelis to support this Call, for the sake of justice and genuine peace.
>
> These non-violent punitive measures should be maintained until Israel meets its obligation to recognize the Palestinian people's inalienable right to self-determination and fully complies with the precepts of international law by:

---

[80] Palestinian Civil Society, "Palestinian Civil Society Call for BDS," BDS, 9 July 2005, https://bdsmovement.net/call.

52 PROMOTING JUSTICE ACROSS BORDERS

1. Ending its occupation and colonization of all Arab lands and dismantling the Wall
2. Recognizing the fundamental rights of the Arab-Palestinian citizens of Israel to full equality; and
3. Respecting, protecting and promoting the rights of Palestinian refugees to return to their homes and properties as stipulated in UN resolution 194.[81]

Of course, insofar as they advocate for governments to sanction the Israeli state, BDS's participants *do* interact with Israel's formal political institutions. A substantial portion of their campaign, though, is focused on encouraging economic, cultural, and academic boycotts and divestment from companies that profit from Israeli occupation and settlement.[82] These modes of opposition take place outside Israel's formal political institutions and don't directly interfere with their operation. Thus, these elements of BDS also belong in a gray area: they operate neither through nor against the authority of Israeli institutions. Instead, they operate outside those institutions.

Many boycott-centered movements similarly operate neither through nor against the authority of existing institutions in the society they seek to change. So how we understand the ethical significance of this condition could have wide-reaching implications for our moral judgments about global politics. Again, though, prominent thinking on the ethics of intervention focuses on interventions that are outright adversarial with respect to recipients' institutions. There are certainly adversarial elements to boycott movements like BDS, but there are conciliatory elements as well. That an intervener chooses to act outside of rather than interfere with the operation of recipients' institutions is morally significant. It calls into question the traditional picture of intervention as an attempt to undermine those very institutions. But existing scholarship leaves us without many resources to make principled distinctions among interventions that take more or less adversarial stances with respect to recipient institutions.

Finally, interveners may engage in *intra-systemic intervention*, trying to achieve their ends by working *through* recipients' existing institutions—as did, for instance, the states that submitted amicus briefs opposing SB 1070 to

---

[81] Ibid.
[82] See BDS, "What Is BDS?," accessed 26 July 2017, https://bdsmovement.net/what-is-bds; BDS, "Get Involved: Know What to Boycott," accessed 26 July 2017, https://bdsmovement.net/get-involved/what-to-boycott.

the US Supreme Court. Intra-systemic interventions like the submission of these briefs challenge the common assumption that intervention must aim to undermine or overthrow recipients' political institutions even more radically than extra-institutional interventions like BDS do.

Which of these four options—regime change, oppositional, extra-institutional, or intra-systemic—describes a given intervention may affect the chances of its failing to show due respect for recipients' legitimate political institutions. For example, justifying *regime change* or *oppositional* interventions, which operate in direct opposition to recipients' political institutions, may require furnishing an account of why those institutions are illegitimate.

The case isn't so clear for extra-institutional interventions. Though they seek to produce change in recipient institutions, they don't directly interfere with their operation. They certainly exert influence but aren't *obviously* premised on a denial of recipient institutions' legitimacy. Do legitimate regimes have valid objections to extra-institutional intervention? Are they conclusive objections? Do the answers to these questions depend on interveners' identities—for example, whether they are state or nonstate actors? I, for one, think many would be quite differently disposed to BDS if it were orchestrated by another state—Lebanon, let's say—rather than by people within Palestinian civil society. This is (at least partly) because, while states' treatment of other states on the global stage is widely recognized as an indicator of the latter's status in the international community, the same isn't obviously true of civil society groups' treatment of states. For better or worse, public disapproval from members of civil society doesn't carry the same suggestion of illegitimacy as does public disapproval from a state's fellow states. How this affects the morality of civil-society-led interventions is an open question that the state-centric literature on the ethics of intervention isn't well placed to answer. What we need, then, is further investigation into when and why would-be interveners' obligations to recognize or treat a recipient state as legitimate preclude (or don't) the moral permissibility of their proposed intervention.

Intra-systemic intervention, on the other hand, seems clearly compatible with recipient institutions' legitimacy. This kind of intervention, after all, operates only via political channels recipient societies themselves have opened to foreign influence. This insight is not so much denied as it is obscured by the prominent literature's focus on interventions that interact adversarially with recipients' institutions.

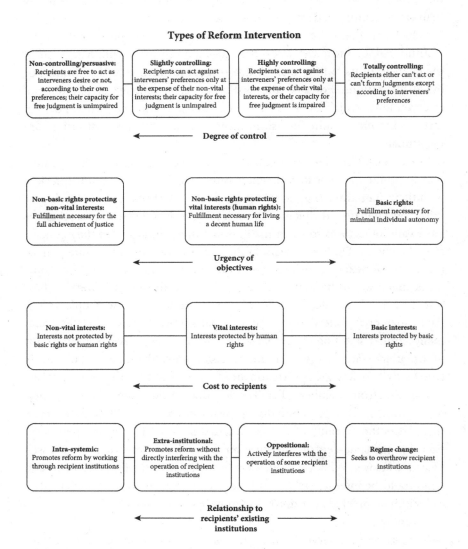

Figure 1.1 A typology of reform intervention.

A Note on Case Selection

The typology constructed above (and summarized in Figure 1.1) gives us a new conceptual framework within which to explore the moral questions raised by different kinds of reform intervention. It highlights the wide range of forms reform intervention can take—many of which prominent scholarship neglects. It gives us the resources to understand why different types of reform intervention aren't always subject to the same moral objections, and therefore why one type of reform intervention may be permissible when another is not (and vice versa). The following chapters take the typology as a starting point, drawing on it to determine when the different types of reform intervention it picks out are morally impermissible, permissible, or obligatory. Before jumping into this analysis, though, it's worth saying a few words about those real-world cases that figure most prominently in the book.

Some may worry that the cases introduced above—the central (though not the only) cases this book will concern itself with—don't constitute a representative picture of the goings-on in world politics. This is probably right but not, I think, a problem. Military intervention, for example, may be underrepresented in the cases I've discussed, compared to how often it occurs in the real world. On the other hand, interventions that rely on persuasion and education alone to accomplish their aims may be overrepresented here—as may interventions undertaken by actors with comparatively little geopolitical power.

My purpose in introducing the cases I have, though, is not to support an account of what intervention *generally* or *usually* looks like or what the average intervention that's actually undertaken looks like. Doing that would certainly require me to draw on a representative sample from the universe of actual cases. Instead, my purpose is to help illustrate the wide range of forms reform intervention can take, to highlight especially those forms under-treated by existing literature, and to introduce some empirical facts to help us understand more concretely both the moral problems posed by reform intervention and their possible solutions.

Some may object further that focusing on the cases I have will skew our normative conclusions about reform intervention, making us adopt an overly permissive attitude toward it. If we mainly discuss cases of reform intervention immune from (or at least less vulnerable to) the weighty moral objections often leveled against it (which are, after all, often leveled against state-led forceful and coercive interventions—precisely the types

56 PROMOTING JUSTICE ACROSS BORDERS

underrepresented here), we will end up mistakenly thinking reform intervention is *generally* immune from these objections. Again, though, I'd ask readers to remember the central aims of this work, as well as the context in which it's being put forth. I don't seek to give an account of what the average reform intervention actually undertaken looks like or how morally problematic it is. I seek to develop ethical standards to guide our judgments about the many different kinds of reform intervention there are—and especially to guide our judgments about the kinds often neglected in current thinking. Given this goal, it's reasonable to give special attention to the sorts of cases prominent literature on the ethics of intervention tends to overlook.

Readers should also remember that this book hasn't appeared in a vacuum but in the context of an already-existing literature. Viewed as a corrective to extant literature—which focuses on the most violent and risky types of intervention, giving the false impression that intervention is permissible only in exceptional circumstances—my focus on less violent and risky types of intervention is not misleading but illuminating. It will help us see that intervention is not always as dangerous (morally or otherwise) as we're used to believing. And, combined with the typology I've developed—which includes the full range of forms reform intervention can take and identifies their morally significant differences—my present focus will help us see precisely what kinds of intervention escape the usual dangers under what circumstances. I make no claims, however, about proportionally how often interventions actually do meet the standards I lay out, thereby escaping the usual dangers. In essence, I hope to develop an account of what kinds of reform intervention are permissible or obligatory under what circumstances. For the most part, I'll leave it to others to take positions on how often the standards I develop have been met in the past or are likely to be met in the future.

What *is* essential for my present purposes is that the cases I discuss (1) illustrate the different conceptual and normative distinctions my theory of the ethics of reform intervention relies on, (2) illustrate what it would look like to apply that theory to the real world, and (3) show that the theory can guide our judgments about many different kinds of cases. Thus, I've chosen focal cases that exemplify the different categories in my typology (e.g., the different levels of control interveners might exercise and the different ways they might interact with recipients' existing institutions), that span different regions and means of intervention (from persuasion to military force), and that involve different sorts of actors (e.g., states, NGOs, corporations, and activist networks). My analysis shows how one would go about applying my

BEYOND THE STATE, BEYOND WAR   57

theory to these cases, thereby demonstrating it can guide our judgments in the wide range of different cases they represent.

That said, one final caveat is in order. My training and expertise is in political theory, and this book's primary contribution is theoretical: a set of ethical principles to guide our moral judgments about reform intervention. When I apply these principles to a given case of reform intervention and reach a verdict about whether it is or is not morally permissible, the verdict is based not only on the theory but also on a certain interpretation of the empirical facts of the case. I fully admit to the possibility that my interpretation of the empirical facts of any given case may be contested or mistaken—or that new evidence or analyses may come to light over time, rendering my interpretation less plausible than it once was.[83] This would not, however, nullify the ethical principles I develop and defend, nor would it render my theory obsolete. If readers disagree with my interpretation of the salient empirical facts, they should not simply reject my principles. Rather, they should apply these principles to the case given the facts as *they* understand them. This book highlights certain moral questions raised by reform intervention and gives a theoretical account of how we should address those questions. One can disagree with how I apply this theory to a particular case without rejecting the theory itself.

Summary

The foregoing discussion has, I hope, illustrated several things. First, a recent proliferation of global political actors and of their capacities to exert influence beyond their own societies has transformed global politics, making it the site of important moral puzzles as yet unsolved—and in some cases unidentified—by currently prominent thinking on the ethics of intervention. Much of the literature on the ethics of intervention was written for a world in which states were the only actors on the global stage capable of carrying out interventions—or at least the only ones capable of doing so in ways that required moral scrutiny—and in which coercion and force were their primary means of intervention. But our world is not like that. Thus, received notions about the ethics of intervention cry out for reconsideration. If our ethical

---

[83] For a similar perspective on the limits of political theory and philosophy, see Blake, *Justice and Foreign Policy*, 5, 10.

58 PROMOTING JUSTICE ACROSS BORDERS

standards are to speak to actors in the real world of global politics—a world in which many different kinds of actors trade influence using many different means—they must address cases other than those in which states undertake interventions using coercion or force. The typology developed here will help us construct ethical standards sufficiently broad in scope.

Second, appreciating the full range of forms reform intervention can take and the moral issues each raises will also help us better understand what our natural duty of justice requires of us—when and how we are required to pursue justice in foreign societies. This is another use to which we'll put our typology.

Third, once we do appreciate the full range of forms reform intervention can take (again, by referring to our typology), we will find that some forms are immune to the standard objections leveled against intervention. The following chapters compose an argument to this effect. In fact, they will argue that it's generally the case (not only in emergency conditions but in the everyday circumstances of global politics) that at least one kind of reform intervention will be a permissible response to a given injustice. Sometimes reform intervention will even be obligatory. The upshot of these overarching conclusions is that the promotion of justice beyond one's own society is generally an acceptable, and sometimes a morally necessary, goal of global political contestation. In other words, the pursuit of justice is not something only co-citizens should undertake together. It is, and should be, humanity's collective project.

2

Toleration as Engagement

Introduction

According to conventional wisdom, international toleration requires people in different societies to stay out of each other's politics—and certainly to refrain from promoting their preferred conceptions of justice abroad.[1] Hence the first standard objection to reform intervention: that it treats recipients with intolerance. I'll call this the toleration objection.

Here, I'll assume a principled commitment to international toleration as a starting premise, but I'll argue that the conventional view of international toleration is deeply mistaken and encourages undue complacency in the face of global injustice. In this chapter, I develop principles to determine when reform intervention does and doesn't treat recipients with intolerance (and to identify those extraordinary cases in which even interventions that do so are, all things considered, justifiable). In so doing, I not only offer normative recommendations for would-be interveners; I also offer a distinctive vision of what international toleration requires, arguing that commitment to toleration as a moral ideal doesn't always preclude—and sometimes even generates reason *in favor of*—reform intervention.

The temptation to adopt the conventional view of international toleration is understandable. It has its basis in the historical settlement of Europe's religious wars (establishing that each people should be allowed to seek salvation in their own way) and in the intuitive idea that people in other societies have their own values, different from ours. Toleration, so the thinking goes, requires we leave them alone to pursue their values on their own.

Michael Walzer endorses the conventional view, saying international toleration is embodied in the concept of sovereignty, which "guarantees that no one on *that* side of the border can interfere with what is done on *this* side."[2]

---

[1] E.g., John Rawls, *The Law of Peoples with "The Idea of Public Reason Revisited"* (Cambridge, MA: Harvard University Press, 1999); Michael Walzer, *On Toleration* (New Haven, CT: Yale University Press, 1997); Michael Walzer, *Thick and Thin: Moral Argument at Home and Abroad* (Notre Dame, IN: University of Notre Dame Press, 1994).

[2] Walzer, *On Toleration*, 19.

Promoting Justice Across Borders. Lucia M. Rafanelli, Oxford University Press. © Oxford University Press 2021.
DOI: 10.1093/oso/9780197568842.003.0003

60 PROMOTING JUSTICE ACROSS BORDERS

Walzer suggests *any* attempt to limit a foreign state's sovereignty constitutes "intolerance," even if it involves only noninvasive tactics, like cultural boycotts or public criticism ("collective condemnation").[3] Elsewhere, Walzer holds that international toleration requires a multiplicity of different "tribes," each allowed to govern itself "within its own modest bounds."[4] He writes, "[T]his is the political equivalent of toleration for every church and sect."[5]

Rawls too endorses the conventional view, arguing that, to treat foreign societies with toleration, liberal peoples must not pressure them to adopt a liberal conception of justice.[6] Like Walzer, Rawls thinks even soft forms of foreign influence exercised to this end, like diplomatic pressure, financial incentives for liberalization, or (on some interpretations)[7] public criticism from a foreign state's government, constitute intolerance.[8] Unlike Walzer, Rawls thinks only societies meeting his standards of liberalism or "decency" deserve toleration.[9] However, Rawls still endorses the conventional view in saying that, to practice toleration, liberal peoples must refrain from pressuring other societies to adopt their preferred conceptions of justice. That he claims liberal peoples need practice toleration only in their relations with other liberal and decent peoples doesn't change this. Though not writing about international politics specifically, Godfrey-Smith and Kerr take up a position consonant with the conventional view, defining tolerance as a disposition toward non-interference and therefore suggesting, prima facie, that international toleration requires staying out of other societies' politics.[10]

I argue, against the conventional view, that practicing international toleration doesn't always preclude promoting justice in foreign societies. In fact, some reform interventions (which by definition aim at justice promotion) both treat recipients tolerantly and encourage (or at least don't discourage) tolerant treatment *within* recipient societies—and are therefore immune from the toleration objection. Ultimately, I argue for a novel account of toleration that I call *toleration as engagement*. According to this account, we can practice toleration even while (1) engaging with people in other societies. (2) in an attempt to change their behavior, (3) even if we do so to ensure they

---

[3] Ibid., 21–2.

[4] Walzer, *Thick and Thin*, 79.

[5] Ibid.

[6] Rawls, *Law of Peoples*, 59–62.

[7] For discussion, see note 31 in Chapter 3.

[8] Rawls, *Law of Peoples*, 9–10, 54–9, 61–3, 82–5, 92–3, 121–3.

[9] Ibid., 59–62.

[10] Peter Godfrey-Smith and Benjamin Kerr, "Tolerance: A Hierarchical Analysis," *Journal of Political Philosophy* 27, no. 4 (2019): 403–21, 405.

realize the full requirements of justice (as opposed to some more minimalist standard). Moreover, if we endorse toleration as a moral ideal, this sometimes gives us *positive reason* to engage with people in other societies in this way. In other words, commitment to toleration sometimes generates a reason *in favor* of reform intervention. More specifically, some reform interventions *both* promote justice in ways that also encourage recipients to treat each other more tolerantly *and* do so using tolerant means. In these cases, our commitment to toleration generates a reason in favor of reform intervention.

Contrary to the conventional view, my account of international toleration holds that there are some cases of engagement with people in other societies, meant to change their behavior, for which our commitment to toleration generates a reason. In some of these cases (those that constitute reform intervention), the engagement aims to make recipient societies more just. That justice promotion is its aim doesn't preclude a commitment to toleration from generating a reason for a particular intervention. Further, in some of *these* cases, the aim of intervention is to remedy a relatively minor injustice. My arguments for the thesis that our commitment to toleration sometimes generates reason in favor of reform intervention don't depend on the relevant injustice being especially severe. Thus, a commitment to toleration sometimes generates reason in favor of promoting justice in another society even if its present injustice doesn't drop it below, say, the requirements of Rawlsian "decency"[11] or Walzerian "thin morality."[12] Hence my conclusion: a commitment to toleration sometimes *gives us reason to* (1) engage with people in other societies (2) in an attempt to change their behavior, (3) even if we do so to ensure they realize the full requirements of justice (as opposed to some more minimalist standard).

Other critics of the conventional view have defended similar positions. For example, both Blake and Tan argue that the moral commitment (to individual autonomy) underlying our commitment to toleration gives us reason to pursue certain ends in foreign societies—to promote liberal policies that will protect individual autonomy.[13] Blake and Tan therefore avoid one main pitfall of the conventional view: encouraging complacency in the face of injustice abroad.

---

[11] Rawls, *Law of Peoples.*

[12] Walzer, *Thick and Thin.*

[13] See Michael Blake, *Justice and Foreign Policy* (Oxford: Oxford University Press, 2013); Michael Blake, "Tolerance and Theocracy: How Liberal States Should Think about Religious States," *Journal of International Affairs* 61 (2007): 1–17; Kok-Chor Tan, *Toleration, Diversity, and Global Justice* (University Park: Pennsylvania State University Press, 2000).

62 PROMOTING JUSTICE ACROSS BORDERS

However, prominent alternatives to the conventional view are plagued by two serious problems. First, they suggest that a commitment to toleration doesn't give us *principled* reason to respect foreigners' domestic political choices when (we think) they create injustice (though there may be other reasons to refrain from interfering with foreigners' domestic politics). This is troubling because we are fallible judges about justice. Recall the fact of moral uncertainty discussed in the previous chapter, which any credible ethics of intervention must take into account. When foreigners adopt policies we think unjust, this may be the result of a good-faith disagreement about justice—and we may be in the wrong. Part of acknowledging this is respecting others' political choices, even if they aren't the ones we would make.

The second problem with prominent alternative views is that they (like the conventional view itself) say little about the means by which we might promote (our ideas of) justice abroad. But the means used affect whether a reform intervention is compatible with a principled commitment to toleration. My account of toleration takes the question of means as central. And the typology developed in Chapter 1 perfectly equips us to investigate the moral significance of interveners' chosen means, thus allowing me to address normative issues that both proponents of the conventional view and its prominent alternatives largely overlook.

I argue, if we are committed to toleration as a moral ideal, this gives us reason to do two kinds of things. It gives us reason, *on the first order*, to ensure individuals treat each other tolerantly in their day-to-day interactions. And it gives us reason, *on the second order*, to pursue this end only in ways that themselves treat people tolerantly. Blake and Tan may contend that when we promote (liberal) justice abroad, we promote tolerant treatment (because individuals treat each other more tolerantly in more liberal societies). But they don't acknowledge that practicing toleration also requires abiding by the second-order constraint that, when intervening in another society, we treat its members tolerantly (*even if* we could more effectively promote tolerant treatment in their society by treating them intolerantly). So Blake and Tan get only half the picture. Promoting liberalism abroad may help ensure foreigners treat each other tolerantly, but this doesn't tell us whether the *means* by which this end is pursued themselves treat foreigners tolerantly. Not knowing this impedes our ability to determine whether a given attempt to promote liberalism abroad is morally justifiable. Blake and Tan miss something on the conceptual level (our commitment to toleration gives us reason to do two kinds of things) that renders their normative judgments unreliable.

My account of toleration remedies these problems. Moreover, my discussion of what a commitment to toleration requires on the second order—by identifying the specific means interveners must use to treat recipients tolerantly—shows how interveners can express respect for recipients' political choices (which they do when they opt for means that treat recipients tolerantly) without becoming complacent in the face of recipient societies' injustices.

My analysis of international toleration reveals that enacting a commitment to toleration on the global stage doesn't require simply leaving people in other societies alone but rather engaging with them in ways that both encourage (or at least don't discourage) tolerant treatment as an end and use tolerant means. Below, I'll argue that some reform interventions promote justice in ways that also encourage (or at least don't discourage) tolerant treatment in recipient societies and that use tolerant means. These reform interventions are therefore immune to the toleration objection.

I will also argue that even some interventions that *are* vulnerable to the toleration objection (i.e., that either treat recipients intolerantly or encourage intolerant treatment within recipient societies) are, all things considered, justifiable. After all, toleration isn't the only value, and it may be overridden in exceptional circumstances.

Showing that some kinds of reform intervention escape the toleration objection (and that others may be morally permissible despite not escaping it) constitutes one step toward discrediting the skeptical view of the natural duty of justice. Thus, this chapter begins to show that not all kinds of reform intervention involve the serious moral wrongs the skeptical view suggests: not all kinds of reform intervention involve unjustifiably treating recipients with intolerance. Furthermore, if this is right, our global duty of justice may give us reason to pursue the achievement of justice in other societies after all. Of course, to fully discredit the skeptical view more needs to be said about the other serious moral wrongs (besides objectionable intolerance) reform intervention might involve. This is a topic for future chapters.

In order to fully understand the normative implications of the natural duty of justice, we'll also need to say more about when (if ever) it *requires us* (rather than simply *permits us* or *gives us reason*) to engage in reform intervention. I'll discuss this issue at the end of this chapter, but this discussion, too, will develop fully only over the course of subsequent chapters.

64 PROMOTING JUSTICE ACROSS BORDERS

International Toleration as a Moral Ideal

Taking inspiration from Andrew Jason Cohen, I assume *practicing toleration* requires limiting one's use of power to change the behavior of others, despite disapproving of that behavior.[14] As Creppell notes, the view that toleration involves withholding one's power to avoid imposing one's judgments or values on another is widely held.[15] Thus, this assumption should be uncontroversial. Cohen adds two further conditions: first, to practice toleration, the agent withholding their power must do so *based on a principled commitment to showing the proper regard for the other's independent choices*.[16] Second, they *must believe themselves to have power to interfere further with the disapproved behavior*.[17] (Not exercising power one neither has nor believes oneself to have does not, on Cohen's view, count as practicing toleration.) However, I will leave aside discussion of these conditions. This is because I'm concerned with assessing the moral permissibility of actions, not the moral characters of actors (except insofar as this is determined by whether they act permissibly).

In particular, I want to determine what reform interveners would have to do in order to act in ways compatible with a principled commitment to toleration. To do this, reform interveners need not adopt any particular motivation. Assuming they act as a principled commitment to toleration would require them to, their intervention will not be rendered impermissible because it involves objectionable intolerance (it will not be vulnerable to the toleration objection). This is true whether or not interveners are actually motivated by a principled commitment to showing the proper regard for other's independent choices; and it is true whether they don't exercise certain powers over others because they consciously choose not to or because they can't (or believe they can't).

Perhaps interveners' moral characters would be more admirable if they consciously strove to show respect for others' choices or to forgo available avenues of exercising power over recipients, but, holding their actions constant, the presence or absence of these motivations is irrelevant to determining their actions' permissibility. Thus, even if one believes Cohen is right to include the two conditions listed above in the definition of *practicing*

---

[14] See Andrew Jason Cohen, "What Toleration Is," *Ethics* 115, no. 1 (2004): 68–95.

[15] Ingrid Creppell, *Toleration and Identity: Foundations in Early Modern Thought* (New York: Routledge, 2003), 3.

[16] Cohen, "What Toleration Is," 68–9, 79–85, 94.

[17] Ibid., 69, 72–3, 78–9, 93–5.

toleration, whether an intervener fulfills those conditions has no effect on whether their *actions* are compatible with a principled commitment to toleration. In other words, for the purpose of my analysis, *practicing toleration* is equivalent to *acting as one would if one were practicing toleration*, and I will treat them as equivalent from here on. So, for example, if geopolitically "weak" actors intervening in a geopolitically "strong" recipient state limit their exertion of power over the recipient state as toleration requires, the interveners act as one would if one were practicing toleration. I treat such interveners as practicing toleration even if the causal explanation for their restraint is that they didn't have the resources to intervene in a less restrained way in such a "strong" recipient state. The crucial point for my argument is that (regardless of one's motivations or other available options) practicing toleration involves limiting one's use of power to change another's behavior, despite one's disapproval of that behavior.

This raises the question: *how* must one limit the use of one's power to change another's behavior in order to practice toleration? Cohen—along with most people writing on toleration—answers that one must *not interfere* with the other actor's behavior in order to practice toleration.[18] Perhaps this is true about toleration considered as a purely "descriptive concept," but, I propose, it isn't true about toleration considered as a moral ideal.[19] A descriptive concept of toleration would define toleration in a way that was neutral among different moral values and that entailed no normative implications: saying some action was an act of toleration in the descriptive sense wouldn't imply it was good or (even pro tanto) the right thing to do.[20] But toleration considered as a moral ideal is not value-neutral or normatively inert in this way.[21] Practicing toleration considered as a moral ideal would mean doing something one has moral reason to do. Here, I'm interested in what the proper commitment to toleration as a moral ideal would give international actors reason to do on the global stage. So hereafter, when I refer to "toleration," I mean toleration as a moral ideal.

With this in mind, I return to the question of *how* one must restrain one's power over another's behavior in order to practice toleration *considered as a moral ideal*. My answer is that one need not (necessarily) refuse to interfere

[18] Ibid., 68–9, 85–7, 94.

[19] See ibid., 95; Peter P. Nicholson, "Toleration as a Moral Ideal," in *Aspects of Toleration: Philosophical Studies*, ed. John Horton and Susan Mendus (London: Routledge Taylor & Francis, 1985), 158–73, 161.

[20] See Cohen, "What Toleration Is," 95; Nicholson, "Toleration as a Moral Ideal."

[21] Ibid.

66 PROMOTING JUSTICE ACROSS BORDERS

with the other's behavior. Instead, one may sometimes interfere, but must interfere only in ways that are compatible with the moral reasons for practicing toleration. This is what it means for toleration to be a moral ideal that encodes commitments to certain norms and values.[22] The claim that practicing toleration requires restraining one's power simply by *not interfering* with a given behavior, no matter the reasons for or against interference, may be true about toleration considered as a purely descriptive concept. It cannot be true about toleration as a moral ideal, since practicing toleration as a moral ideal must mean doing something one has moral reason to do.

Perhaps further investigation will reveal there are no ways for international actors to interfere with the behavior of people in foreign societies in ways that are compatible with the moral reasons for practicing toleration. If that were the case, we'd be left with the conventional view—that international toleration requires people in different societies to stay out of each other's politics and refrain from promoting their preferred conceptions of justice abroad. However, I argue this is *not* the case; there *are* ways international actors can interfere with the behavior of people in other societies in ways compatible with the moral reasons for practicing toleration.

So what are the moral reasons for practicing toleration? The answer may differ in different contexts. The context I'm interested in is that of international actors interacting with people in foreign societies, so it is for this context that I propose an answer: we should practice toleration because all people deserve to be treated as if they're presumptively entitled to live lives that are the products of their own (freely made) choices, which reflect their (freely adopted or freely retained) values. In other words, everyone deserves to be treated as if they're presumptively entitled to live by their own lights.

This answer should be uncontroversial, because many prominent theorists of international toleration—even those who otherwise disagree with each other—endorse it in some form. This is clearly true of liberal individualists, like Blake and Tan, who see toleration as valuable because it enables, or insofar as it allows, individuals to live autonomously.[23] It is also true of more "communitarian" theorists of toleration, like Walzer. Though, on Walzer's view, we owe international toleration to political *communities* rather than

---

[22] My position resembles Nicholson's in "Toleration as a Moral Ideal," 169: "The moral ideal of toleration does not require us to put up with everything . . . we should reject whatever contravenes the moral base on which the ideal of toleration rests."

[23] Blake, "Tolerance and Theocracy"; Blake, *Justice and Foreign Policy*; Tan, *Toleration, Diversity, and Global Justice*.

individuals, he ultimately argues that it's valuable because it secures each individual's interest in influencing the common life of their particular political community (their interest in being constrained only by institutions that reflect their own choices and values).[24] Similarly, Rawls, though he takes decent *peoples* to be its primary subjects, justifies international toleration by arguing it's necessary to show the proper respect for their individual citizens.[25] He further suggests that decent peoples deserve toleration because they allow their members a significant role in political decision-making and because practicing toleration toward them helps ensure their members remain "attached to their political culture and . . . take part in its common public and civic life."[26] Thus, for Rawls, too, international toleration is justified with reference to the value of people living under institutions that reflect their own choices and values.

It should be uncontroversial, then, to say that international actors ought to practice toleration because everyone deserves to be treated as presumptively entitled to live by their own lights. Earlier, I argued that, to practice toleration, one must restrain one's power over another's behavior by interfering with it only (if at all) in ways that are compatible with the moral reasons for practicing toleration. We can now conclude: in the international sphere, this means practicing toleration involves restraining one's power by interfering with another's behavior only (if at all) in ways compatible with a commitment to all people (including the interfered-with party) being treated as presumptively entitled to live by their own lights. Since my subject is the ethics of reform intervention and when reform intervention is compatible with a commitment to toleration, I focus on identifying those cases where international actors *do* interfere with others' behavior, but where they nonetheless practice toleration because they interfere in ways compatible with a commitment to all people being treated as presumptively entitled to live by their own lights.

To signal its relationship to toleration, I will from here on refer to treating someone "as presumptively entitled to live by their own lights" as treating them "tolerantly." That said, anyone who objected to this terminology could replace "treating people tolerantly" with "treating people as presumptively

---

[24] Michael Walzer, *Just and Unjust Wars: A Moral Argument with Historical Illustrations*. 5th edition (New York: Basic Books, 2015), 53–4, 86–91; Walzer, *On Toleration*, 19; Walzer, *Thick and Thin*, 67–9, 79.

[25] Rawls, *Law of Peoples*, 61.

[26] Ibid.

68 PROMOTING JUSTICE ACROSS BORDERS

entitled to live by their own lights" throughout this chapter without changing the substance of its main argument: one can practice toleration while trying to change another's behavior, as long as one does so in a way compatible with a commitment to all people being treated as presumptively entitled to live by their own lights.

Note, treating people as presumptively entitled to live by their own lights doesn't mean always letting them do as they please. Not everyone who is constrained (e.g., by a law prohibiting them from doing what they desire) has necessarily been treated intolerantly. After all, presumptions can be overridden. Constraints need not count as "intolerant" if the balance of reasons recommends someone be constrained *despite* the presumption that they are entitled to live by their own lights, and if the constraints are imposed via a process that itself operates according to this presumption. I'll elaborate the latter condition in more detail below. For now, the important (and, I expect, intuitive) thing to remember is that practicing toleration does not require eliminating all constraints on individual behavior.

Note also, interveners who interfere with the behavior of people in another society can fail to treat the recipients of their interference tolerantly *even if* they ostensibly interfere in the name of values the recipients endorse. After all, recipients' judgments regarding how to behave in light of their own values deserve respect, even when interveners think different behaviors would better reflect those values. Interveners don't treat recipients as presumptively entitled to live by their own lights if they simply override recipients' judgments about how to live whenever those judgments diverge from the interveners' own. One consequence of this (elaborated below) is that reform interveners treat recipients tolerantly only when they use means that ensure their desired reform is enacted only if the recipients actually support it.

Some may object to my assumption that would-be interveners committed to toleration should treat the *individuals* in recipient societies tolerantly, proposing instead that they should treat recipient *societies,* considered as group agents, tolerantly. The objection continues: the way to accomplish this is to treat each *society*'s representatives in the international community tolerantly, which may or may not necessitate treating individual members of those societies tolerantly. For example, as highlighted above, Rawls and Walzer both think international toleration is owed to groups—liberal and decent peoples or political communities, respectively—each of which is represented in the international community by its government officials. One might interpret their views to say practicing toleration toward these groups requires treating

TOLERATION AS ENGAGEMENT 69

the *groups* (rather than their individual members) tolerantly. Since the groups are represented to the international community by their government officials, this requires treating these officials (considered as representatives of their respective groups) tolerantly.

In response, I'd point out that Rawls and Walzer think global political actors should practice toleration in their relations with the relevant groups (liberal and decent peoples, political communities)—and by extension the officials who represent them—because these officials in turn represent the individual members of their societies in a morally important sense. Rawls thinks a liberal or decent people's officials represent the people's members because they protect individual members' human rights and govern in accordance with a conception of justice that constitutes a reasonable account of the (members') public good, and because members have had the opportunity to contribute to officials' policymaking process.[27] Similarly, Walzer thinks a political community's officials can be said to represent the community's members because individual members have acted in concert to create the public culture the officials embody.[28]

My account of toleration leaves open the possibility that, when some official adequately represents the members of their society, treating individual members tolerantly can be accomplished by treating their group's representative tolerantly. As it happens, I doubt both Rawls' and Walzer's theories of representation—I'm not certain the officials of Rawls' decent peoples or Walzer's political communities really do adequately represent their societies' members. But that's immaterial at the moment. It is beyond this book's scope to argue for a particular theory of representation. The important point for now is that nothing in my account of toleration rules out an arrangement like the one Rawls and Walzer envision, where global actors practice toleration by treating the officials of sufficiently representative governments tolerantly.

Toleration: A Two-Level Problem

The previous section established that international actors can practice toleration even if they interfere (as reform interveners do) with the behavior

---

[27] Ibid., 62–80.

[28] See Walzer, *Just and Unjust Wars,* 54; Michael Walzer, "The Moral Standing of States: A Response to Four Critics," *Philosophy and Public Affairs* 9, no. 3 (1980): 209–29.

of people in other societies—as long as they do so in ways compatible with a commitment to all people being treated as presumptively entitled to live by their own lights (i.e., treated tolerantly). Imagine an intervener promoting some behavioral change in a foreign society. To practice toleration, the intervener must not discourage people in the recipient society from treating each other tolerantly. Additionally, the intervener must promote their desired change in a way that itself treats people in the recipient society tolerantly. This is because, to practice toleration, the intervener must act in ways compatible with a commitment to all people being treated tolerantly. If they discouraged tolerant treatment within the recipient society or promoted their desired change in a way that didn't treat recipients tolerantly, the intervener would clearly fail to meet this standard and would therefore not count as practicing toleration. So, given that an international actor has decided to engage in reform intervention, to practice toleration they must both (1) not discourage tolerant treatment within the recipient society and (2) intervene in a way that itself treats people tolerantly. Failure to do either would constitute failure to practice toleration.

Further, if a would-be intervener endorses toleration as a moral ideal, this gives them *positive reason* to promote certain kinds of reforms in foreign societies. When someone endorses toleration as a moral ideal, we can assume they endorse the underlying moral reason for practicing toleration: that everyone deserves to be treated as presumptively entitled to live by their own lights (i.e., treated tolerantly). This is part of what it means to endorse toleration as a moral ideal—rather than simply as a convenient convention or a pragmatic guideline. This means they have positive reason to help ensure people everywhere are treated tolerantly. And this, in turn, means they have positive reason to promote tolerant treatment, including in foreign societies.

That said, the second-order constraint, that international actors, including reform interveners, should promote reform in foreign societies *only in ways that treat the people there tolerantly,* still applies. This is true even in cases where an intervener promotes a reform that would encourage people in the recipient society to treat each other more tolerantly. This is because it is pro tanto objectionable for interveners to treat recipient populations intolerantly *even if* doing so brings about a world in which people treat each other tolerantly more often than they would otherwise. Every person has a claim to be treated tolerantly, and we have reason to pursue states of the world in which more people's claims to tolerant treatment are satisfied. But the fact that some action is an effective means to this end doesn't erase anyone's claim to be treated tolerantly in the meantime. Thus, we should generally treat people tolerantly even if not doing so could bring about a world in which people treated each other tolerantly more often. (The word "generally" here indicates there are cases in which we're, all things considered, justified in treating people intolerantly, though I won't discuss those cases just yet.)

Some ways interveners could promote first-order tolerant treatment may fail to abide by the second-order constraint that they treat recipients tolerantly, and vice versa. Consider a "benevolent conqueror" who forcibly implements a law that perfectly prevents intolerant behavior—without so much as a pretense of input or influence from those subject to it and against their vocal objections. In implementing the law, the conqueror fails to treat their conquered subjects as presumptively entitled to live by their own lights. That would *at least* require not forcing them to submit to constraints they had no say in designing or opportunity to contest. Thus, in imposing the law, the conqueror doesn't act in a way compatible with a commitment to all people being treated as presumptively entitled to live by their own lights, and therefore fails to practice toleration. Though preventing intolerant behavior is a worthy goal, if the conqueror is committed to practicing toleration as a moral ideal, they shouldn't pursue this goal via means that treat people intolerantly.

Similarly, we can imagine a political system that abides by the second-order constraint without promoting first-order tolerant treatment. Let's posit that abiding by the second-order constraint requires implementing first-order rules only after they've survived a sufficient amount of public scrutiny, such that those to be constrained by the rules have had some opportunity to influence their content. We needn't endorse a full account of what specific institutions would be necessary. But, as above, we can assume that treating people as presumptively entitled to live by their own lights (which is what the second-order constraint requires) *at least* requires giving them some input into and some opportunity to change those constraints limiting the choices actually available to them. Certainly, a political system could meet these criteria but still allow or even encourage first-order intolerant treatment. Take, for example, the US military's until recently long-standing policy "Don't Ask, Don't Tell" and some American states' continued attempts to allow discrimination against LGBT citizens. Indeed, citing North Carolina's elimination of local non-discrimination law, the same state's law requiring that transgender people use bathrooms corresponding to the sex they were assigned at birth, Mississippi's law permitting religion-based discrimination against LGBT people, and Tennessee's law allowing therapists to turn away LGBT patients

72 PROMOTING JUSTICE ACROSS BORDERS

as examples, Human Rights Watch reports that American "state legislatures introduced a record number of bills" limiting the rights of LGBT citizens in 2016.[29] (Though these examples are from the domestic rather than the international context, they still illustrate the possibility of establishing policies that encourage first-order intolerant treatment via means that nonetheless treat people tolerantly when considered independently of the ends for which they're used.)

Thus, accounts of toleration that focus on promoting first-order tolerant treatment get only half the picture. For example, adding in the second-order constraint outlined above serves to complicate some prominent liberal views, like Blake's and Tan's. They argue that the moral commitment (to individual autonomy) underlying our commitment to toleration gives us reason to promote tolerant treatment both at home and abroad, by encouraging and supporting liberal regimes (which encourage tolerant treatment) and reforming illiberal ones (which allow intolerant treatment) wherever they occur.[30] They say little, though, about the second-order question of *how (using what means)* we should support liberal regimes and oppose illiberal ones.

Below, I argue that, when interveners promote reform in another society, to abide by the second-order constraint that they treat the recipient population tolerantly, they must use means that ensure their reform is enacted only if the recipient population supports it. Importantly, I argue that abiding by this second-order constraint does *not* require interveners to refrain from persuading or incentivizing the recipient population to adopt reforms they (the recipients) don't *currently* support. Though abiding by the second-order constraint precludes interveners from *imposing* unwanted reforms on recipients, they can persuade or incentivize recipients to adopt reforms they wouldn't have adopted absent intervention *while still treating recipients tolerantly*.

Some may object that abiding by what I've called the second-order constraint isn't really a requirement of toleration. They may say ensuring that people subject to constraints have sufficient influence over their content is not part of the practice of toleration but is rather a matter of respecting some other value—like collective self-determination or legitimacy.[31] To this, I'd

---

[29] Human Rights Watch, "United States: Events of 2016," *World Report 2017*, https://www.hrw.org/world-report/2017/country-chapters/united-states#e81181.

[30] See Blake, *Justice and Foreign Policy*, esp. 43–4, ch. 3; Blake, "Tolerance and Theocracy"; Tan, *Toleration, Diversity, and Global Justice*.

[31] Thank you to Charles Beitz, Anna Stilz, and Bas van der Vossen for posing this objection.

say that the resemblance between what it looks like to treat people tolerantly (which one must do in order to practice toleration) and what it looks like to establish collective self-determination is no accident. On my view, one reason we have to value collective self-determination is a toleration-based reason. Specifically, our commitment to toleration as a moral ideal gives us reason to treat people as presumptively entitled to live by their own lights whenever we interact with them. Trying to constrain their behavior by instituting certain public policies is surely a way of interacting with others. Therefore, if we try to constrain others' behavior in this way, our commitment to toleration gives us reason to do so in line with the presumption that they're entitled to live by their own lights. And, as outlined above, this requires giving people some say over the content of the constraints to which they'll be subject. Constraining them without giving them a say would summarily disqualify them from making important decisions about how their lives will proceed; this would be incompatible with the presumption that they're entitled to live by their own lights.

This toleration-based reason is not the *only* reason we have to value collective self-determination, and enabling genuine collective self-determination may require more than treating the recipients of our influence tolerantly. My view doesn't entail that the values of toleration and collective self-determination are identical, nor does it conflate them. Rather, my view highlights one way in which they're connected: fulfilling one condition for collective self-determination (giving the people subject to constraints sufficient influence over their content) is also a requirement of toleration (we must do it in order to treat people as presumptively entitled to live by their own lights and, therefore, in order to practice toleration).

Similarly, objectors may say abiding by the second-order constraint is a requirement of legitimacy rather than toleration. Thus, we should criticize actors like the "benevolent conqueror" described above because their refusal to abide by the second-order constraint makes their political power illegitimate, not because they treat people intolerantly. In reply, I'd say it may very well be true that, on the correct theory of legitimacy, the "benevolent conqueror" is not a legitimate ruler. However, whether or not this is true is irrelevant to this chapter's arguments. I have argued that (at least in the international context) imposing laws on someone without giving them any say in the matter treats them intolerantly (and actors who impose laws in this way therefore fail to practice toleration in their relations with those subject to their impositions). This claim is not undermined in the least by the further claim that imposing

74 PROMOTING JUSTICE ACROSS BORDERS

laws on someone without giving them a say in the matter is also an "illegitimate" way to exercise political power.

With all this in mind, I'll now turn to the question of how reform interveners must behave in order to count as practicing toleration in their relations with recipient populations.

Toleration in Reform Intervention: Degrees of Control

Drawing on the account of toleration developed above and the typology developed in Chapter 1, this section argues that it's possible for reform interveners to practice toleration toward recipients even as they intervene— that some types of reform intervention are immune to the toleration objection.

Let us begin with *non-controlling* or *persuasive* intervention. Persuasive interventions produce change only conditional upon interveners' proposals being voluntarily taken up by people within the recipient population.

As noted earlier, Tostan's work in western Africa is a striking example of persuasive intervention. Though Tostan unapologetically advocates for significant social and political changes in recipient communities (ending child marriage, ending FGC, giving women prominent roles in community decision-making, and recognizing human rights, for example), it promotes these changes through educational programs, by encouraging community members to disseminate information to their friends and family, and by encouraging the formation of grassroots community organizing committees that may work themselves to pursue local sustainable development.[32] Though Tostan clearly has an agenda, its representatives don't simply impose it on recipient communities. Instead, preserving recipients' ability to live according to their own choices and values, Tostan seeks to convince them to make certain choices and adopt certain values. Indeed, Bicchieri characterizes Tostan as encouraging recipients to explore the implications of their own deeply held value commitments—an exploration that (at least sometimes) culminates in the conclusion that they should change some existing practice because

---

[32] Tostan's own description of their programs can be found on their website: *Tostan: Dignity for All*, http://www.tostan.org. For more in-depth information about Tostan in Senegal in particular, see Nafissatou J. Diop et al., "The TOSTAN Program: Evaluation of a Community Based Education Program in Senegal" (Washington, DC: US Agency for International Development, 2004).

TOLERATION AS ENGAGEMENT   75

they've determined it's inconsistent with those value commitments.[33] Tostan's curriculum was even collaboratively designed—having been revised early on in response to participants' feedback—and is centered around interactive learning, demonstrating a commitment to engaging with participants as autonomous agents rather than passive recipients of knowledge.[34] In fact, on certain occasions, Tostan has failed to achieve its aims because its representatives were rejected by recipient communities, demonstrating the conditionality of its success on recipient support.[35] Moreover, Mackie reports that the original impetus for trying to end FGC in one of Tostan's early client communities came from the community itself—not from Tostan.[36]

Persuasive reform interventions like Tostan's needn't presume recipients are incapable of making or unqualified to make their own decisions about how their lives should proceed. Quite the opposite: if recipients weren't presumptively entitled to shape their lives around their own choices and values, they wouldn't need to be persuaded. Thus, persuasive interveners *can*, at least, treat recipients tolerantly—thus abiding by the second-order constraint identified in the previous section, which they must do to practice toleration—even as they advocate change in foreign communities.

Arguably, Tostan's involvement in a community can also promote first-order tolerant treatment there by encouraging community members to empower each other to live according to their own choices and values. For instance, insofar as it helps limit child marriage and FGC and promotes other women's rights protections, it may increase the degree to which recipient populations enable women and girls to effectively make their own choices about their bodies, family life, and life more generally.

Admittedly, it is easier to maintain that a persuasive intervention is compatible with a commitment to toleration when, like Tostan's, it aims to engage a relatively broad swath of the recipient population at the grassroots level and to make social change conditional upon *their* acceptance. What if, instead, an

[33] Cristina Bicchieri, *Norms in the Wild: How to Diagnose, Measure, and Change Social Norms* (Oxford: Oxford University Press, 2017), 159–60.

[34] See Beniamino Cislaghi, Diane Gillespie, and Gerry Mackie, "Expanding the Aspirational Map: Interactive Learning and Human Rights in Tostan's Community Empowerment Program," in *Human Rights Education: Theory, Research, Praxis*, ed. Monisha Bajaj (Philadelphia: University of Pennsylvania Press, 2017): 198–209; Diane Gillespie and Molly Melching, "The Transformative Power of Democracy and Human Rights in Nonformal Education: The Case of Tostan," *Adult Education Quarterly* 60, no. 5 (2010): 477–98.

[35] Diop et al., "The TOSTAN Program," 35.

[36] Gerry Mackie, "Social Norms Change: Believing Makes It So," *Social Research: An International Quarterly* 85, no. 1 (2018): 141–66, 145.

76 PROMOTING JUSTICE ACROSS BORDERS

intervener persuaded a repressive elite in an authoritarian regime to adopt a reform that encouraged tolerant treatment in their society? There may still be grounds to call the intervention intolerant (with respect to non-elite members of the recipient population) despite its persuasive nature.

Imagine, for instance, that a foreign government persuaded the Chinese political elite to pass and enforce laws against discrimination based on sexual orientation and gender identity.[37] On one hand, this would promote first-order tolerant treatment within China by helping eliminate the intolerant behavior of would-be discriminators. Recall, though, that encouraging (or at least not discouraging) first-order tolerant treatment is only one thing our commitment to toleration gives us reason to do. It also gives us reason to do so in a way that itself incorporates the presumption that people are entitled to live by their own lights. As in the case of the benevolent conqueror, if the Chinese elite impose this (desirable, required-by-justice) policy (that encourages tolerant behavior) on their constituents without giving them any input or opportunity to reject it, they fail to treat the non-elite as if they're presumptively entitled to live by their own lights. Such is the nature of authoritarianism—even its righteous triumphs are also moral failures.

So the question remains whether the interveners who persuaded the elite to change their ways behaved intolerantly toward the non-elite of China. After all, though their intervention was *persuasive*, it persuaded the elite to impose a policy on the subjugated in a way that disregarded their presumptive entitlement to live by their own lights. The interveners were complicit in this imposition.

This may be true, but I propose it doesn't necessarily mean the interveners acted intolerantly. The interveners did act *through* a set of institutions that disregarded subjects' presumptive entitlement to live by their own lights, but there is a way in which the interveners might have done this without themselves behaving intolerantly. Namely, interveners could have done so in a way that subverted, rather than reinforced, elites' ability to impose policies on the general populace without their consultation or approval (i.e., in a way that subverted elites' ability to disregard their subjects' presumptive entitlement to live by their own lights).

---

[37] There have been some international efforts to change Chinese attitudes toward LGBT citizens. For example, the Dutch and French embassies and the Beijing American Center have hosted film screenings in China related to LGBT awareness and acceptance. See Tabitha Speelman, "Tiptoeing Out of the Closet: The History and Future of LGBT Rights in China," *Atlantic*, August 21, 2013, http://www.theatlantic.com/china/archive/2013/08/tiptoeing-out-of-the-closet-the-history-and-future-of-lgbt-rights-in-china/278869/.

Imagine there were a substantial popular movement within China in support of laws against sexual orientation– and gender identity–based discrimination.[38] By presumption, this popular movement would ordinarily have no way to effectively lobby elites to adopt their preferred policies. But if interveners are in a position to lobby elites on behalf of the non-elite, they may provide a channel through which popular preferences can exert influence on otherwise elite-driven policy. That is, instead of simply continuing the elite practice of imposing policy on non-elites without their consultation or approval, the interveners could co-opt typically elite-driven power structures in order to make them responsive to non-elite voices. They could embody a commitment to toleration on the first order by promoting a policy that encourages tolerant treatment, and on the second order by doing so in a way that accounts for (and induces recipient elites to account for) the recipient population's political views (thereby treating the latter as presumptively entitled to live by their own lights and, in turn, to have input into the content of laws that constrain them).

If, on the other hand, the interveners used existing power structures to impose a non-discrimination policy on the Chinese public regardless of popular sentiment, they would arguably act intolerantly—not toward the elites, whom they would have merely persuaded, but toward the public, whom they would have effectively constrained without allowing them any input into the nature of the constraints. Moreover, "popular sentiment" in such a case may include popular preferences about *who* brings on a particular political change. Imagine that the Chinese population favored the anti-discrimination laws interveners advocated but that they *opposed* foreigners playing any significant role in the laws' adoption.[39] In such a case, a foreign intervention that acted through non-representative political elites to impose these anti-discrimination laws would, I take it, treat the non-elite intolerantly—again because it would effectively constrain non-elites without allowing them the right kind of input into the nature of the constraints.

Note, this doesn't mean interveners should disengage from any political struggle the outcome of which recipient populations don't want to be determined by foreigners. Rather, it means interveners should prefer to engage directly with recipient populations (or sufficiently representative governments

---

[38] Though the government has been slow to act, there is arguably growing social support for LGBT rights in China. See ibid.; Human Rights Watch, "China: Events of 2015," *World Report 2016*, https://www.hrw.org/world-report/2016/country-chapters/china-and-tibet.

[39] I'm grateful to Anna Stilz for bringing my attention to this issue.

78   PROMOTING JUSTICE ACROSS BORDERS

authorized to act on their behalf) instead of engaging with non-representative elites. At least, interveners should wait to engage with non-representative elites unless and until they convince recipient populations not only to support the policies they advocate but also that it's acceptable for foreigners to play a significant role in bringing those policies about.

After all, if interveners try to persuade a recipient population directly (or through their sufficiently representative government), the recipient population retains the power to refuse whatever course of action interveners advocate. But this option isn't open to recipients when interveners engage with non-representative elites who don't respond to popular preferences. To put it in terms of our hypothetical, if interveners tried to persuade Chinese citizens directly to adopt some anti-discrimination measure, and Chinese citizens opposed either the measure or foreigners' involvement in its advocacy, they could simply refuse. But if interveners persuaded non-representative elites to adopt the same policy, citizens who opposed either it or foreigners' involvement in its adoption would have no way to refuse. Hence the conclusion that interveners' persuading a recipient population directly (or through their sufficiently representative government) to adopt a certain policy wouldn't treat them intolerantly, even when interveners' persuading non-representative elites to adopt the same policy would. So interveners should prefer to engage directly with recipient populations (or sufficiently representative governments authorized to act on their behalf), as opposed to engaging with non-representative elites.

In addition to guarding against intolerance, interveners' engaging directly with recipient populations (or their sufficiently representative governments) has another benefit: it reduces the risk that interveners will lend credibility to authoritarian regimes by treating them (erroneously) as their people's rightful representatives in international relations.

What we have come to, then, is the conclusion that persuasive interventions need not be intolerant. In fact, I argued above that, if they're committed to toleration as a moral ideal, reform interveners have reason to promote tolerant treatment in recipient societies *on the condition* that they do so in a way that itself treats recipients tolerantly (i.e., as if they're presumptively entitled to live by their own lights). This insight together with the analysis of persuasive reform intervention above yields the conclusion that reform interveners' commitment to toleration generates a reason in favor of persuasive intervention when interveners (a) encourage tolerant treatment in a recipient society and (b) do so by either by trying to persuade a representative segment of the recipient society to adopt some reform or by trying to persuade an elite to adopt a reform favored by a representative segment of the society (where what they "favor" includes their preferences about *who* achieves their preferred policy outcomes).

Above, I refer to a "representative segment" of the recipient society to acknowledge that recipients may disagree with each other regarding the reform interveners advocate, and on the assumption that treating people with toleration doesn't require enacting or encouraging reforms in their society only when they are *unanimously* endorsed. (Someone subject to a political reform they don't endorse hasn't necessarily been treated intolerantly.) I assume there's some way for a subset of a population to be sufficiently *representative* of the population as a whole, such that this subset could enact reforms applicable to the population as a whole without treating its members—even those who opposed the reforms—intolerantly. This assumption is widely shared; it is not unique to my account of toleration. Indeed, denying this assumption would mean affirming that any government doing anything not unanimously endorsed by its constituents is *necessarily* treating them intolerantly. So I'll continue with the assumption that it's possible for a subset of a population to be *representative* of the population as a whole. That said, developing an account of *representativeness*—for example, what a group would have to look like or do, or how it would have to be chosen, in order to be representative of the population from which it was drawn—is beyond this book's scope. My arguments here don't depend on a particular account of representativeness—only on the assumption that *some* such account is true. As such, whenever I reference a "representative segment" of some population, readers should feel free to interpret this phrase in light of their preferred theory of representation.

Precisely, then, commitment to toleration as a moral ideal generates a reason to intervene if the intervention meets conditions (a) and (b). Meeting condition (a) ensures the intervention promotes tolerant treatment in the recipient society, while meeting condition (b) ensures that, in so doing, it treats recipients tolerantly. As argued above, endorsing toleration as a moral ideal involves endorsing the underlying moral reason to practice toleration: that everyone deserves to be treated tolerantly. This, in turn, gives one reason to promote tolerant treatment for all people, including in foreign societies— albeit subject to the second-order constraint that one do so in ways that treat the subjects of one's influence tolerantly. Thus, international actors committed to toleration as a moral ideal have prima facie reason to intervene (including via reform intervention) in other societies when this will promote tolerant treatment there. They have this prima facie reason in virtue of their endorsing toleration as a moral ideal (which includes endorsing the underlying moral reason for practicing toleration: that everyone deserves to be treated tolerantly).

This doesn't entail that they should, all things considered, intervene in any given case. In fact, a commitment to toleration generates genuine (as opposed to prima facie) reason in favor of intervention that will promote tolerant treatment in recipient societies only *on the condition* that it uses means that treat recipients tolerantly. If an intervention promotes tolerant treatment, but does so in a way that treats recipients intolerantly (if it meets condition (a) but not condition (b)), a commitment to toleration generates a reason against it. Again, this reason may or may not be conclusive, as we'll see later.

Further, a commitment to toleration doesn't generate reason in favor of interventions that treat recipients tolerantly (that meet condition (b)) but that neither encourage nor discourage tolerant treatment in the recipient society. Interveners in such a case practice toleration because their influence is compatible with a commitment to everyone being treated tolerantly: they neither discourage tolerant treatment nor treat recipients intolerantly. However, a commitment to toleration doesn't generate positive reason *in favor* of intervention that doesn't promote tolerant treatment. Therefore, if an intervention meets condition (b), but neither encourages nor discourages tolerant treatment among recipients, then a commitment to toleration doesn't generate a reason for or against the intervention.

Recall also that, in order to practice toleration, interveners must not discourage tolerant treatment in recipient societies. Thus, a commitment to toleration generates reason against interventions that discourage tolerant treatment in recipient societies, even if they use means that treat recipients tolerantly (if they meet condition (b)).

All told, persuasive reform intervention can sometimes embody a commitment to toleration on both the first and second orders. The question remains, though, whether other kinds of reform intervention can meet these criteria. Take, for example, *slightly controlling* intervention—during which interveners impose some cost, but not an unreasonable cost, on recipients who refuse to adopt interveners' desired reforms. In such cases, interveners leave recipients able to act against interveners' preferences, but only at the cost of some non-vital interest.

TOLERATION AS ENGAGEMENT   81

Consider the case of the US-Oman trade negotiations described in the previous chapter. In this case, the US conditioned its signing a preferential trade agreement with Oman upon the latter's adopting several progressive workers' rights reforms.[40]

At the very least, we can say this intervention *didn't discourage* tolerant treatment in Oman. One might further argue that the intervention *encouraged* tolerant treatment in Oman. It's plausible, after all, that employers subjecting their workers to indecent working conditions (excessive risk or unreasonable working hours, for example) were impeding workers' abilities to live by their own lights, and that the intervention did something to remedy these conditions. However, what follows doesn't depend on readers taking this further position. For the purposes of our analysis, it's sufficient to say the intervention didn't discourage tolerant treatment in Oman. The remaining question, then, is whether the American intervention abided by the second-order constraint that it treat recipients tolerantly—whether it promoted its political goals in Oman in a way compatible with the presumption that Oman's citizens are entitled to live by their own lights.

I propose that it did. Oman's officials[41] were put in a position to choose between neglecting workers' rights, on the one hand, and signing a trade agreement with the US on the other. Put another way, they were forced to absorb a cost (the loss of an advantageous trade deal with the US) if they wished to neglect workers' rights. As noted earlier, Oman would certainly have been able to bear losing the trade deal. Oman's interests would be advanced considerably if it won the trade deal—because its economy was at the time heavily dependent on oil reserves, which were projected to potentially run out in the coming decades, and because a trade deal with the US would have allowed it to diversify its economy.[42] But the situation wasn't so grave that Oman had no choice but to agree to whatever terms the US proposed in order to secure a trade deal.

---

[40] Emilie Hafner-Burton, *Forced to Be Good: Why Trade Agreements Boost Human Rights* (Ithaca, NY: Cornell University Press, 2009), 146–9.

[41] I assume *arguendo* that Oman's political institutions are sufficiently representative such that we can take their officials' preferences to be the preferences of a representative segment of Oman's people. If we were to reject this assumption, the US-Oman trade negotiations would look more like the hypothetical pro-LGBT-rights intervention in China described above: the US would have been negotiating with a political elite that didn't represent Oman's populace, and whether the US treated Oman's people with toleration would depend on *their* attitudes toward the policies the US was incentivizing.

[42] Hafner-Burton, *Forced to Be Good*, 147.

82 PROMOTING JUSTICE ACROSS BORDERS

Thus, though the intervention did force Oman's officials to *choose* between maintaining a certain political stance on workers' rights and making a trade deal with the US, there is no meaningful sense in which they were forced to abandon this political stance regardless of their preferences—the paradigm case of intolerance. Note here the contrast with the Latin American countries subject to structural adjustment programs in the 1980s, which *were* made to adopt "free market" reforms regardless of their preferences because the cost of refusal was devastating economic collapse that would have endangered their populations' vital interests. Instead, Oman's officials were forced to rank their preferences, to decide which they valued more: maintaining a certain political stance on workers' rights or a beneficial trade agreement with the US. Both maintaining their political stance and accepting the trade deal were perfectly viable options.[43]

In general, making it such that someone must absorb a reasonable cost in order to act as they please doesn't constitute intolerance. (It doesn't constitute forcing them to live a certain way regardless of their preferences.) After all, treating someone tolerantly doesn't require making it *costless* to live however they like. Indeed, it would be difficult to understand what it meant to say someone valued a certain way of life if they were unwilling to accept *any* costs to continue it.

There is nothing, then, about the characteristic means of slightly controlling reform interventions that make them especially or inherently intolerant. Thus, we can apply the criteria laid out above for persuasive interventions to slightly controlling ones as well. Commitment to toleration generates a reason in favor of slightly controlling interventions when they (a) encourage tolerant treatment in a recipient society and (b*) do so either by incentivizing a representative segment of the recipient society to adopt some reform or by incentivizing an elite to adopt a reform favored by a representative segment of the society.[44] This means (among other things) that Walzer is wrong to suggest that incentivizing a foreign society to reform using economic sanctions is necessarily intolerant.[45] Similarly, Rawls is wrong to say the same about liberal peoples incentivizing others to liberalize with financial subsidies.[46]

---

[43] That is, Oman could have accepted either option without putting its citizens' vital interests or basic rights at additional risk, compared to the pre-intervention status quo. Of course, opting to neglect workers' rights would still have constituted an injustice.

[44] Again, if interveners incentivize a non-representative elite in the recipient society to adopt a particular policy over the recipient populations' objections (even if a representative segment of the population would support the same policy were it introduced by their compatriots), I'm inclined to think the intervention doesn't meet condition (b*).

[45] Walzer, *On Toleration*, 21–2.

[46] Rawls, *Law of Peoples*, 84–5.

TOLERATION AS ENGAGEMENT 83

Even given this, some might still think highly and totally controlling interventions must be intolerant. These interventions either literally force recipients to act in line with interveners' preferences, create a situation in which complying with interveners is recipients' only reasonable option (by making noncompliance possible only at the expense of some vital interest), or make recipients' compliance involuntary (by manipulating information or the psychological conditions to which they are subject such that they cannot freely choose to act in one way or another). Whereas persuasive and slightly controlling interventions promote change only on the condition that it's accepted by recipients freely acting on their freely made judgments (including, in the case of slightly controlling interventions, judgments about the costs they are willing to absorb in order to continue some practice of theirs, when multiple different such judgments would be reasonable), highly and totally controlling interventions circumvent recipients' ability to act or judge freely. These interventions effectively single out one option as the only reasonable option open to recipients, regardless of their preferences. Thus, the argument continues, these interventions are paradigmatically intolerant: they promote changes in recipient societies independently of recipients' preferences.

While this characterization is generally true, there are some circumstances under which highly or totally controlling interventions could be compatible with a commitment to toleration. Namely, if (a) they encourage tolerant treatment in the recipient society, (b**) they implement the will of a representative segment of the recipient population,[47] and (c) they don't manipulate the recipient population. Under these circumstances, interveners arguably behave just as a representative state would (having available to it the full range of violent and coercive means), taking into account the preferences of its citizens while enforcing its laws. As suggested earlier, as long as a state operates on the presumption that people are entitled to live as they choose (which at least means taking account, in some way, of their preferences as to how they should be governed), it may arguably constrain people's choices— even by violent or coercive means—without treating those people intolerantly. Similarly, interveners, if they are truly responsive to the input of those their interventions seek to constrain, may employ highly or totally controlling means without treating recipients intolerantly. Clearly, a highly or totally

---

[47] In this case, too, if a representative segment of recipients objects to *interveners* being the ones to impose a particular policy, interveners don't implement the will of a representative segment of the recipient population (condition (b**) isn't met).

84   PROMOTING JUSTICE ACROSS BORDERS

controlling intervention will be unnecessary to enact the will of the would-be recipient population when their own state is sufficiently representative. When this isn't the case, though, if interveners are more reliable enactors of recipients' preferences than the recipients' own state, the mere fact that they are outsiders shouldn't make us think them intolerant.

Some, like Walzer, may object that would-be interveners won't likely be able to accurately judge whether they'd be more reliable enactors of recipients' preferences than recipients' own states. Walzer argues that interveners generally won't have access to the kind of information necessary to make this determination: except in very extreme circumstances, such as when a government perpetrates genocide, enslavement, or mass expulsion, outsiders won't be able to gauge whether the government sufficiently represents its subjects' preferences, and therefore whether outsiders would do a better job.[48]

Walzer arguably overestimates the difficulty of getting reliable, "close to the ground" information about the preferences of people in foreign societies and whether they align with their governments' activities. Even in 1980, David Luban was right to criticize Walzer's dismissal of foreigners' epistemic resources, writing, "There are, after all, experts, experienced travelers, expatriates, scholars, and spies; libraries have been written about the most remote cultures."[49] His sentiments are probably even more true now, in the age of information.

That said, I take Walzer's basic point. It may often be difficult to reliably judge whether interveners would do a better job of fulfilling recipients' preferences than recipients' own states, especially given the unpredictability and potential gravity of a proposed intervention's side effects—which may be accentuated when the intervention is highly or totally controlling. Historically, interveners using highly or totally controlling means have often failed to enact recipients' preferences. Again, the structural adjustment programs of the 1980s—whereby the US, IMF, and World Bank imposed "liberalized" trade policy on recipient populations, often over local opposition[50]—are an illustrative case. One reason we should object to these programs is precisely that interveners essentially forced recipients to adopt interveners' desired policies against recipients' own preferences—thereby

---

[48] Walzer, "The Moral Standing of States," 209–29, 212, 216–8.

[49] David Luban, "The Romance of the Nation-State," *Philosophy and Public Affairs* 9, no. 4 (1980): 392–7, 395.

[50] See Richard W. Miller, *Globalizing Justice: The Ethics of Poverty and Power* (Oxford: Oxford University Press, 2010), 136–41.

TOLERATION AS ENGAGEMENT 85

treating recipients intolerantly. Far from denying this position, the view I defend here helps us make sense of it.

In fact, that I identify the IMF's and World Bank's exertion of control to subvert recipients' policy preferences as a morally distinguishing feature of their structural adjustment programs, and a key reason we should criticize them, allows me to account for the moral importance of geopolitical hierarchies in a way not everyone does. For example, Fabre's analysis of whether the IMF and World Bank were justified in conditioning aid to economically vulnerable countries (e.g., Bolivia and Tanzania) on the privatization of their public water systems hinges largely on whether this choice produced "egregiously unjust outcomes."[51] By contrast, my view explains why *the mere fact* that the IMF and World Bank took advantage of aid or loan recipients' extreme vulnerability in order to impose policies the recipients themselves opposed made the IMF's and World Bank's actions morally objectionable, regardless of how likely they were to produce good or bad consequences. My approach gives us the resources to criticize such exploitative uses of geopolitical power *as such*, without needing to evaluate the utility of their consequences.

Pattison also (like Fabre) underestimates the moral significance of interveners capitalizing on recipients' extreme vulnerability to advance their desired ends against recipients' own preferences. Since he thinks any offer that enlarges recipients' option set—even when they have no reasonable choice but to accept the offer—enhances recipients' freedom,[52] he's committed to seeing the IMF's and World Bank's conditional offers as freedom-enhancing. After all, these offers gave recipients an option (to avoid economic collapse by agreeing to interveners' political conditions) they didn't have before. However, this assessment obscures the way in which the IMF and World Bank leveraged their disproportionate power to get recipients to adopt their preferred reforms against recipients' own preferences—thereby interfering with recipients' ability to live by their own lights. For Pattison, like for Fabre, the most promising route to the conclusion that the IMF and World Bank acted objectionably is through an assessment of their intervention's aftereffects. My view, on the other hand, gives us the resources to criticize the IMF's and World Bank's intervention without

[51] Cécile Fabre, *Economic Statecraft: Human Rights, Sanctions, and Conditionality* (Cambridge, MA: Harvard University Press, 2018), 126.
[52] James Pattison, *The Alternatives to War: From Sanctions to Nonviolence* (Oxford: Oxford University Press, 2018), 141–2.

86 PROMOTING JUSTICE ACROSS BORDERS

tracing complex and contestable causal chains or evaluating dubious counterfactuals about how things would have played out absent intervention. On my view, this intervention was intrinsically morally objectionable because the fact that the interveners exerted a high degree of control over recipients to get them to act contrary to their own preferences means interveners treated recipients intolerantly.

To be fair, Pattison does consider one circumstance under which offers like the IMF's and World Bank's could be intrinsically morally objectionable—namely, when they are exploitative.[53] But even considering this, his account fails to identify all morally objectionable offers as such. This is because of how narrowly he defines exploitation. According to Pattison, exploitation occurs when the agent incentivizing some behavior takes advantage of recipients' vulnerable situation to offer less of an incentive than they would if the recipients were less vulnerable.[54] But interveners offering incentives can exert objectionable degrees of control over recipients even without engaging in exploitation so defined. Imagine that, had the recipients of structural adjustment programs not been teetering on the edge of economic collapse, the IMF and World Bank wouldn't have offered them loans at all. But seeing that they *were* so vulnerable, the IMF and World Bank saw an opportunity to leverage this vulnerability to get recipient populations to adopt neoliberal reforms against their own preferences. So the IMF and World Bank offered loans to incentivize recipients to adopt these reforms. On this description of the case, the IMF and World Bank didn't "exploit" recipients in Pattison's sense because they didn't offer recipients less—in fact, they offered recipients more—than they would have had the recipients been less vulnerable. But, as my account of toleration helps us see, the IMF and World Bank still interfered with recipients' ability to live by their own lights by putting them in a position where their only reasonable option was to enact interveners' preferences at the expense of their own. That Pattison can't account for the inherently objectionable nature of this action is a point against his view.

Ultimately, all this tells us that, while some highly and totally controlling interventions may, in principle, treat recipients tolerantly, there is a real danger that highly and totally controlling interventions will treat recipients intolerantly by making them adopt interveners' preferred reforms against

---

[53] Ibid., 142.
[54] Ibid.

their own preferences. We thus have good reason to prefer less rather than more controlling interventions, *ceteris paribus*. This is a preference that, as we'll see, there's plenty of other reason to adopt as well.

Moreover, highly and totally controlling interventions that manipulate recipient populations cannot treat recipients tolerantly. Manipulative interventions prevent policies from responding to or representing the freely made choices and freely adopted values of those constrained by them, because they prevent those constrained from making choices and adopting values freely. Thus, they promote political changes independent of the free choices and freely adopted values of people constrained by the relevant policies. In other words, they treat recipients intolerantly.

Before moving on, it's worth saying more about the requirement that interventions help enact policies approved by a "representative segment" of recipient societies, and what this means for interventions meant to advance minority rights. In particular, some may object that requiring interventions to be constrained by the will of a representative segment of recipient societies will preclude interventions meant to protect the rights of minorities not recognized by the population as a whole. This is a problem, the argument continues, because many cases in which we intuitively think reform intervention most appropriate will involve a need to protect minority rights. There are two main things to say in response to this concern. First, failure to meet the standards laid out above only means a commitment to toleration generates a reason against an intervention, not necessarily that it isn't, all things considered, justified. Thus, if a representative segment of people in a recipient society reject some measure for the protection of a minority's rights, an intervention advancing that measure could be justified even if it isn't compatible with a commitment to toleration (if the case is one in which the value of toleration is overridden, the conditions for which I'll discuss below).

Second, *persuasive* and *slightly controlling* interventions aimed at getting a popular base (a representative segment) of a recipient society to adopt a given policy treat recipients tolerantly even if the popular base doesn't support the policy pre-intervention. The idea is that, when interveners use persuasive or slightly controlling means, recipients will adopt interveners' desired policies only if they judge for themselves (albeit in response to external persuasion or incentives) that they should. In these cases, interveners can try to persuade or incentivize a popular base in a recipient society to adopt their agenda, but the popular base still gets to decide for themselves whether or not to do so.

88   PROMOTING JUSTICE ACROSS BORDERS

Thus, even if the intervention promotes a currently unpopular policy (such as protecting a marginalized minority's rights), it doesn't treat recipients intolerantly, because the decision about whether to adopt this policy still lies with the popular base.

This isn't so when interveners bypass means of popular control in implementing their desired policies—when they directly implement them using highly or totally controlling means or when they (as in the hypothetical case of LGBT rights in China) implement them via elite-run political institutions that aren't themselves representative. It is only in these cases, then, that practicing toleration requires interveners' ends to reflect the *already formed* will of a representative segment of the recipient society. In other cases—when they employ persuasive or slightly controlling means directed at a popular base in the recipient society—interveners can promote policies the base doesn't currently support, in the hopes of convincing them to change their views. Thus, while the standards laid out above may restrict intervention in support of minority rights somewhat, they by no means eliminate it as a meaningful option.

A New Account of International Toleration

The foregoing analysis of the implications a commitment to toleration has for the ethics of reform intervention yields a new account of international toleration, which I will call *toleration as engagement*. I've argued that practicing international toleration requires *not discouraging tolerant treatment in other societies* and *treating people in other societies tolerantly*. When international actors do both these things, they practice toleration, even if they also attempt to change the behavior of those in other societies. Moreover, I have shown that commitment to toleration as a moral ideal sometimes gives us reason to (1) engage with people in other societies (2) in an attempt to change their behavior, (3) even if we do so to ensure they realize the full requirements of justice (as opposed to some more minimalist standard).

The first aspect of toleration as engagement may seem unsurprising. After all, intuitively, one paradigmatic manifestation of toleration is people of differing beliefs peacefully coexisting, often engaging in dialogue. Some, however, do seem to consider the paradigm of toleration a kind of "leaving alone." Recall Walzer's characterization of toleration in the international sphere: it is embodied in the concept of sovereignty, which "guarantees that no one on *that* side of the border can interfere with what is done on *this* side."[55] Similarly, Godfrey-Smith and Kerr (though not discussing international toleration specifically) define tolerance as a disposition toward non-interference.[56] My view of toleration stands in opposition to these views and others like them: contrary to the conventional view, we should understand practicing toleration as a kind of principled engagement rather than as keeping one's distance.

Toleration as engagement also stands in opposition to views that characterize practicing toleration as a kind of engagement narrowly aimed at understanding others rather than changing their behavior. Oberdiek, for example, tends to characterize efforts to produce change in a culture[57] other than one's own as a sign that toleration has reached its limits.[58] But even in the case of persuasive reform intervention, arguably the least intrusive kind of reform intervention, the dialogue between interveners and recipients isn't merely exploratory. Interveners don't set out only to understand recipients' behavior—their primary aim being self-education, with intervention, in Oberdiek's words, as a "reluctant last resort."[59] Instead, interveners try to promote social change in line with a particular conception of justice. (If they didn't, they wouldn't be engaged in reform intervention.)

Another distinctive feature of toleration as engagement, then, is that it says we can practice toleration *even as* we try to change the behavior of people in other societies—if we seek to change their behavior so as to make it more tolerant (or at least not less tolerant) and if we do so in ways that treat them as presumptively entitled to live by their own lights. Seeking to change recipients' behavior isn't mutually exclusive with treating them tolerantly—and a commitment to toleration as a moral ideal may even give positive reason to seek such change.

This brings us to the third distinctive feature of toleration as engagement: it says not only that reform interveners attempting to produce change in other societies can treat recipients tolerantly (and can thus practice

[55] Walzer, *On Toleration*, 19.

[56] Godfrey-Smith and Kerr, "Tolerance," 405.

[57] See Hans Oberdiek, *Tolerance: Between Forbearance and Acceptance* (Lanham, MD: Rowman & Littlefield, 2001), 134–9. Oberdiek tends to use the term "culture" to describe the nature of the boundaries across which we ought to tolerate each other. I usually refer to "societies," because I am interested in what toleration requires of people in different political communities, regardless of their cultural identities.

[58] Ibid., 135.

[59] Ibid., 136. It is unclear whether Oberdiek means only forceful intervention, but the conceptual point still stands: dialogue-as-learning is toleration; intervention happens when you reach the limits of toleration.

90   PROMOTING JUSTICE ACROSS BORDERS

toleration in their relations with recipient societies), but that this can be true even if their interventions are based on and justified in reference to what Walzer calls "thick" moral judgments about recipient societies' practices, or judgments that those societies are unjust despite having already achieved a threshold level of justice (like Rawls' standard of "decency"). After all, none of my arguments for the thesis that reform interveners can practice toleration in their relations with recipient societies even as they intervene, or that a commitment to toleration sometimes generates reason in favor of reform intervention, has depended on the presumption that the injustice interveners seek to remedy is especially severe. Reform interveners who live up to the standards I've developed here treat recipients tolerantly (and the interveners therefore count as practicing toleration as long as they don't discourage tolerant treatment in the recipient society), even if they seek to remedy an injustice whose continuation is consistent with the recipient society being "decent" and living up to the requirements of Walzer's "thin morality." Thus, toleration as engagement opposes views that say interveners who try to reform a recipient society in line with a fully fleshed out theory of justice (as opposed to a less demanding standard like "decency" or "thin morality") necessarily treat recipients with intolerance.

The contrast is especially stark with Walzer, who, during his discussion of international toleration in *Thick and Thin*, says it requires a multiplicity of different "tribes," each allowed to govern itself "within its own modest bounds."[60] Walzer's understanding of these "bounds" rests on a distinction he makes between *thick* (maximalist) and *thin* (minimalist) morality. Thin moral principles are so general and abstract that even people who don't share broader cultural commitments can identify with and affirm them. A general commitment to "truth and justice," or an opposition to brutal oppression, for example, would be a minimalist commitment. Minimalist ideas are always contained and situated within maximalist ones—for example, full theories of what truth, justice, and freedom from oppression consist in—but it is only minimalist morality that Walzer makes the focus of international ethics. He argues that in times of crisis, minimalist commitments become salient, and people in different societies can identify with and support each other's struggles for upholding minimalist standards.[61] These standards, he

[60] Walzer, *Thick and Thin*, 79.
[61] For a brief summary of this position, see ibid., 1–6.

TOLERATION AS ENGAGEMENT   91

suggests, define the bounds within which the world's different "tribes" must operate in order to deserve toleration.[62]

On this view, it seems, as long as a society doesn't run afoul of widely held minimalist moral principles, it should be treated with toleration, which means outsiders should leave it alone to organize its own internal affairs. Attempts to change some law or practice in a foreign society based not merely on one's *thin* moral commitments but on a *thick* view about whether that society is adequately achieving justice (for example) appear to constitute intolerance.

One source of Walzer's skepticism toward reform intervention based on thick moral principles seems to be the idea that commitments to such principles arise only among people who share a common life—culture, language, history, customs, territory, etc.—and that people in general (people around the globe, people in separate political communities) don't share such a life.[63] Therefore, any attempt to induce a foreign society to conform to one's own preferred thick principles would constitute an imposition on people of a morality they couldn't possibly accept as their own. Not only would this constitute intolerance (because it would straightforwardly amount to preventing people from living according to their own values), but taking this project to its logical end—attempting to bring about worldwide conformity to a single set of thick moral principles—could only be credibly attempted by a level and kind of coercion that would be both morally condemnable itself and unlikely to succeed.[64]

There is, I propose, a threefold response to this worry. First, we would be mistaken to think only people who shared political communities could share thick moral commitments. Even accepting Walzer's position that these commitments (their content, as well as people's allegiance to them) are socially constructed by those who share a common life, we shouldn't think that *no* such common life is possible across borders. There are clearly cultural, linguistic, affinity, and interest groups whose memberships cross borders.[65]

Moreover, reform intervention of the kinds I've been discussing will, simply by occurring, tend to increase the degree to which interveners and recipients share a common life in the relevant sense. After all, intervention

---

[62] See ibid., 67–9, 79–81.

[63] See, e.g., ibid., 60–1.

[64] Ibid., 69.

[65] See, for example, Seyla Benhabib on the ubiquity of cross-border relationships and identities of various kinds, in her "*The Law of Peoples*, Distributive Justice, and Migrations," *Fordham Law Review* 72, no. 5 (2004): 1761–87, esp. 1769–76.

92 PROMOTING JUSTICE ACROSS BORDERS

will make it more likely that interveners and recipients will experience significant consequences as the result of each other's choices. Further, reform intervention constitutes a kind of public moral criticism. Insofar as it is tolerant, it involves a reciprocal exchange of information and ideas between interveners and recipients, which results (or doesn't) in some policy change, depending on *both* interveners' and recipients' contributions. In the case of persuasive intervention, interveners engage recipients as partners in dialogue, and their desired policies are implemented only if recipients endorse and adopt them as their own.

Other kinds of reform intervention that treat recipients tolerantly also involve a kind of exchange between interveners and recipients such that both sides influence the policies ultimately adopted in recipient societies. Recall, the slightly controlling interventions that treat recipients tolerantly produce interveners' desired policy changes only if recipients agree to them (which they remain free not to do). And highly or totally controlling interventions that treat recipients tolerantly only advance policies favored by a representative segment of the recipient population. To ensure this, interveners must gather information from recipients about their values and policy preferences, and then work to see them instantiated in political institutions. If interveners wish to promote a policy contrary to recipients' values or preferences, they must (in order to treat recipients tolerantly) first get recipients to adopt different values or preferences. Tolerant reform intervention thus creates an occasion for interveners and recipients to reflect, together, on what justice requires and how it should be implemented. Reform intervention isn't always a rash attempt to uniformly impose a set of moral principles on otherwise disconnected people, because it can actually *facilitate* the development of shared moral concepts and language and a shared moral world.

This leads us to a second response, which is that (as I've been arguing) not all kinds of reform intervention amount to an imposition on others of practices and values they cannot accept as their own. Indeed, when it meets the standards laid out above (encouraging, or at least not discouraging, tolerant treatment in recipient societies and treating recipients tolerantly), reform intervention is not merely an "imposition." Persuasive intervention in particular constitutes an attempt to convince people to act on a particular view about how justice requires them to behave. It is precisely an attempt to persuade them to adopt certain reforms on the condition that they *can* accept them as their own. The fact that the persuaders are foreign or that they advance a view about what "thick" morality prescribes does nothing to change

TOLERATION AS ENGAGEMENT 93

this. We can apply similar logic to the other types of reform intervention I've argued are compatible with a commitment to toleration. When interveners limit the changes they actually produce in recipient societies to those supported by recipient populations (though they may *encourage* changes not supported by recipient populations without forcing recipients to adopt those changes), they signal that they respect recipients' own assessments of what policies should govern their society.

Interveners' refusal to forcibly impose policies rejected by a representative segment of recipient populations indicates, again, that their attempts to promote change are conditioned on recipients being able to accept that change as reflecting their own preferences. Thus, we should reject the view that any intervention motivated by thick moral commitments is intolerant because it must constitute an imposition on recipients of practices or values they can't recognize as their own. To the contrary, if a reform intervention meets the criteria developed here, its results will in a very real way reflect recipients' own preferences.

Third, Walzer is surely right that enforcing adherence to a single conception of justice worldwide, if it were even possible, would require a frightening and perhaps unsustainable level of coercion on the part of currently weak or nonexistent global institutions. However, thinking reform intervention is sometimes compatible with a commitment to toleration—and could sometimes be justified—does not commit us to thinking a single conception of justice should be forcibly imposed on everyone the world over.

True, advocating reform intervention may commit us to the view that deciding and implementing what justice requires is a project even people who don't share political communities should undertake jointly. Indeed, assuming there is a natural duty of justice requiring all persons to support just institutions where they exist and help establish them where they don't, showing that some kinds of reform intervention are impervious to the usual objections—for example, showing that they don't involve intolerance—goes some way toward showing reform intervention can be a morally permissible way to discharge our natural duty. If this is the case, we may also sometimes be morally *required* to engage in reform intervention—if, for instance, it is both morally permissible and the most effective way to fulfill our natural duty of justice. Similarly, citizens might be morally required to open up their political communities to certain kinds of reform intervention, making official political channels available for some forms of justice-promoting foreign influence—if they can do so without suffering unreasonable costs and

94 PROMOTING JUSTICE ACROSS BORDERS

if doing so will help them better discharge their natural duty of justice by supporting the emergence of (more) just institutions in their own society.

I'll discuss the nature and extent of these moral requirements at greater length later on in the book. But for now, it suffices to say that even accepting there are such requirements doesn't commit us to the view that anyone who has the insight to perceive the one "true" conception of justice also has the right to enforce global compliance with it by any means and at any cost. This is surely a position we should reject, but it isn't entailed—or even suggested— by the views I've defended here. In fact, one major contribution of this book is to show that there are significant moral constraints on how anyone ought to pursue justice on the global stage, *even assuming* they're right about what justice requires, and to give an account of what these constraints are. If it were true that anyone with the correct view of justice were morally permitted to promote it by any means necessary and at any cost, we wouldn't need an ethics of reform intervention like the one I develop here. If this were true, any effort (perhaps any successful effort) to implement the true conception of justice would be morally justified, and the questions I address regarding which *ways* of promoting justice are or aren't permissible wouldn't even arise. Thus, if anything, the present work is premised on the assumption that even someone who knows what justice *really* requires doesn't have the right to enforce global compliance with its requirements by any means and at any cost.

Some may further object to toleration as engagement, warning that it perverts the value of toleration—meant to safeguard people's freedom to make diverse choices about the course of their lives—making it into the tool of those who would brazenly replace the central norms and practices of others' communities with those of their own. To alleviate this worry, I suggest we recall the limited range of reforms a commitment to toleration gives interveners reason to pursue—those that reduce *intolerant* practices, thus allowing *more* room for the development of individuals' diverse life plans, and that use tolerant means in pursuit of this end. Additionally, an account of toleration that distinguishes between tolerant and intolerant attempts at promoting social change in foreign societies may constrain (not only encourage) would-be interveners. After all, if we are convinced that any attempt at producing change in another society is intolerant—or that it occurs in a social space without toleration, beyond the "limits" of toleration—we may be more inclined to think, once we decide such change is necessary, that any means of producing it will show an equal (lack of) respect for recipients' ability to live by their own lights. If, once we decide change is needed, we are already

TOLERATION AS ENGAGEMENT 95

beyond the limits of toleration, no way of bringing about that change can be considered any more or less tolerant. If, on the other hand, we recognize that a commitment to toleration is compatible with *some* but not other ways of bringing change, we will have a principled basis on which to critique those means that don't allow people constrained by the proposed changes to give their input or approval. If toleration is still "on the table" as a legible standard we can use to evaluate change promotion, we can call these means "intolerant." If we've written off all change promotion as intolerant, though, we will have to look elsewhere for a principled reason to distinguish between means that account for the preferences of those to be constrained by new policies and those that don't.[66]

Overall, this examination of reform intervention has left us with a new, distinctive account of toleration: toleration as engagement. On this view, toleration doesn't simply require leaving alone those who engage in practices to which we object, nor does it require that we engage with them only in order to understand or come to appreciate the value in their activities. Instead, a commitment to toleration on this understanding is compatible with—and in fact gives us positive reason for—trying to get others to change their ways, as long as this is done toward the right end (getting others to behave more tolerantly themselves) and via the right means (tolerant means, which are responsive to the preferences of those whose behavior is to be changed). Further, if such an attempt to produce change is based on a "thick" moral commitment, or promotes justice in a society that has already reached the threshold of "decency," this does not make it intolerant.

Contrary to the conventional view, toleration as engagement says that a commitment to toleration sometimes gives us reason to (1) engage with people in other societies (2) in an attempt to change their behavior, (3) even if we do so to ensure they realize the full requirements of justice (as opposed to some more minimalist standard). Since this account of toleration illustrates how interveners can advocate for justice in other societies without treating recipients intolerantly, it avoids the main pitfall of the conventional view: that it encourages undue complacency in the face of global injustice.

As noted earlier, other alternatives to the conventional view also avoid encouraging complacency by arguing that a principled commitment to

---

[66] G. E. M. Anscombe notes a parallel concern with pacifism—that its denial of any moral difference between limited and undiscriminating violence encourages those who think they can't avoid violence altogether to engage in the latter rather than the former—in her "War and Murder," in *Nuclear Weapons and Christian Conscience*, ed. Walter Stein (London: Merlin Press, 1961): 47–62, 56.

96 PROMOTING JUSTICE ACROSS BORDERS

toleration is compatible with promoting justice abroad.[67] But this comes at a cost—denying we have principled reason to respect foreigners' domestic political choices, even when (we think) they create injustice. These alternative views argue that toleration doesn't give us principled reason to show such respect (though there may be other reasons to refrain from interfering with foreigners' domestic politics). My view, on the other hand, explains how we can avoid complacency without abandoning our principled respect for foreigners' political choices.

Indeed, when interveners follow the standards I've outlined here—when they use only means that treat recipients tolerantly—they express respect for whatever support recipients show toward their own existing political arrangements, *even as* the interveners try to reform those arrangements. Thus, my view allows me to maintain the position—which Blake[68] abandons—that it matters morally whether a local population supports their current political arrangements, *even if these arrangements don't achieve liberal democratic equality*. In other words, the presence or absence of local support can change how outsiders ought to treat even inegalitarian, illiberal regimes—and this is true for principled, not merely prudential, reasons. Further, I can maintain this position *without* denying that conscientious people should oppose injustice and inequality wherever it occurs. Blake worries that if we accept that local populations' support of their inegalitarian political arrangements is "worthy of our principled respect," we'll have to deny that "[w]e [as foreigners] have reason to speak out against this sort of injustice."[69] But my account of toleration shows otherwise. When reform interveners treat recipients tolerantly, they show respect for recipients and the choices they make for themselves about their own political arrangements. Thus, by showing that reform interveners can (when they use certain means) treat recipients tolerantly, I show how foreigners can demonstrate principled respect for locals' choices to support their illiberal regimes *all the while* speaking and acting against those regime's injustices. This allows us to avoid the twin dangers of discounting recipients' legitimate interests in designing their own political arrangements, and complacency in the face of injustice.[70]

---

[67] E.g., Blake, *Justice and Foreign Policy*; Blake, "Tolerance and Theocracy"; Tan, *Toleration, Diversity, and Global Justice*.

[68] Michael Blake, "Justice and Foreign Policy: A Reply to My Critics," *Ethics & International Affairs* 29, no. 3 (2015): 301–14, 308–13.

[69] Ibid., 313.

[70] For discussion, see ibid., 308–13; Anna Stilz, "Against Democratic Interventionism," *Ethics & International Affairs* 29, no. 3 (2015): 259–68.

My account (unlike Blake's) recognizes both the moral importance of a population supporting its regime (even if it's unjust) and of opposing injustice abroad (even if it enjoys local support).

Toleration as engagement's two-level structure[71] also gives us the resources to determine both what *end* a commitment to toleration gives interveners reason to pursue in recipient societies—encouraging tolerant treatment there—and by what *means* they should pursue this end: those that treat recipients tolerantly. (By definition, reform interveners always pursue justice promotion, but, as above, I assume some justice-enhancing reforms also encourage tolerant treatment in recipient societies. Commitment to toleration generates reason for interveners to pursue *these particular reforms,* whatever other reasons they may have to pursue justice-promotion more generally.) This allows us to move beyond the deceptively simple question of *whether* reform intervention is compatible with a commitment to toleration and to answer the more complex and politically salient question of *what specific kinds of cross-border political engagement* are compatible with this commitment.

According to toleration as engagement, practicing toleration doesn't require simply staying out of other societies' politics. On the contrary, commitment to toleration as a moral ideal sometimes argues in favor of reform intervention. When foreigners advocate reforms that encourage recipients to treat each other tolerantly, and when they ensure the content of the reforms adopted is sufficiently responsive to recipient populations' input, they treat recipients as if they're presumptively entitled to live by their own lights and encourage recipients to treat each other as such—thereby fulfilling the core requirements of international toleration. Rethinking toleration as engagement, rather than as leaving alone, reveals that we need not turn away from other societies' injustices to properly respect their members.

Toleration in Reform Intervention: Urgency and Cost

Of course, deciding whether an intervention is compatible with a commitment to toleration doesn't tell us whether it is, all things considered, justified. Toleration is not the only value, and it must sometimes be traded off

---

[71] Godfrey-Smith and Kerr, "Tolerance" also proposes a two-level account of toleration, but it doesn't account for the fact that interference with another's behavior can be more or less tolerant because of the means one employs.

98 PROMOTING JUSTICE ACROSS BORDERS

against others. The metrics I have developed for evaluating the urgency of an intervention's objectives and its potential costs to recipients will help us decide when, if ever, reform interventions are justified even when a commitment to toleration generates reason against them.

For example, treating people with intolerance may be easier to justify when they engage in behavior so clearly repugnant that anyone who defends or undertakes it is guilty of a clear moral error. We might think, for instance, reform intervention against a government on the verge of committing genocide would be justified even if interveners discouraged tolerant treatment among recipients[72] or used means that treated recipients intolerantly. We might think this especially true when interveners could stop the impending atrocity without subjecting recipients to comparable harms. Avoiding a massive loss of human life or preventing the eradication of a particular ethnocultural group—especially when this can be done at relatively little cost—is arguably more important than practicing toleration. Given this insight, it is tempting to claim that the more urgent an intervention's objectives, and the better the trade-off between their urgency and the intervention's likely costs, the more intolerant it can be, while still being, all things considered, justified.

It is important, though, that we not overlook the normative significance of the fact that people disagree about how urgent any particular objective of a proposed intervention is and about how costly the intervention is likely to be. This may be because they disagree about the conditions on the ground in a recipient society or the probable consequences of intervention, or because they agree about these conditions and predictions but disagree about their moral importance (i.e., about whether they constitute urgent problems or morally significant costs). This disagreement is normatively important, first, because it may lower the confidence interveners can justifiably place in their judgments of urgency and cost. Moreover, if interveners pursuing sufficiently urgent objectives at sufficiently little cost may be permitted to treat recipients intolerantly (i.e., to disregard recipients' preferences about which policies they are subject to and which practices they take part in), then we

---

[72] It is perhaps unlikely that a genuinely justice-promoting reform intervention would discourage tolerant treatment among recipients. However, this is not *impossible*. One could imagine a scenario like the one described above, of impending genocide, where interveners could most effectively prevent the atrocity by encouraging intolerant treatment of the would-be perpetrators. Moreover, there certainly may be interventions *presented as* justice-promoting interventions, even if they don't actually promote justice, that discourage tolerant treatment among recipients. As I argued earlier, we have good reason to treat all interventions *presented as* justice-promoting as reform interventions, and to want our principles to guide us in assessing their permissibility. For these reasons, I don't rule out the possibility of a reform intervention that discourages tolerant treatment among recipients.

TOLERATION AS ENGAGEMENT 99

ought to be concerned about cases in which interveners and recipients disagree about the relative urgency and cost of a proposed intervention. After all, interveners should *generally* practice toleration and should *generally* treat recipients tolerantly because they ought to treat recipients' claims about how their own lives, institutions, and practices should be organized as weighty. This would mean little, however, if interveners were permitted simply to disregard the value of toleration (and therefore disregard recipients' claims) whenever they alone asserted the stakes were high enough.

Thus, Pattison's suggestion that interveners can show recipients proper respect simply by sufficiently accounting for (interveners' interpretation of) their interests in interveners' own deliberations is mistaken.[73] Granted, sufficiently accounting for recipients' interests is *one thing* interveners must do to treat recipients with proper respect. This follows from my analysis in Chapter 1 of what it means to treat others as our moral equals. But interveners must also practice toleration in their relations with recipients, unless something other than interveners' own discretion indicates that they find themselves in one of the exceptional circumstances in which the value of toleration is overridden. To illustrate why, consider: one reason interveners should treat recipients tolerantly (where treating recipients tolerantly is one element of practicing toleration) is that interveners should limit their interference so its effects are at least partially determined by recipients' preferences. But if interveners can permissibly disregard the requirements of toleration at will, this won't be accomplished.

How, then, should we go about determining whose judgments regarding urgency and cost should take precedence under what conditions? Recall that our interest in asking this question is determining when interveners are permitted to disregard a concern for toleration—that is, determining when intervention may be permissible[74] despite discouraging tolerant treatment among recipients or itself treating recipients intolerantly.

A reform intervention that a commitment to toleration generates reason *against*, according to the criteria we have laid out, is one that discourages

---

[73] See Pattison, *The Alternatives to War*, 48–50. Here, Pattison discusses only a small range of cases (where interveners use economic sanctions to avert atrocities or stop significant military aggression), but his underlying ideas could have implications for other kinds of intervention, too.

[74] I say we want to determine when an intervention "may be" permissible, because the goal of this section is to discover when toleration gives reasons against an intervention (the intervention is intolerant), but those reasons aren't decisive (the intervention isn't impermissible *because* it's intolerant). That said, there may be other reasons against intervention, unrelated to toleration, that make a given intervention impermissible.

100 PROMOTING JUSTICE ACROSS BORDERS

tolerant treatment among recipients, manipulates the recipient population, and/or implements (via highly or totally controlling means or via an unrepresentative political elite in the recipient society) a policy not desired by a representative segment of the recipient population. Our question is when this might be justified. Our germ of an answer is that when the trade-off between the urgency of the problems the intervention will address and its expected costs to the recipients is good enough, the intervention may be justified irrespective of its intolerance.

But this leaves open an important question that we must answer if we seek to develop a set of principles potential interveners can use to decide when and how to intervene—and that the rest of us can use to evaluate interveners' actions. Namely, when interveners' and recipients' judgments about the urgency-cost trade-off differ, under what conditions can interveners defensibly conclude their own judgments to be decisive such that they can permissibly override the value of toleration and may permissibly intervene, opposition of the recipient population notwithstanding?

I propose interveners may permissibly intervene in ways that discourage tolerant treatment among recipients or treat recipients intolerantly only under a narrow set of circumstances. Specifically, (i) the proposed intervention must protect either basic rights or vital interests; (ii) the urgency of the objectives it will predictably achieve must exceed the costs it will predictably impose on recipients; and (iii) interveners must be justifiably confident that their judgments that the intervention meets conditions (i) and (ii) would hold even for those who don't share their predictable biases. (I will sometimes refer to those unlikely to share interveners' predictable biases as "epistemically diverse" actors.)

The hypothetical foreign attempt to persuade a non-representative Chinese political elite to adopt anti-discrimination laws protecting LGBT populations could meet conditions (i)–(iii), depending on the exact content of the laws. After all, the interest in having an adequate range of options with respect to marriage and family life is a vital interest. Laws that enable LGBT persons to pursue romantic relationships without fear of reprisal protect this interest. Arguably, a persuasive intervention aimed at Chinese political officials would be unlikely to endanger either basic or vital interests (though in a real, as opposed to hypothetical, case this would be an empirical question). And that people should be immune from discrimination based on their sexual orientation or gender identity is relatively widely—though certainly not universally—accepted. This position has been affirmed by multiple human rights treaty bodies and is considered part of international human rights law.[75]

The three-part standard proposed here conforms to the intuition that toleration may be overridden when those being treated with intolerance are behaving in ways that constitute clear moral errors according to a wide variety of moral views. Since people's basic rights and vital interests must be protected in order for them to enjoy even minimal levels of individual autonomy and to live even minimally decent human lives, there can't be reasonable disagreement about whether people are morally entitled to have these rights and interests protected.[76] Nor will there be reasonable disagreement about whether action should be taken to protect basic rights or vital interests when this can be accomplished without risking any comparable harm.[77] Thus, interventions meeting conditions (i) and (ii) will target only behaviors that constitute clear moral errors.

The inclusion of condition (iii) addresses the potential problem flagged earlier—of interveners being able to permissibly disregard the value of toleration at will. Condition (iii) essentially requires that interveners be *justifiably* confident in their own estimations of the urgency-cost trade-off for a given intervention in order to override toleration. Acquiring this justifiable confidence requires interveners to account for their predictable biases, taking care to ensure their judgments aren't parochial in the sense of simply reflecting interveners' particular idiosyncratic mindsets, interests, or political contexts. Thus, interveners may not simply assert that the urgency-cost trade-off justifies intolerant intervention in order to permissibly disregard toleration. Instead, they must be able to show that this judgment would remain justifiable even to those who didn't share their predictable biases.

---

[75] United Nations Free and Equal, "Factsheet: International Human Rights Law and Sexual Orientation & Gender Identity," accessed 23 September 2018, https://www.unfe.org/wp-content/uploads/2018/05/International-Human-Rights-Law-English.pdf.

[76] I can't fully defend a particular account of "reasonableness" here, but the general idea is that having one's basic rights protected and vital interests attended to is necessary for living out a wide variety (virtually all kinds) of life plans, independent of the specific goals and values in which they consist. Thus, even people with widely varying practical and value commitments should be able to agree on the importance of basic rights and vital interests.

[77] I don't mean to suggest there isn't controversy over whether outsiders should make protecting these rights and interests their business. That is indeed controversial, and it's the question I'm trying to answer here. All I mean to say is that the moral desirability of basic rights and vital interests being protected, putting aside the question of who should do the protecting, is relatively uncontroversial. That is, the end goals of interventions that seek to protect basic rights and vital interests are endorsed by a wide variety of moral views, even if the interventions themselves remain controversial.

102   PROMOTING JUSTICE ACROSS BORDERS

Of course, these biases will vary from intervener to intervener. For-profit corporations, for instance, may try to justify interventions that would increase profits, regardless of their actual likelihood to benefit recipients. Even well-intentioned corporate actors' judgments might be unconsciously skewed by a desire to uncover the advantages of interventions that would also happen to augment their profits. (We might think European drug companies' refusal to export drugs they suspected would be used for lethal injections is striking, and admirable, in that it represents an acceptance of a potential loss in profits for the sake of a worthy cause.)

States (and international organizations populated by states' representatives) may have similar interests in profit, in improving their geopolitical standing, or in promoting some other element of their "national interest." For example, the US was partly motivated to broker its 2006 trade deal with Oman in order to solidify its relationship with an important strategic ally in the Middle East, especially with respect to the "war on terror."[78] US insistence that Oman leave the Arab League boycott was presumably similarly strategically motivated.

State interveners' judgments may also be biased because certain moral or social-scientific concepts or theories hold disproportionate sway in their domestic institutions and society. The structural adjustment programs imposed on many Latin American countries in the 1980s may exemplify this kind of bias. One could argue that they were spearheaded largely by representatives of developed, industrialized countries, especially the US, where certain theories within economics (that valued government austerity and "free-market" capitalism as methods of promoting economic growth) were predominant.[79] Indeed, President Ronald Reagan described structural adjustment programs as introducing recipient societies to "the magic of the marketplace."[80] Arguably, because pro-free-market ideas held disproportionate sway in countries capable of intervening effectively in Latin America during this period, those countries' claims that governance in accordance with these ideas would improve Latin American growth and stability should have had to meet higher evidentiary standards than would similar claims made by others.

Nonprofit information-gathering and advocacy organizations (such as Human Rights Watch and Amnesty International) and other NGOs may sometimes be less subject to these sources of bias than corporations or states.

[78] Hafner-Burton, *Forced to Be Good*, 147–8.
[79] For discussion, see Miller, *Globalizing Justice*, 136–41.
[80] Ibid., 137.

But even they have agendas of their own, often connected to attracting large and high-profile donors,[81] which may create a perverse incentive to focus interventions on the causes that generate the most publicity or public support at the expense of those that are most critical to promoting justice.[82]

None of this is particularly novel. In fact, the underlying thought is quite familiar. Say a potential reform intervener makes a claim about the trade-off between the urgency of the problem they want to solve and the costs recipients will likely suffer as a result of the intervention. That claim can justifiably override the competing claims of the recipients themselves only if its truth is reasonably certain. But when evaluating certainty, we (and interveners) must be careful to compensate for any biases we (and they) might have that would predictably skew an assessment of their claim's truth.

The question remains how to translate this thought into action— especially, how to do so on a global stage that (to a large degree, anyway) lacks institutions capable of effectively regulating reform intervention. That is, we can't rely on some global institution to make authoritative judgments about the reliability of any would-be interveners' claims about cost and urgency and to prevent those whose claims don't pass muster from intervening in foreign societies over their populations' objections. In such a world, what resources do we have to determine if an intervener's claims are "certain enough" to justify reform intervention even if it will run afoul of toleration?

Before we begin to answer this question, it is worth reiterating that interveners' claims about the desirability of an intervention's urgency-cost trade-off are based on both empirical and moral judgments. Thus, they can be subject to all three types of uncertainty discussed in Chapter 1: factual uncertainty (about the conditions on the ground in the recipient society), political uncertainty (about the intervention's likely consequences), and moral uncertainty (about the relative moral significance of the intervention's potential costs and benefits).

---

[81] For a brief discussion of the need for organizations supporting nonviolent intervention to attract donors, see Yeshua Moser-Puangsuwan and Thomas Weber, "Nonviolent Humanitarian Intervention: A Framework for the Future," in *Nonviolent Intervention across Borders: A Recurrent Vision*, ed. Yeshua Moser-Puangsuwan and Thomas Weber (Honolulu: Spark M. Matsunuaga Institute for Peace, University of Hawaii Press, 2000), 319–37, 326–7.

[82] For one account of this danger in the context of the human right to healthcare, see William Easterly, "Human Rights Are the Wrong Basis for Healthcare," *Financial Times*, 12 October 2009, https://www.ft.com/content/89bbbda2-b763-11de-9812-00144feab49a. For a lengthier discussion in the context of humanitarian INGOs more generally, see Jennifer C. Rubenstein, *Between Samaritans and States: The Political Ethics of Humanitarian INGOs* (Oxford: Oxford University Press, 2015).

104   PROMOTING JUSTICE ACROSS BORDERS

Factual and political uncertainty can be alleviated especially well via consultation with the many organized interest groups, activist networks, and information-gathering apparatuses that already participate in global politics—what some have called global civil society. International organizations, such as the UN's various commissions, can also play this consultative role. After all, skewed perceptions of factual information about the conditions in a recipient society or the likely effects of a proposed intervention can be corrected by gathering information from multiple sources with different kinds of expertise, different resources, and different agendas (and that are therefore unlikely to share predictable biases).[83]

Moral uncertainty is perhaps more difficult to alleviate in this way. We should generally be wary of using consensus as evidence of the truth of (or justifiable confidence in) moral claims. After all, widespread belief in the acceptability of immoral practices makes them no less immoral. Moreover, it seems there are at least some moral stances of which we shouldn't be disabused even if we are their only surviving proponents—that slavery and wanton murder are wrong, for example. Thus, while we may be able to sufficiently reduce factual and political uncertainty by acquiring ample information from diverse sources about the factual and political claims at stake, we may not be able to sufficiently reduce moral uncertainty by surveying a similarly wide variety of sources (because the sum of people's beliefs about a moral claim isn't evidence of its truth or falsity in the same way the sum of qualified observers' findings is evidence of an empirical claim's truth or falsity).

It's worth saying a bit more about why this is—why there is such a disconnect between how we should evaluate moral versus empirical claims. Indeed, one might argue that everything I've said about moral claims is also true about empirical facts: widespread belief in incorrect "facts" makes them no more correct, and there are at least some empirical facts (perhaps facts about our own experiences, directly observable to us) we should continue to believe even if everyone else disavows them. Why is it, then, that we should typically take the sum of qualified observers' beliefs about empirical facts to be decisive, but not do the same for moral claims?

One possible reply is that some people are privileged when it comes to knowing the empirical truth about certain topics—they have more or better

---

[83] In holding that interveners can obtain accurate information about recipient societies despite being foreign to them, I take a position like David Luban's in "The Romance of the Nation-State," 394–5 and against Michael Walzer's in "The Moral Standing of States," 212.

TOLERATION AS ENGAGEMENT   105

access to more reliable knowledge about these issues than others. In other words, they are experts. The same isn't true, I propose, for the moral truth (assuming there is one). There aren't moral experts in the same way there are experts about the conditions on the ground in Syria or the likely effects of removing Bashar al-Assad. Thus, consulting others (the experts, who know better than us) can and should convince us that certain empirical claims are true or false. When it comes to morality, though, at least prima facie, there is no one with a similarly epistemically privileged position.[84]

That said, one source of moral uncertainty—the possibility that an intervener's moral view is derived from or applicable only to some idiosyncratic feature of the intervener's identity or context, and thus is not applicable to the recipient society—*can* be reduced by consultation with others (who don't share the relevant idiosyncrasies).

This will often—but perhaps not always—be the primary form of moral uncertainty associated with a proposed reform intervention. So goes the common criticism that intervention is often simply a means by which broadly speaking affluent, liberal, Western countries impose their parochial values on others. This is a species of the more general claim that intervention is usually a means by which powerful political actors impose values, priorities, decisions, etc. that may be appropriate for their own society on other societies for which they are inappropriate.

The moral uncertainty that arises from this possibility, I propose, can be sufficiently alleviated if interveners consult with others who don't share the idiosyncrasies—that is, the predictable sources of bias—alleged to be coloring their moral judgments. Such consultation doesn't necessarily entail multilateral intervention. It does entail interveners getting feedback on their moral claims related to an intervention's urgency and costs from people and groups who don't share their biases. This might mean literally consulting with others in real time, or perhaps consulting their publicly stated positions.[85] For example, if epistemically diverse societies have publicly recognized a certain entitlement as a basic human right, interveners who claim its protection is an urgent moral matter are unlikely to be merely channeling their narrow interests or prejudices.

---

[84] I can't offer a defense of this position here, though we should note its concomitance with an idea at the core of our notion of toleration, that everyone is presumptively entitled to decide for themselves which moral values to live by.

[85] I'll discuss the importance of this kind of consultation in more detail in Chapter 5.

106   PROMOTING JUSTICE ACROSS BORDERS

What, though, if the world at large commits an egregious moral error, such that almost all societies fail to condemn an extreme injustice, such as slavery or ethnic cleansing? Are interveners seeking to avert these harms over the objections of would-be recipients bound to conclude that they are not justified in disregarding toleration (and so must let the atrocities happen) because they can't confirm their judgments about the situation's urgency with others who don't share their predictable biases? To alleviate this worry, I should first note that such a scenario is unlikely to actually occur—both because the worst atrocities and human rights abuses are already widely condemned internationally, as evidenced by the wide ratification of prominent human rights treaties and the acceptance of *jus cogens* norms, and because the would-be recipients of an intervention actually meant to save them from such a grave situation would be unlikely to object to it.

Still, the situation is theoretically possible, so it's worth saying something else about it. Thus, I propose that some moral claims are so minimalist that they are much more likely to reflect universal truths about the human condition than they are to reflect the cultural or contextual idiosyncrasies of a would-be intervener's judgment. Interveners could be justifiably confident in these claims even if they weren't actually confirmed by other sources. Much more could be said about which claims belong in this category, but certainly those that have appeared in some form in an extraordinary variety of moral systems—such as those condemning the massive and avoidable loss or devaluing of human life (what current international legal practice might call "supreme emergency" conditions)—are good candidates.[86]

If interveners are to meet condition (iii) from above, then, their factual claims about the cost-urgency trade-off must be confirmed by reliable sources unlikely to share their biases, and their moral claims must either be sufficiently minimalist or be confirmed by reliable sources unlikely to share their biases.

Summary

Here, I've put forth a novel view of toleration—*toleration as engagement*—on which, under certain circumstances, a commitment to toleration gives us

---

[86] We might also think the abstract propositions of Walzer's moral minimalism are good candidates; see his *Thick and Thin*.

reason to *engage* with others rather than simply leave them alone to act as they please. More than that, on this view, our commitment to toleration can give us reason to engage with others *in an attempt to change their behavior* rather than in an attempt to simply learn about or come to appreciate their current behavior. And even more than that, our commitment to toleration can give us reason to engage with others in an attempt to change their behavior even if we do so to ensure they realize *the full requirements of justice* (rather than, say, a less demanding account of what would be required to fulfill basic human rights, Rawlsian standards of "decency," or Walzerian "thin morality").

In developing this account of toleration, I've explored whether and under what conditions reform interveners could practice toleration in their relations with recipients (even as they intervene). That is, I've explored how reform interveners could do what a principled commitment to toleration gives them reason to do. I have also examined the conditions under which an intervention might be justified despite its being incompatible with toleration.

This has produced the following conclusions:

1. Commitment to toleration generates a reason in favor of an intervention when it (A) encourages tolerant treatment in the recipient society; (B) does so by either trying to persuade or incentivizing a representative segment of the recipient society to adopt some reform, by trying to persuade or incentivizing an elite to adopt a reform favored by a representative segment of the society, or by directly implementing a reform favored by a representative segment of the society; and (C) it does not manipulate the recipient population.

2. If an intervention neither encourages nor discourages tolerant treatment but still meets conditions (B) and (C), commitment to toleration doesn't generate a reason for or against the intervention, but interveners do treat recipients with toleration. (They accomplish this by adhering to conditions (B) and (C).)

3. Commitment to toleration does generate a reason against some interventions, either because they discourage tolerant treatment among recipients or because they fail to meet either condition (B) or (C). Such an intervention may nonetheless be morally permissible if (i) it protects either basic rights or vital interests; (ii) the urgency of the objectives it will predictably achieve exceeds the costs it will predictably impose on recipients; and (iii) interveners are justifiably confident

108 PROMOTING JUSTICE ACROSS BORDERS

that their judgments that the intervention meets conditions (i) and (ii) would hold even for those who don't share their predictable biases. In other words, a commitment to toleration doesn't generate *decisive* reasons against intolerant interventions if they meet conditions (i)–(iii) (though it of course generates reasons against them).

Further, the foregoing analysis of toleration has generated some important insights into how reform intervention could fit into and transform our existing global society. First, reform intervention constitutes a kind of inter-societal moral criticism and brings about inter-societal interaction centered around deciding what justice requires and how to implement its requirements. As such, reform intervention facilitates the creation of a common life—a shared moral world, whose members share concepts, history, and experiences—that exceeds the boundaries of established political communities. This is especially true when interveners treat recipients tolerantly—because interveners are then responsive to recipients' preferences about how their institutions should be organized. When it treats recipients tolerantly, reform intervention is therefore a genuine give-and-take between interveners and recipients—a genuinely multisided engagement aimed at redressing injustice. As such engagement happens more and more—as the global common life gains substance (more shared concepts, history, and experiences)—future interveners will arguably be more likely to invoke this substance as a justification for pursuing their objectives.

Interveners will be better able to rely solely on the conceptual and normative resources of the common life they share with recipients in order to articulate justifications for and carry out their interventions. Thus, the risk that intervention will amount to the imposition of some moral scheme on people who don't share in the kind of common life needed to make it salient or appropriate for them will be reduced. We might say the conscientious practice of reform intervention in the world as it is now will encourage the formation of a shared moral world that encompasses multiple political communities, which will in turn make future interventions more likely to appropriately reflect norms, ideas, etc. shared by both interveners and recipients.

Second, existing international legal bodies, global civic organizations, and other international organizations have a significant role to play in ensuring reform intervention is undertaken in morally acceptable ways. Not only may they engage in reform intervention themselves, but they also provide valuable resources without which we may not be able to assess whether interveners

TOLERATION AS ENGAGEMENT 109

are justified in acting on their judgments about the relative urgency and costs of a particular intervention. Through the involvement of global society at large (when epistemically diverse global political actors verify interveners' judgments about cost and urgency), even intolerant interventions may become the instantiation of widely shared commitments rather than the unilateral imposition of one intervener's idiosyncratic preferences on the rest of the world.

Both these insights should help alleviate one common worry about justice promotion on the global scale—namely, that it is hopelessly utopian, because at best it denies the normative importance of politics-as-lived-practice and at worst it ultimately aims at a world without it. Globalized justice promotion as I've envisioned it here is neither premised on nor directed toward the end of politics. Instead, it involves engaging with the vast array of people and organizations already active in global politics, and in fact expands the boundaries of existing sites of political contestation to include political actors worldwide.

Moreover, by showing that some kinds of reform intervention escape the toleration objection—and that some may be permissible despite not escaping it—I have begun to cast doubt on the skeptical view of the natural duty of justice. I've shown that reform intervention doesn't always involve one serious moral wrong the skeptical view alleges it does—namely, unjustifiably treating recipients with intolerance. Of course, I haven't yet said enough to determine whether reform intervention always involves the *other* serious moral wrongs skeptics are wont to associate with it. If reform intervention does involve these other wrongs—like failing to properly recognize or respect recipients' legitimate institutions or undermining recipients' collective self-determination—it may be, all things considered, impermissible, even if it isn't vulnerable to the toleration objection. If so, the skeptical view will be right after all.

I'll argue that reform intervention need not involve these other wrongs either, but this argument will only fully develop over the course of the next chapters, as I discuss the other standard objections (from legitimacy and collective self-determination) to reform intervention.

And if there *do* turn out to be some, all things considered, permissible kinds of reform intervention, as I'll argue there are, it may also be the case that some of them are (some of the time) morally *required*. After all, I argued in Chapter 1 that the natural duty of justice requires us to do our part to ensure people live in just conditions, and that this requirement is global in scope: we're required to help ensure people *everywhere* (not only within our own societies) live in just conditions, as long as we can do so without inordinate cost—and without committing serious moral wrongs. Since they aim to promote justice in recipient societies, reform interventions are attempts to help ensure people in those societies live in just conditions. Thus, if a reform intervention can be accomplished without inordinate cost and is morally permissible (and therefore wouldn't involve committing serious moral wrongs), it may be required by the natural duty of justice.

Of course, it's not clear at this point how often it will be the case that a reform intervention is both feasible at reasonable cost and morally permissible. So it's not clear how often reform intervention will turn out to be required by the natural duty of justice. At the very least, to get a handle on this I'll have to finish identifying the criteria for reform intervention's all-things-considered permissibility. This will happen over the course of the next few chapters.

For now, I'll just make one preliminary remark about how frequently reform intervention is likely to be morally required. Rather than think each instance of morally permissible and feasible-at-reasonable-cost reform intervention is morally required, I want to suggest that what's required is adopting a set of projects in which promoting justice, including via reform intervention, enjoys a sufficiently prominent place. This suggestion is intentionally vague, and I'll fill it out with more specifics as the book continues and our ethics of reform intervention becomes more complete. At the moment, I only want to emphasize that many instances of reform intervention could be both morally permissible and not too costly when undertaken individually. However, undertaking them all together could still prove inordinately costly. We wouldn't want to say each intervention was morally required, because then the conjunction of actions required by the natural duty of justice would indeed be inordinately costly. But the natural duty of justice requires us to help ensure everyone lives in just conditions only when this *isn't* inordinately costly.

Hence my suggestion—that we're required to adopt a set of projects in which promoting justice, including via reform intervention, enjoys a sufficiently prominent place. "Adopting a set of projects" may mean different things in different contexts and for different actors. For individuals, it may mean adopting certain life projects; for states, adopting certain policy priorities; for NGOs, undertaking certain missions; for corporations, holding themselves to certain standards (e.g., related to working conditions in their often global supply chains).

Ultimately, then, I'm not so committed to showing that any specific reform intervention is morally required. Rather, I want to show that political actors are morally required to take on a particular political stance—one that involves adopting the pursuit of justice in other societies as a sufficiently central goal. This moral requirement is not activated only in extraordinary circumstances—in what the world of international relations might call "emergency" conditions. It is not activated only when grave atrocities or massive human rights violations are imminent. This moral requirement binds all political actors in the conduct of their everyday political activities. We are all required to make the achievement of justice, everywhere, a sufficiently central end of our everyday political struggles.

3

Degrees of Legitimacy

Introduction

Drawing on the typology developed in Chapter 1, this chapter argues that some types of reform intervention—such as consumer boycotts, civil-society-led divestment campaigns, and state-led boycott or divestment campaigns that challenge existing geopolitical hierarchies—are justifiable even when recipient states are fully legitimate. This is contrary to Tesón's position that intervention in a fully legitimate state can be justified only if the legitimate government of that state authorizes it.[1] Other types of reform intervention—such as those meant to obstruct a particular government agency or stop the enforcement of a particular law, but that stop short of seeking regime change—don't show recipient states the respect owed *fully* legitimate states. But since they stop short of seeking regime change, they do show recipient states *some* degree of respect. Thus, these kinds of interventions aren't justified in fully legitimate recipient states, but they may be justified in recipient states that are neither fully legitimate nor fully illegitimate.

This chapter also offers an important corrective to prominent understandings of legitimacy. Whereas the existing literature overwhelmingly treats legitimacy as a binary quality that states either have (in full) or don't (at all), I argue we should understand legitimacy as something states can possess (or lack) in degrees. This will allow us to better analyze much of what goes on in global politics and to develop a more nuanced understanding of the relationship between legitimacy and reform intervention.

Despite the disagreement I've just flagged, the view I defend here in some ways resembles Tesón's. He rightly criticizes "statists" for treating state sovereignty as an "all-or-nothing concept"[2] and argues we should instead recognize

---

[1] Fernando R. Tesón, *A Philosophy of International Law* (Boulder, CO: Westview Press, 1998), 60–2. It is perhaps doubtful whether Tesón would categorize all the activities I've listed here as "interventions." That said, it is plausible to think he would at least call state-led boycott and divestment campaigns "interventions," since he is careful (60) to say "intervention" need not involve coercion.

[2] Ibid., 39.

Promoting Justice Across Borders. Lucia M. Rafanelli, Oxford University Press. © Oxford University Press 2021.
DOI: 10.1093/oso/9780197568842.003.0004

114 PROMOTING JUSTICE ACROSS BORDERS

that "sovereignty admits of degrees."[3] He goes on to say that only fully legitimate states deserve "the complete protection of state sovereignty provided by international law."[4] On the other hand, states where the "horizontal" social contract binding individuals to each other in a unified society is legitimate, but the "vertical" social contract binding the population to its government is *illegitimate*, deserve "less protection of [their] sovereignty."[5] And in fully illegitimate states, where both the horizontal and vertical contracts have lapsed, Tesón tells us, "sovereignty considerations no longer apply."[6] This three-way distinction mirrors the distinctions I make among fully legitimate, partially legitimate, and fully illegitimate states and their differential liabilities to intervention. (Though, since I don't take a position on what makes a state legitimate or illegitimate, I remain agnostic about whether Tesón's account of the role "horizontal" and "vertical" social contracts play in determining a state's legitimacy is correct.)

That said, there is a crucial element Tesón's analysis overlooks, but that mine provides. (And it is from this omission that my disagreement with Tesón, flagged above, arises.) Namely, Tesón does not acknowledge the morally significant distinction between interventions that challenge recipient institutions' domestic authority and those that don't—because he assumes all interventions *do* challenge recipient institutions' domestic authority.[7] However, making use of the typology I developed in Chapter 1, I explicitly examine this distinction and its moral significance. This is not only to say Tesón hasn't evaluated the ethics of intervention in the exact terms suggested by my typology—of course he hasn't, but this alone isn't a reason to criticize his view. Rather, my point is that Tesón's analysis obscures morally important distinctions among different kinds of intervention, and it is precisely these distinctions that my typology is designed to reflect. For example, below I argue that not all interventions challenge recipient institutions' domestic authority and those that challenge it don't all do so to the same degree. The way my typology differentiates between interventions based on the ways in which they relate to recipients' established political institutions is well suited to capture these distinctions. And insofar as domestic authority is something legitimate states are entitled to, these distinctions can make the difference

[3] Ibid., 40.
[4] Ibid., 58.
[5] Ibid. For definitions of the "horizontal" and "vertical" social contracts, see 57.
[6] Ibid., 64.
[7] Ibid., 47.

DEGREES OF LEGITIMACY   115

between an intervention being permissible or not in (fully or partially) legitimate states.

This brings me back to the main task of this chapter: though one standard objection to reform intervention—the legitimacy objection—says that it involves unjustifiably denying or disregarding the legitimacy of recipients' established political institutions, here I contend that some types of reform intervention escape this objection. The reasoning behind the legitimacy objection should be familiar enough. For example, Walzer argues that, except under very extreme circumstances—such as massacre, enslavement, mass expulsion, or mass starvation—outsiders should treat foreign states[8] as if they are legitimate.[9] In his words, these states have "presumptive legitimacy."[10] Intervention, the argument continues, is impermissible against legitimate (including presumptively legitimate) states.[11] Intervening in a state thus means treating it as if it's illegitimate; any credible assertion that an intervention was justifiable would have to be premised on a denial of the recipient state's legitimacy. But if existing states are rendered illegitimate only under the extreme and comparatively rare circumstances enumerated above, intervention must be generally impermissible.

Others hold that states are rendered illegitimate when they commit wrongs less grievous than those Walzer identifies.[12] But virtually no one holds that only fully just states can be legitimate.[13] Thus, one might think intervention aimed at promoting justice in general (reform intervention), rather than at alleviating only the most serious injustices, is especially likely to risk treating actually (or at least presumptively) legitimate states as illegitimate—and therefore especially likely to be impermissible.

---

[8] Though both states and nonstate actors can engage in reform intervention, this chapter will often identify the recipients of intervention as "states" because I assume political legitimacy is a feature possessed (or not) by states. Though foreigners could intervene in the affairs of groups not subject to states, their cases wouldn't raise the issues surrounding legitimacy I address here. For the same reason, when I refer to "institutions," I mean formal political institutions (the kind that comprise states).

[9] Michael Walzer, "The Moral Standing of States: A Response to Four Critics," *Philosophy and Public Affairs* 9, no. 3 (1980): 209–29, 217–8 and "Beyond Humanitarian Intervention: Human Rights in Global Society," in *Thinking Politically: Essays in Political Theory*, ed. David Miller (New Haven, CT: Yale University Press, 2007), 251–63, 257–8.

[10] Walzer, "Moral Standing," 214–8.

[11] Ibid.

[12] See, e.g., Andrew Altman and Christopher Heath Wellman, *A Liberal Theory of International Justice* (Oxford: Oxford University Press, 2009); David Luban, "Just War and Human Rights." *Philosophy and Public Affairs* 9, no. 2 (1980): 160–81.

[13] Tesón is a possible exception. He at times suggests a state must fully achieve liberal justice in order to be legitimate (*A Philosophy of International Law*, 1–9, 15–6, 21, 40, 43–5, 149–50, 172–3, 177).

116 PROMOTING JUSTICE ACROSS BORDERS

But here, I'll argue that once we appreciate the full range of forms reform intervention can take—and once we appreciate that legitimacy can occur in degrees—we'll see that some types of reform intervention are immune to the legitimacy objection. Moreover, I'll identify the kinds of reform intervention that are justifiable only when recipients' institutions are entirely illegitimate, those justifiable when recipients' institutions are partially legitimate, and those justifiable even when recipients' institutions are fully legitimate.

Note, I say "justifiable" rather than "justified" because this chapter will focus on determining which kinds of reform intervention are and aren't vulnerable to the legitimacy objection—in other words, which kinds of interventions would be objectionable when directed at legitimate institutions *for the reason that* they denied or disregarded those institutions' legitimacy. An intervention that escapes this particular objection is (potentially) justifiable, but it could of course be, all things considered, unjustified for reasons unrelated to the need to properly respect recipients' legitimate institutions. Just as the previous chapter focused on explicating our toleration-based reasons to refrain from or engage in reform intervention, this chapter will focus on our legitimacy-based reasons. That said, at the end of this chapter, I'll examine how the ethical standards developed in this and the previous chapter apply to my focal cases. In so doing, I'll begin to discuss how to make all-things-considered ethical judgments about reform interventions—a discussion I'll add to successively throughout the book.

The Concept of Legitimacy

Different accounts of legitimacy understand the criteria states must fulfill in order to be "legitimate" differently. Some think states must do an adequate job of protecting their subjects' human rights in order to be legitimate; some think they must have been consented to; some think they must represent the public culture of their subjects; some think they must not dominate their subjects; some think they must be sufficiently responsive to subjects' input, and so on.[14] I won't adjudicate among these alternatives here, as this

---

[14] For human-rights-based theories of legitimacy, see Altman and Wellman, *A Liberal Theory of International Justice*; Luban, "Just War and Human Rights." For a consent-based theory of legitimacy, see A. John Simmons, "Justification and Legitimacy," *Ethics* 109, no. 4 (1999): 739–71. For a view on which legitimate institutions must represent their subjects' public culture, see Walzer, "Moral Standing," especially the notion of "fit." For a non-domination-based theory of legitimacy, see Phillip Pettit, *On the People's Terms: A Republican Theory and Model of Democracy* (Cambridge: Cambridge

DEGREES OF LEGITIMACY   117

exceeds the scope of the present project. In other words, I won't take a position on what makes a state legitimate or illegitimate. I will simply assume that there exist some criteria such that, when states fulfill those criteria, they are "legitimate."

I'll further assume (along the lines of the legitimacy objection) that there are limits on how outsiders can permissibly behave toward legitimate states. Theorists disagree about what these limits are, but all plausible views share some basic features: they hold that, if a state is legitimate, it is justified in making and enforcing policy within its jurisdiction and it deserves a certain elevated international status. Thus, I'll assume that outsiders to a legitimate state ought to (1) grant it authority to decide and implement policy within its jurisdiction (policymaking authority, for short) and (2) grant (or at least not deny) it "good standing" in the international community.[15] I'll assume outsiders to a legitimate state ought to meet both these conditions *even if* they could, by refusing to do so, effectively promote justice in that state. In other words, when a would-be recipient state is legitimate, this places constraints on how foreigners may permissibly intervene there, even when their aim is justice promotion. This is a widely held and generally uncontroversial view. It also means that, in order to treat a state *as if* it is legitimate (regardless of whether it is *in fact* legitimate), outsiders must meet conditions (1) and (2)—they must grant it policymaking authority and grant (or at least not deny) it "good standing" in the international community. If interveners fail to meet these conditions, they treat the recipient state as if it is (at least partly) illegitimate. If the state is *in fact* illegitimate, this may be justified—and, of course, deciding whether it's justified in a particular case would require taking a

---

University Press, 2012), especially ch. 3. Finally, Rawls presents responsiveness to citizens' input as a criterion of legitimacy when he sets out the consultation procedure non-liberal societies must adopt in order to qualify as "decent" and therefore as members in good standing of the international community; see John Rawls, *The Law of Peoples with "The Idea of Public Reason Revisited"* (Cambridge, MA: Harvard University Press, 1999), 62–78. So does Anna Stilz in *Liberal Loyalty: Freedom, Obligation, and the State* (Princeton, NJ: Princeton University Press, 2009), 88–96. See also her discussion of "maker" interests in "Against Democratic Interventionism," *Ethics and International Affairs* 29, no. 3 (2015): 259–68.

[15] I leave open the possibility that a single area (physical or otherwise) could be under the jurisdiction of multiple legitimate institutions, which might even issue contradictory directives. In such a case, perhaps neither institution is entitled to *exclusive* policymaking authority, as Allen Buchanan discusses; see his "Institutional Legitimacy," in *Oxford Studies in Political Philosophy*, ed. David Sobel, Peter Vallentyne, and Steven Wall (Oxford: Oxford University Press, 2018), 4:53–78, 58–9. Since I aim to assess the permissibility of reform intervention in more- or less-legitimate states irrespective of the independent legitimacy of the intervening institutions, I leave the discussion of this possibility aside.

118 PROMOTING JUSTICE ACROSS BORDERS

position on what makes a state legitimate or illegitimate. Since, again, I will remain agnostic on this question, my primary interest here is in whether there are ways to conduct reform intervention that treat recipient states *as if* they're legitimate.

Intuitively, it may seem that reform interveners, by the very nature of reform intervention, must fail to meet conditions (1) and/or (2). If this were true, one wouldn't be able to engage in reform intervention while acting toward the recipient state as one ought to act toward a legitimate state. Thus, on this reasoning, any credible assertion that a reform intervention was justifiable would have to be premised on a denial of the recipient state's legitimacy. Moreover, recall that reform interventions must aim to redress injustice but need not aim to redress any specific *kind* of injustice. Therefore, a reform intervention may very well seek to remedy an injustice that doesn't undermine the recipient state's legitimacy (that doesn't prevent the state from fulfilling the criteria of legitimacy, whatever those are). Hence the legitimacy objection: reform intervention involves treating recipient states as illegitimate, but often targets actually (or presumptively) legitimate states, and so is often impermissible.

But this is too coarse-grained a picture. Now that we have a better understanding of the different types of reform intervention, we can see that, though some types are justifiable only when recipient states are totally illegitimate, others may be justifiable when recipient states are partially or fully legitimate.

Legitimacy and Reform Intervention

Regime-Change Interventions

Recall that reform interveners can interact with recipient societies' established institutions in a variety of ways. In extreme cases, their interventions may seek regime change, as was the case with NATO's 2011 intervention in Libya, to take one example.

Justifying a *regime-change intervention* would require a total denial of the recipient state's legitimacy.[16] To say a regime-change intervention was

---

[16] One could try to justify a regime-change intervention without denying the recipient state's legitimacy by denying that the state's legitimacy had any implications for how outsiders ought to behave toward it. However, this option isn't open to me, because I've stipulated a state's legitimacy *is*

justified would be to straightforwardly deny the existing state had *any* policymaking authority. Moreover, we haven't explored precisely what it means to grant (or at least not deny) a state "good standing" in the international community. But on any plausible understanding of what granting this status involves, it must necessitate refraining from regime-change intervention. Thus, those engaging in regime-change intervention won't be able to meet either condition (1) or condition (2) from above. One can't simultaneously engage in regime-change intervention *and* act toward the recipient state as one ought to act toward a legitimate state. The thinking behind the legitimacy objection, which says reform intervention is permissible only when the recipient state is illegitimate, is right—when we're talking about *regime-change interventions*. But these are only one of many types of reform intervention.

Oppositional Interventions

Oppositional intervention, in which reform interveners interfere somewhat with recipients' established institutions without seeking to overthrow them entirely, may involve (for example) interfering with the enforcement of certain laws or obstructing the operation of certain government agencies. Here, I'll argue that oppositional intervention can be justified only when recipient states are at least partially illegitimate. But it may (unlike regime-change intervention) be justified when recipient states are not *entirely* illegitimate. As I suggested above, this will involve introducing a nonbinary notion of legitimacy.

Let's illustrate with a few cases.

Arguably, the European refusal to sell lethal injection drugs to the US is an oppositional intervention. We can interpret it as an attempt to stop the US from enforcing laws that call for the death penalty. I recognize some may contest this interpretation. Ultimately, though, what matters most for the success of my arguments is that readers accept the broader theoretical framework I put forward (the contours of the typology I develop and the general normative recommendations I make) for understanding the ethics of reform

---

normatively significant for outsiders: it means they ought to (1) grant it policymaking authority and (2) grant (or at least not deny) it "good standing" in the international community. Moreover, I'll assume for the rest of the chapter that any intervention that fails to adequately recognize or respect recipient institutions' (actual level of) legitimacy isn't justifiable (though some might argue that such an intervention could be, all things considered, justified if its goals were important enough).

120 PROMOTING JUSTICE ACROSS BORDERS

intervention, rather than that you accept my categorization and evaluation of each specific case. Much like those who agree on what the correct principles of justice are may still disagree on the specific policies and institutional arrangements they require, people who adopt my standards for ethical reform intervention may disagree about how to apply them to specific cases. Nonetheless, here, I offer some considerations in favor of my interpretation of the Europeans' actions as oppositional reform intervention.

Objectors may argue that the European actors in question have no obligation to trade with the US at all, let alone to trade in any specific goods (like lethal injection drugs). Therefore, the objection continues, Europeans' refusal to export lethal injection drugs isn't an "intervention" meant to interfere with the enforcement of US law. The Europeans in this case simply exercise a moral permission (to refuse to trade in a certain good) so as not to materially support a practice (execution) they wouldn't engage in themselves.[17]

On the contrary, I propose we *should* think of the Europeans' refusal to trade in lethal injection drugs as a reform intervention, mainly because, as previously noted, it was publicly justified as an attempt to bring an end to the death penalty. The policy's architects easily could have said they wanted not to be actively involved in carrying out the death penalty—that they simply wanted to wash their hands of the practice. But they went further than this, instead positioning their refusal to export the necessary drugs as an expression of moral opposition to the death penalty—and, more than that, as part of a campaign seeking its abolition.

As for the claim that Europeans have no obligation to trade in general, and no obligation to trade in lethal injection drugs in particular, accepting it doesn't imperil my interpretation of this case as a reform intervention. As I've defined "reform intervention," it need not involve failing to perform some typically binding moral obligation. It need only involve a deliberate attempt to promote justice in a society other than one's own. And if we take seriously the words of the people involved, this case certainly involves that.

Objectors who remain unconvinced may imagine, for the duration of the present argument, a slightly modified version of the European export ban case—one in which the Europeans not only refused to sell lethal injection drugs to the US but also tried to stop US officials from getting them elsewhere (perhaps by incentivizing others to join Europe in refusing to sell the drugs).

---

[17] I thank Anna Stilz for posing and discussing this objection.

DEGREES OF LEGITIMACY   121

In any case, if we interpret the Europeans' actions as I suggest—as attempts to stop the US from enforcing laws that call for the death penalty, and therefore as oppositional interventions—we should see them as a refusal to grant the US government *exclusive* authority to make and implement policy in its jurisdiction. After all, US laws calling for the death penalty are laws the government has passed and tries to implement each time it tries to carry out an execution. If outsiders to the US were to grant its government exclusive policymaking authority in its jurisdiction, they would have to let it implement these laws unimpeded. So, in order for the Europeans' intervention to be justified, the US must not have a claim to exclusive policymaking authority in its jurisdiction. Of course, it may still have *some* claim to policymaking authority. If regime-change interventions can be justified only when recipient states have *no* claim to policymaking authority in their jurisdictions, oppositional interventions like this one can be justified if the recipient states have *some* claim to policymaking authority—but not a claim to *exclusive* policymaking authority—within their jurisdictions.

What does this mean for whether those engaging in oppositional intervention (in this case, the Europeans refusing to sell lethal injection drugs) can meet condition (1)—whether they can grant the recipient state (in this case, the US) domestic policymaking authority? If, as argued above, interveners grant recipient states *some* authority to decide and implement policy within their jurisdictions, but not *exclusive* authority, this suggests that the standard laid out in (1) can be achieved in degrees. In this case, the European interveners haven't refused to grant the US *any* domestic policymaking authority; they haven't tried to overthrow the US government and replace it wholesale. But they have—by attempting to prevent it from enforcing some of its laws—refused to grant the US *exclusive* domestic policymaking authority. They have met condition (1) to a degree, but not fully.

And remember that the standard laid out in condition (1) is a standard for how outsiders ought to behave toward legitimate states. To say that interveners have partially, but not fully, met the standard is to say they've treated the relevant recipient states as partially, but not fully, legitimate. To make sense of this, we'll need to adopt a nonbinary notion of legitimacy—one that says legitimacy can be possessed in degrees. I'll proceed for now on the assumption that this is sensible and continue to examine what it would mean for our thinking about the ethics of reform intervention. Thinking through some more cases will help us better understand what it would mean

122 PROMOTING JUSTICE ACROSS BORDERS

to adopt a nonbinary notion of legitimacy and, in the end, will help establish the desirability of doing so.

So, for now, let's continue exploring some illustrative cases.

The work of international tribunals, as well as attempts to enforce human rights treaties and trade agreements containing human rights protections (protective trade agreements, for short), may also fall into the category of oppositional intervention. After all, this work may interfere with the enforcement of certain laws in the societies subject to the relevant international bodies or agreements, or with the operation of some of these societies' governmental bodies. International tribunals and attempts to enforce human rights treaties and protective trade agreements serve (or at least attempt) to arrest certain kinds of political activity in the societies subject to them when the subject societies transgress agreed-upon standards. They therefore serve (or at least attempt) to transfer *some* policymaking authority from the subject societies to the relevant international bodies, but they don't aim to replace subject societies' political institutions wholesale. The logic from above holds: if regime-change interventions can be justified only when recipient states have *no* claim to domestic policymaking authority, the work of international tribunals and attempts to enforce human rights treaties and protective trade agreements can be justified when recipient states have *some* claim to domestic policymaking authority—but not a claim to *exclusive* domestic policymaking authority. And, as above, interveners who grant recipient states *some*, but not *exclusive*, domestic policymaking authority treat them as if they are partially, but not fully, legitimate.

This characterization fits with plausible understandings of historical cases. The operation of tribunals like the Nuremberg trials or the International Criminal Tribunal for the former Yugoslavia, for example, arguably did call into question the legitimacy of certain institutions in the societies whose agents they investigated. After all, these agents, as subjects of the tribunals, were taken to be potentially guilty of culpable wrongdoing and potentially liable to punishment, even if they'd only ever acted within the bounds of their roles as defined by their societies' political institutions.

Tribunals like these are not called for because some political actors are suspected of egregiously violating their domestic institutions' rules or norms, but because they are suspected of committing atrocities whose performance should be discouraged and punished regardless of whether they were legally permitted by established political institutions. Moreover, in the case of international tribunals, this determination is made by actors outside

DEGREES OF LEGITIMACY   123

the society of the accused, and the authority of the tribunals' decisions is taken to supersede that of the political institutions in the society of the accused. Those judged guilty and perhaps punished by one of these tribunals wouldn't be excused if they could show their actions to be judged acceptable by the standards of the political institutions in place in their own society at the time of their transgressions. Thus, it seems fair to say those who operate international tribunals and carry out their decisions treat institutions within the societies of the accused as if their legitimacy is somewhat diminished. Domestic institutions are taken to lack the authority to determine if certain of accused parties' actions are permissible, and this authority is lodged instead in the international body of the tribunal. It need not, however, be the goal of such a tribunal to overturn the institutions of the accused parties' societies wholesale. (Participants in the tribunal need not treat these institutions as if they are *entirely* illegitimate.)

Similarly, those who try to enforce international agreements, such as human rights treaties and trade agreements containing human rights protections (protective trade agreements),[18] may aim to interfere with the operation of parties' political institutions when they violate agreed-upon standards—thereby effectively depriving them of the authority to license certain behaviors and transferring some policymaking authority to treaty bodies or arbitrators tasked with enforcing the protective provisions of a trade agreement. Indeed, one major contribution of the human rights project to global politics has been the introduction of norms and practices justified with reference to the idea that states' legitimacy is conditioned on their treating their citizens in accordance with certain standards.[19]

[18] I don't mean to suggest these two things are the same. They differ in important respects, which Emilie Hafner-Burton discusses in *Forced to Be Good: Why Trade Agreements Boost Human Rights* (Ithaca, NY: Cornell University Press, 2009), especially ch. 6. However, attempts to enforce human rights treaties and to enforce what Hafner-Burton calls "preferential trade agreements" can both involve transferring a limited amount of authority from domestic to international institutions, and it is this shared feature that places them in the same category of reform intervention with respect to the metric I'm currently examining (an intervention's relationship to recipients' established institutions).

[19] See, e.g., International Development Research Centre, *The Responsibility to Protect: Report of the International Committee on Intervention and State Sovereignty* (Ottawa: International Development Research Centre, 2001); United Nations General Assembly, Resolution Adopted by the United Nations General Assembly on 16 September 2005: 60/1, 2005 World Summit Outcome, 2005, http://www.un.org/en/development/desa/population/migration/generalassembly/docs/globalcompact/A_RES_60_1.pdf, esp. paras. 138–40; Charles R. Beitz, *The Idea of Human Rights* (Oxford: Oxford University Press, 2009), 106–17; Rawls, *The Law of Peoples*, 78–80; Henry Shue, "Limiting Sovereignty," in *Humanitarian Intervention and International Relations*, ed. Jennifer M. Welsh (Oxford: Oxford University Press, 2004), 11–28.

124 PROMOTING JUSTICE ACROSS BORDERS

Trade agreements containing human rights provisions are not uncommon in global politics.[20] Some of these agreements have "soft" human rights provisions that establish some standard to which parties are supposed to adhere but don't necessarily include enforcement mechanisms; others, such as the US agreement with Oman, contain what Hafner-Burton calls "hard" standards.[21] Rather than a vague, unenforceable commitment to human rights, the US-Oman agreement, for example, offers specific benchmarks for both parties to meet (both must follow their domestic laws protecting workers' human rights and must avoid weakening those protections) and clear avenues for redress should they fail (a tribunal will be tasked with enforcing compliance if there are any violations, and both the US and Oman are guaranteed the ability to seek remedies if they suffer abuses).[22] In cases like this one—of trade agreements with "hard" human rights standards—it is especially clear that enforcement would transfer some of the political authority once belonging to states parties to international bodies instead. Thus, much like operating an international criminal tribunal, enforcing these agreements reflects a judgment that insofar as parties perpetrate certain human rights violations, their political institutions aren't fully legitimate (though again, they may not be fully illegitimate either).

Some may object that the enforcement (or attempted enforcement) of human rights treaties and the human rights protections contained in some trade agreements shouldn't count as oppositional intervention because states voluntarily sign onto these treaties and agreements. Objectors may argue that, since the agreements are voluntary, they don't really involve a transfer of policymaking authority from states parties to the relevant international bodies. It's true that a body charged with monitoring compliance with a human rights treaty or enforcing the human rights protections in a trade agreement may try to interfere with the operation of some institution within a society subject to it. But this is true only because that subject society previously agreed to the arrangement making this possible. Therefore, the objection continues, the operation of the international body doesn't deny the subject society any policymaking authority; it only respects the policymaking authority that society exercised when signing onto the original agreement.[23]

---

[20] For some examples, see Hafner-Burton, *Forced to Be Good,* 144–6.
[21] Ibid.
[22] Ibid.
[23] I thank Anna Stilz for raising this objection.

To someone convinced by this objection, the work of such an international body might seem more like *intra-systemic* rather than *oppositional* intervention. Recall that intra-systemic interventions operate *through* the recipient society's established political institutions. An advocate of the present objection might argue that an international body like the ones we've been discussing does exactly that: when the societies subject to it voluntarily agreed to be subject, they opened up an officially sanctioned channel through which the international body could exert influence over them. Thus, one could argue, we should see any exercise of influence through that channel as an intra-systemic intervention. On this view, the work of human rights treaty bodies would be more like the foreign countries' submission of amicus briefs to the US Supreme Court than like the work of an international criminal tribunal.

If correct, this objection may be normatively important, because whether we identify a given case of reform intervention as oppositional or intra-systemic could affect our assessment of its permissibility. As I've already suggested, oppositional interventions are justifiable only when recipient states are at least partially illegitimate. However, as I'll argue later, intra-systemic interventions are justifiable even when recipient states are fully legitimate. Thus, if we categorize attempts to enforce human rights treaties and trade agreements with built-in human rights protections as oppositional interventions, we will have to conclude that they are justified only when recipient states are at least partially illegitimate.

We could take this to mean enforcing human rights treaties and protective trade agreements will be "harder to justify" if we see it as oppositional (rather than intra-systemic) intervention. (It will be justified only when recipient states are partially illegitimate, as opposed to intra-systemic intervention, which may be justified even when recipient states are fully legitimate.) Or we could take it to tell us something about cases in which we already accept that attempts to enforce human rights treaties and protective trade agreements are justified; in these cases, we must *also* accept that the recipient states are partially illegitimate. Either way, how we decide to categorize attempts to enforce human rights treaties and protective trade agreements (as oppositional or intra-systemic interventions) will affect how we assess normatively important elements of real-world cases (either how easy it is to justify attempted enforcement or how legitimate states parties to justifiably enforced agreements are).

In order to fully respond to the objection at hand, a clarification is in order. I don't mean to suggest that *the mere act of signing onto* a human rights treaty or protective trade agreement is justifiable only when the states parties are partially illegitimate, or that the act of signing somehow signals parties' (partial) illegitimacy. On the contrary, the mere act of *offering* a foreign state the opportunity to sign onto a human rights treaty or protective trade agreement would, I take it, count as an intra-systemic intervention—one meant to induce change by working through the recipient states' existing institutions.

However, *once a party breaches* such an agreement, if any attempt is made to interfere with the operation of the party's political institutions, in an effort to arrest the breach, *this* reflects a judgment that—and is justifiable only when—those institutions are at least partially illegitimate. It may, more specifically, reflect a judgment that the current government is partially illegitimate, even if the underlying institutional structure known as the "state" is legitimate, or a judgment that a particular law, policy, or decision the state (or government) has taken is illegitimate (because it mandates behavior the state has no authority to mandate).

The important point for us is that an attempt to interfere with the operation of political institutions in a state party to a human rights treaty or a protective trade agreement, meant to arrest a breach of that agreement, reflects a judgment that—and is justified only when—the state party lacks exclusive domestic policymaking authority (i.e., is at least partially illegitimate). Those trying to enforce the human rights treaty or protective trade agreement treat the state against which they bring enforcement as if it lacks exclusive policymaking authority within its jurisdiction (i.e., as if it is at least partially illegitimate). This remains true even if the treaty or agreement they try to enforce was entered into voluntarily by the same state whose legitimacy the enforcement brings into question.

Thus, even leaving aside cases in which states parties to human rights treaties or protective trade agreements don't freely agree to them, but instead are made to do so by geopolitical forces beyond their control, submitting to those charged with enforcing the agreements still involves transferring authority to an international body in a way opening up a domestic political channel to foreign actors doesn't. In the paradigm case of intra-systemic intervention, interveners will exercise influence within the recipient society's domestic political institutions; they will not be granted freestanding authority to pass judgment on those domestic institutions' operation, interfering with it when they see fit.

DEGREES OF LEGITIMACY   127

Take the case of the Latin American countries that submitted amicus briefs to the US Supreme Court. They exercised influence over US policy via a channel the US itself opened to them. But the US didn't cede any of its policymaking authority to the Latin American countries (and the Latin American countries didn't seek to deny the US any policymaking authority). It was still the US court system that ultimately decided what US policy would be. Contrast this with the case of the US-Oman trade agreement. In this case, a tribunal—not the government of the US or Oman—would be tasked with adjudicating disputes over violations of the agreement's human rights protections.[24] Even if the US and Oman both agreed to this arrangement, what they agreed to was (in the case of an alleged violation) ceding some policymaking authority to the tribunal. In the event of a dispute, it would be the tribunal—not the US's or Oman's domestic institutions—that would decide whether the disputed policy or practice should be retained or eliminated.

There does seem to be a reasonably clear distinguishing line between cases in which foreign actors exercise influence through recipient societies' established domestic institutions (as in intra-systemic intervention) and those in which foreign actors take on some of the policymaking authority that would otherwise belong to recipient societies' domestic institutions (as in oppositional intervention). Perhaps someday it will be hard to tell whether a given intervention falls on one or the other side of this line. Perhaps someday we will see the international bodies a state has signed onto as simply an extension of its domestic institutions, making it hard to distinguish foreign influence exercised within those domestic institutions from the independent authority of the international bodies. But today is not that day. Until the apparatuses of international law and global governance become much more integrated with domestic politics, it will often be easy to tell the difference between intra-systemic and oppositional intervention as I've conceived of them here. Surely, the amicus briefs and Oman cases are ones in which it's easy to tell.

The foregoing discussion has shown that oppositional intervention— exemplified by the European refusal to sell lethal injection drugs to the US, the work of international criminal tribunals, and the attempted enforcement of human rights treaties and protective trade agreements—involves a partial denial of policymaking authority to recipient states. Thus, those engaged in oppositional intervention don't act toward recipient states as if they're fully

---

[24] Hafner-Burton, *Forced to Be Good,* 144–6.

128 PROMOTING JUSTICE ACROSS BORDERS

legitimate. For oppositional intervention to be justified, recipient states must be at least partially illegitimate, though they need not be fully illegitimate.

Extra-Institutional Interventions

Extra-institutional reform intervention, remember, seeks to encourage political change in a recipient society without directly interacting with its established (formal, political) institutions. Boycott and divestment campaigns exemplify this type of intervention. Take the BDS movement. Insofar as it advocates for governments to sanction the government of Israel, it does interact with Israel's formal political institutions. A substantial portion of its campaign, though, is focused on encouraging economic, cultural, and academic boycotts, and divestment from companies that profit from Israeli occupation and settlement.[25] These parts of the campaign are certainly political and seek to bring about legal and political changes in Israel, but they don't engage directly with the country's formal institutions. Though they obviously aim to subject Israeli officials to pressure, they don't aim to interfere with the enforcement of Israeli law or otherwise remove Israeli policymaking authority to international bodies.

I propose that extra-institutional reform interventions like this don't involve a failure to meet condition (1) from above—interveners don't deny recipient states any degree of domestic policymaking authority. (This is contrary to Tesón's claim that any "act of intervention impinges on the monopoly of coercive power that a government wields in its territory.")[26] The claim that an extra-institutional intervention is justified is compatible with the claim that its recipient state should have exclusive domestic policymaking authority. After all, the modus operandi of extra-institutional interventions is to influence the actions taken by officials within established institutions, but only by means that are themselves compatible with the institutions' continued existence and normal operation.[27]

---

[25] See BDS, "What Is BDS?," accessed 26 July 2017, https://bdsmovement.net/what-is-bds.

[26] Tesón, *A Philosophy of International Law*, 47. This disagreement with Tesón is, at least in part, semantic. In the same book, he defines an "intervention" as "any act that punctures the sovereignty of the target state" (60). My point is that attempts to promote justice in a foreign society can raise (some of) the moral questions central to an ethics of "intervention" even when they do not challenge the recipient state's domestic policymaking authority.

[27] The requirement that an intervention not interfere with the normal operation of recipient institutions in order to qualify as "extra-institutional" is important. One could imagine a boycott movement that so devastated the recipient state's economy that its established political institutions were unable to function adequately. Such an intervention would count as "oppositional." One could

DEGREES OF LEGITIMACY   129

There is one exception to this conclusion—namely, extra-institutional interventions that use force.[28] Interveners who use force attempt to directly (forcefully) implement their own preferred policies in recipient societies. They therefore deny recipient states an exclusive claim to domestic policy-making authority. They fail to meet condition (1), at least to a degree. (This aligns with the intuition that forceful action is typically forbidden against fully legitimate institutions.)

Does this mean those engaging in *non-forceful* extra-institutional intervention treat recipient states as they ought to treat fully legitimate states? In other words, can non-forceful extra-institutional interventions be justified when recipient states are fully legitimate? I haven't yet said enough to answer these questions. Recall that there are two conditions outsiders to a given state must meet in order to treat it as a fully legitimate state. We have established that extra-institutional intervention (as long as it doesn't use force) doesn't involve a failure to meet the first of these conditions (granting recipient states domestic policymaking authority), but what about the second?

The second condition requires that outsiders grant (or at least not deny) the state in question "good standing" in the international community. The question, then, is whether or not engaging in non-forceful extra-institutional intervention involves denying recipient states "good standing." If extra-institutional intervention does constitute a denial of good standing, it will be justifiable only when recipient states are at least partially illegitimate; if it doesn't constitute a denial of good standing, it may be justified even when recipient states are fully legitimate.

The answer to our question will depend on what it means to be a member in good standing of the international community. Note, I don't mean "good standing in the international community" to signify only that a state is legally

---

also imagine an intervention that prevented its recipient state from fulfilling the criteria it would need to in order to be legitimate. Depending on the specifics of the case, this sort of intervention, too, could count as interfering with the normal operation of recipients' institutions, and therefore could count as "oppositional." And even if this *weren't* true, such an intervention might undermine recipients' collective self-determination. (Some think one criterion of legitimacy is that a state channels or expresses its people's collective self-determination.) If this were the case, even an intervention that didn't fail to recognize or respect recipients' already legitimate institutions could be objectionable because it undermined their collective self-determination. I'll discuss this possibility in the next chapter.

[28] I take it that, generally, forceful interventions will target recipients' established political institutions directly (and will therefore be oppositional). However, I leave it open, as a conceptual possibility, that a forceful intervention may be extra-institutional.

130 PROMOTING JUSTICE ACROSS BORDERS

recognized as such by other states or international legal institutions. I assume that entities legally recognized as states can lack good standing in the sense in which I use the term here. That said, what it means to have "good standing in the international community" must reflect in some way conventional understandings of what this means that are actually accepted in real-world global politics. This is because "good standing" is a status; part of enjoying a status is enjoying recognition as having that status; and the form that recognition takes depends on the shared norms of the relevant community (in this case, the international community).

Just as one person might deny another the status of a moral equal by refusing to recognize them as a moral equal (even though they are, in fact, a moral equal), one state might deny another state the status of member in good standing of the international community (whether or not the latter deserves this status). In the interpersonal case, which actions count as refusing to recognize another as a moral equal depends at least in part on the accepted conventions of the relevant community. And the same is true in the international case: which actions count as granting or denying a state the status of member in good standing depends at least in part on the accepted conventions of the international community.

So what does it mean for a state to enjoy good standing in the international community? Rawls offers quite an extreme view. He argues that in order for a people[29] to enjoy good standing in the international community, other peoples must refrain from *any* deliberate attempts to influence its domestic policymaking, even (perhaps especially) if their aim is to promote justice. Rawls' view seems to be that if a people employs any means—including, strikingly, diplomatic pressure—to encourage political reform in another, the intervening people denies the recipient people status as a full member of international society.[30]

Arguably, Rawls even holds that one people officially and publicly *criticizing* another with the aim of encouraging it to adopt more just policies domestically amounts to a denial of good standing—as evidenced by his apparent position that liberal peoples shouldn't officially, publicly criticize decent peoples with the aim of liberalizing them, lest the former deny the latter

---

[29] I use the language of "peoples" rather than states here because it's the language Rawls uses. Note, however, that a "people" is simply a particular kind of society governed by a particular kind of political institutions (Rawls, *Law of Peoples*, 23–5).

[30] Ibid., 59.

DEGREES OF LEGITIMACY   131

their due respect as full members of the Society of Peoples (the international community).[31]

That said, though Rawls thinks *peoples* encouraging other *peoples* to adopt justice-enhancing reforms constitutes a denial of good standing, similar encouragement undertaken by individuals, activist networks, NGOs, or corporations (for example), as opposed to (states representing) peoples, might *not* constitute a denial of good standing. This is because, on Rawls' view, good standing in international society is something *peoples* enjoy (or not) in virtue of how they are treated by other *peoples*.[32] The myriad other political actors that aren't proper members of Rawls' "Society of Peoples" arguably could try to influence a people's domestic politics without denying it good standing in the Society. These other political actors are simply incapable of granting or denying standing, and their treatment of peoples is therefore no indication of those peoples' standing.[33]

---

[31] Rawls' views on the role of public criticism (as such—that is, detached from any material or coercive sanction) in the Society of Peoples are somewhat ambiguous. However, the textual evidence strongly suggests that if a liberal people launched official public criticism against a decent people with the aim of *bringing about liberal reforms* in the latter, rather than merely registering the liberals' disagreement with the decent people's policies (as allowed on ibid., 84), they would deny the decent people good standing. If a liberal people were, in its official capacity, to criticize a decent people in order to make the decent people more liberal, this could qualify as a "political" or "diplomatic" sanction, which Rawls says are precluded by international toleration (which in turn is required because of the respect owed liberal and decent peoples) (59, 61). Or such public criticism might be one of the further damages members in good standing of the Society of Peoples ought to be immune from, whose existence Rawls reveals when he says that good standing requires more than mere freedom from political sanction (59). Moreover, Rawls holds that making other societies liberal is not a legitimate end of a liberal people's foreign policy (9–10, 62–3, 82–3, 92–3) and that all official activity in the Society of Peoples must be justified in terms of the Society's public reason, which doesn't recognize as valid reasons grounded in the goal of making its members liberal (54–9, 121–3). Both these positions imply that any official activity (including public criticism) on the part of liberal peoples meant to liberalize decent peoples would be unjustifiable according to the Society of Peoples' governing principles. Rawls also suggests that the only way liberal societies may pursue global liberalization is by treating decent peoples with respect (i.e., refraining from trying to induce them to reform) in the hopes that they will eventually liberalize on their own (61–2, 122). Finally, whenever Rawls does talk about permissible persuasive influence meant to bring about liberalizing reforms in other societies, it is an example of an acceptable course of action against a non-decent people—that is, one that can be permissibly denied good standing in the Society of Peoples (38, 93, 93–4n). Prominent interpreters have also read Rawls' ideal in *The Law of Peoples* as precluding liberal peoples officially criticizing decent peoples for being illiberal; see Stephen Macedo, "What Self-Governing Peoples Owe to One Another: Universalism, Diversity, and the Law of Peoples," *Fordham Law Review* 72, no. 5 (2004): 1721–38, 1725; Tesón, *A Philosophy of International Law*, 113–4; Leif Wenar, "John Rawls," in *The Stanford Encyclopedia of Philosophy*, ed. Edward N. Zalta, Spring 2017 edition, https://plato.stanford.edu/archives/spr2017/entries/rawls/.

[32] See, for example, where Rawls explicitly distinguishes between a liberal people's foreign policy and the actions of its citizens or civil society groups (*Law of Peoples*, 85).

[33] Michael Walzer makes a similar point when he argues that individual and nonstate activist groups can "legitimately" promote democracy in foreign societies even when a state's doing the same would be illegitimate. Walzer, though, doesn't cite states' unique ability to deny good standing, instead noting that individuals' interference (unlike states') is "noncoercive, dependent on persuasion, and slow enough in its effects to allow the 'other people' [recipients] time to consider and reconsider

132   PROMOTING JUSTICE ACROSS BORDERS

Others besides Rawls hold that, to enjoy good standing in the international community, a state must be free from *some*—but need not be free from *all*—kinds of deliberate influence from other states. Certainly, subjection to forceful intervention is widely characterized as a denial of good standing. Subjection to coercive but non-forceful intervention is discussed less extensively and less explicitly in political theory, so it isn't especially clear whether it's generally thought to entail a denial of good standing. For example, when Buchanan writes that granting a state recognitional legitimacy means granting it "the full bundle of powers, liberties, rights, and immunities that constitute sovereignty,"[34] it isn't immediately obvious if these include freedom from all coercive interference.

In any case, in order to decide whether extra-institutional interventions deny recipients good standing in the international community, and whether they are therefore justified only when recipient states are at least partially illegitimate, we must continue to develop our view about what it means to enjoy good standing.

Rawls' view is too extreme; it identifies too many kinds of foreign influence as denials of good standing in the international community. It presents the international community as one in which membership in good standing (which is enjoyed, or not, by *peoples*) entails total isolation from any other member's (i.e., any other *people's*) deliberate political influence (at least when it's aimed at promoting justice within the first member's domestic society). Probably the strongest defense of this view would begin by analogizing—as Rawls does—between peoples in international society and individuals in domestic political society.[35] This would at least give us strong reason to value peoples' independence on the international stage, as we value individuals' independence on the domestic stage—which might, in turn, lend credence to the view that peoples who deserve to enjoy good standing in the international community should leave each other be.

However, even accepting this analogy (which I actually think we should reject, except perhaps in some rare circumstances), I propose we shouldn't accept Rawls' account of what it means to be a member in good standing

what they are doing"; see Michael Walzer, "On Promoting Democracy," *Ethics and International Affairs* 22, no. 4 (2008): 351–5, 352.

[34] Allen Buchanan, *Justice, Legitimacy, and Self-Determination: Moral Foundations for International Law* (Oxford: Oxford University Press, 2003), 145.
[35] See Rawls, *Law of Peoples*, 25, 55, 59–60, 122–3.

in international society. After all, enjoying "good standing" in domestic political society doesn't typically require members to be totally free from each other's deliberate influence. In fact, vigorous political contestation, in which members publicly criticize each other, try to get others to support their favorite causes, and perhaps provide material incentives (in the form of campaign contributions or protest boycotts) for them to do so—all activities Rawls prohibits among members in good standing of the international community—is often seen as a sign of a healthy domestic political community.

If we accept the analogy between peoples and individuals—without which Rawls' account of membership in good standing in the international community seems facially much less plausible—why should we think that international and domestic political societies are so different in this respect (what it means for members to enjoy good standing)? Rawls seems to offer two possible reasons. One is that a proper respect for toleration requires members of *international society* specifically to refrain from influencing other members.[36] We have already seen, though, that there are ways to engage in reform intervention compatible with a proper commitment to toleration. A concern for toleration, then, shouldn't make us think any people's attempt to influence another in the name of justice necessarily denies the latter good standing in the international community.

The other reason Rawls might have to think members in good standing of the international community must be totally free from other members' deliberate justice-promoting influence is the distinctive value of political self-determination. The thought goes something like this: one main point of international society is to facilitate the political self-determination of all its members who enjoy good standing, and this is made difficult if not impossible when members seek to influence each other's domestic politics. I address this concern in more detail in the next chapter, but for now it suffices to make two quick observations.

First, it isn't at all obvious what exactly collective self-determination requires in the way of political institutions, or that its achievement will always be frustrated by external influences.[37] As suggested in Chapter 1, we have good reason to think that societies can exert influence on each other in

---

[36] Ibid., 59–62.
[37] For one account of how foreign influence might *enable* collective self-determination, see Allen Buchanan, "Self-Determination, Revolution, and Intervention," *Ethics* 126 (2016): 447–73.

134 PROMOTING JUSTICE ACROSS BORDERS

a variety of ways, not all of which will be equally (or perhaps at all) threatening to recipients' self-determination. Second, pointing out the importance of peoples' self-determination hardly seems promising as a method of distinguishing the international from the domestic political community. After all, we also typically think individuals' self-determination is critically important, yet we *don't* typically take this to mean they must not be subject to any influence from other individuals with whom they share a political community.

If Rawls' view is too extreme, and others have little to tell us about whether (or under what conditions) nonviolent interventions deny recipients "good standing" in the international community, we'll need an alternative.

In the spirit of Buchanan's earlier sentiment,[38] I propose that states enjoy good standing in the international community when no other state denies them the privileges standardly granted to legitimate states, including the privilege to conduct a (non-aggressive) foreign policy of their own choosing. I'll presume for now that *states* in particular are the actors capable of granting or denying good standing. This reflects not a deep, immutable moral truth but a contingent fact about the way the concept of good standing has developed in global politics as practiced (and, often, as theorized). The traditional picture of the international community is one of a society of states; since states are the members of this community, it is states that enjoy good standing or don't, and states that grant others good standing or deny it. Note, I don't claim that any state enjoying good standing is necessarily legitimate or that any state denied it is necessarily illegitimate. Again, I won't endorse any particular view about what makes states legitimate. Instead, I claim that denying a state good standing in the international community is one way for outsiders to treat that state *as if* it is illegitimate, and that only states can deny good standing in the international community to other states.

I'll proceed for now taking this picture of the international community as given. Since, according to this characterization, only state-led interventions even have the capacity to deny recipient states good standing, my discussion will focus (for now) on *state-led* (non-forceful) extra-institutional interventions.

Enjoying good standing, on the view I've proposed, doesn't require that a state's activities never be subject to political contestation on the part of other states. Instead, it puts requirements on the *ways* in which other states undertake this political contestation. For instance, they can't, consistent with

---

[38] Buchanan, *Justice, Legitimacy, and Self-Determination,* 145.

DEGREES OF LEGITIMACY 135

recipients' good standing, intervene such that their sheer military or geopolitical power virtually guarantees recipients will acquiesce, adopting interveners' preferred policies. In other words, state-run totally and highly controlling (extra-institutional) interventions are incompatible with recipient states enjoying good standing in the international community. Recipients of these kinds of interventions are made into mere puppets of their foreign influencers. Whatever enjoying good standing in the international community requires, it must at least require not being the mere instrument of other members' wills.

And even if interveners' military or geopolitical power doesn't *determine* an intervention's outcome—as it doesn't with slightly controlling or persuasive intervention—it will almost certainly affect the course of the intervention. For instance, Hafner-Burton finds that a country's market share in the global economy is a good predictor of whether it will be able to convince other countries to sign onto trade agreements containing restrictive human rights provisions.[39] The US, for example, has an easier job than others recruiting signatories for these agreements because its economic power makes it an extremely attractive trading partner. If an economically less powerful country would lose out on advantageous trading terms with the US unless it agreed to abide by the latter's proposed human rights standards, that could be a significant economic loss.[40] This may be true even if the resulting loss wouldn't be so devastating as to render compliance with the standards the only viable option. Thus, even interventions that leave recipients free to take one of a number of reasonable options (even those that are slightly controlling or persuasive, that is) may bear the mark of disparities in geopolitical power among interveners and recipients.

Of course, as indicated above, the US attaching human rights provisions to trade agreements—and then enforcing them—may qualify as oppositional intervention, which I've taken to constitute at least a partial denial of legitimacy. One could easily imagine a similar case, though, in which, rather than imposing sanctions in response to a trading partner violating some human rights standard, a state supported boycott or divestment movements within its own borders, or divested itself from its dealings with businesses in another country. We could classify such a move as an extra-institutional intervention. Still, though, this would be a far more effective move if there were

[39] Hafner-Burton, *Forced to Be Good*, 30–2, 115–6.
[40] Ibid.

136 PROMOTING JUSTICE ACROSS BORDERS

a significant differential in political or economic power between intervener and recipient.

This raises the question of whether manifest power inequalities between interveners and recipients can render even slightly controlling and persuasive (non-forceful, extra-institutional) interventions indicative of a loss of good standing in the international community. If a state's enjoying good standing means no other state denies it the privileges standardly granted to legitimate states, is good standing compromised when one state leverages its superior geopolitical power[41] to incentivize or encourage political change in another state—even if it's left up to the latter to decide whether to accept the incentive or encouragement?

One might think the fact that geopolitically powerful states will in general be the ones able to effectively intervene and that geopolitically less powerful states will in general be those subject to intervention means that an international politics in which intervention plays a significant role will inevitably be one in which the disempowered are denied good standing. The worry is that patterns of intervention that reinforce existing geopolitical hierarchies consistently establish recipient states as inferiors to other members of the international community. Though these recipient states aren't forced (or even, necessarily, coerced) to do interveners' bidding, the consistent reinforcement of their inferior position amounts to a denial of equal status that *effectively* prevents them from enjoying the standard privileges of a fully sovereign state—and thus prevents them from enjoying good standing in the international community. On this view, the less powerful states repeatedly subject to intervention are, in some sense, puppets of the more powerful interveners. This is, in fact, one prominent objection raised against the "Responsibility to Protect" norm in international relations, and against humanitarian intervention more generally.[42]

This is a serious concern, but there are ways to mitigate it. It is not, after all, the act of reform intervention itself that is problematic but the ways in which its practice instantiates and reinforces global power inequalities. But this would be less of a risk if interveners leveraged their superior power to

---

[41] I can't offer a precise definition of "geopolitical power" or a complete account of all its determinants. This is at least as much a job for empirical social science as it is for political theory. Suffice it to say that I use "geopolitical power" to refer generally to an actor's total power in global politics, including, for example, military and economic power, negotiating power, influence in international institutions, and reputational stature.

[42] For a brief discussion, see Michael Doyle, *The Question of Intervention: John Stuart Mill and the Responsibility to Protect* (New Haven, CT: Yale University Press, 2015), 120–1, 140.

DEGREES OF LEGITIMACY 137

undermine the power structures that advantaged them in the first place. They could achieve this, for example, by (a) opening themselves up to the same kinds of interventions they aimed at others[43] or (b) subjecting their operations to some kind of oversight from other, less powerful states or other actors in global civil society. If it had been accomplished more fully, the international community's adoption of the New International Economic Order (proposed in the 1970s as a way to make the rules of international politics more responsive to the needs of the developing world),[44] and any accompanying enforcement, might have been a good example of powerful states acting so as to undermine the power structures that advantaged them.

Thus, there are arguably some circumstances under which slightly controlling and persuasive extra-institutional interventions, even when undertaken by powerful states and aimed at less powerful recipients, can be compatible with recipients' good standing in the international community—and thus with their full legitimacy. After all, above I stipulated that outsiders to a legitimate state ought to (1) grant it policymaking authority and (2) grant (or at least not deny) it "good standing" in the international community. I've already established that those engaged in (non-forceful) extra-institutional intervention do grant recipient states an exclusive claim to domestic policymaking authority; these interveners therefore fully satisfy condition (1).

What was left to do was to determine whether those engaging in (non-forceful) extra-institutional intervention denied recipients good standing in the international community. If they did, they wouldn't meet condition (2). We would then have to conclude that they didn't treat recipient states as outsiders ought to treat legitimate states; their interventions would be justified only if the recipient states were at least partially illegitimate. I've just argued, though, that *in some cases* slightly controlling and persuasive extra-institutional interventions (even when the interveners are comparatively powerful states and the recipients are less powerful) *don't* constitute a denial of recipients' good standing in the international community.

---

[43] For example, when the US signed the trade agreement with Oman discussed above, the US did agree to be subject to the same human rights standards, and the same potential recourse should it violate them, as Oman (Hafner-Burton, *Forced to Be Good,* 145–6). Of course, this doesn't totally erase the residue of the power asymmetry between the US and Oman; it was still the US that had the economic stature to insist on the terms of the deal in the first place.

[44] See United Nations General Assembly, Resolution Adopted by the United Nations General Assembly: 3201 (S-VI), Declaration on the Establishment of a New International Economic Order, 1 May 1974, http://www.un-documents.net/s6r3201.htm.

138 PROMOTING JUSTICE ACROSS BORDERS

This is because for a state to enjoy "good standing," no other state must deny it the privileges standardly granted to legitimate states. Powerful states deprive others of this ability when they act in ways that reinforce their already disproportionate power in global politics. Engaging in reform intervention may well be one of these problematic actions—but this isn't so if powerful interveners act so as to undermine status quo power hierarchies, thus augmenting, rather than undercutting, less powerful states' abilities to exercise the privileges standardly granted to legitimate states. In working to undermine the power hierarchies that privileged them in the first place, powerful interveners would help make recipients less, rather than more, vulnerable to their power.

We would be mistaken to say that any time a geopolitically powerful state utilized its power to induce less powerful states to change their behavior in some way, it treated them as inferiors. After all, even powerful states find themselves embedded in power structures that aren't easy to dismantle. Whenever they act, they act within these power structures, and it may therefore be virtually impossible for them to act without leveraging their unequal power. There must, though, be some way for states to grant each other good standing even as they are embedded in social and political structures that give them unequal power (lest the concept of good international standing become normatively inert and wholly inapplicable to the real world). Powerful states meet this challenge when, though they leverage their unequal power, they do so in ways that amplify the voices of less powerful states, effectively raising the less powerful states' political stature and undercutting the established hierarchies that subjugate them in the first place.[45]

Let me take stock of what I've argued so far, with respect to those engaging in (non-forceful) state-led extra-institutional interventions: though they don't deny recipient states any policymaking authority, some of them do deny recipient states good standing in the international community. Specifically, those states that engage in totally or highly controlling extra-institutional interventions deny recipients good standing. Those states that engage in slightly controlling or persuasive extra-institutional interventions, where they're more geopolitically powerful than recipient states, also deny recipients good standing *unless* they leverage their superior power to

---

[45] For helpful treatments of the ethics of acting within social structures that instantiate significant power differentials, see A. J. Julius, "Nagel's Atlas," *Philosophy and Public Affairs* 34, no. 2 (2006): 176–92; Iris Marion Young, "Responsibility and Global Justice: A Social Connection Model," *Social Philosophy and Policy* 23, no. 1 (2006): 102–30.

undermine the power structures that advantaged them in the first place. They could achieve this, for example, by (a) opening themselves up to the same kinds of interventions they aimed at others or (b) subjecting their operations to some kind of oversight from other, less powerful states or other actors in global civil society.

Therefore, state-led extra-institutional interventions that are totally or highly controlling are justifiable only when recipient states are at least partially illegitimate. Similarly, state-led extra-institutional interventions where the interveners are more powerful than the recipients, and where the interveners don't do anything to undermine the power structures that advantaged them in the first place, are justifiable only when recipient states are at least partially illegitimate. As long as they are slightly controlling or persuasive, state-led extra-institutional interventions where the interveners are more powerful than the recipients, and where the interveners *do* leverage their superior power to undermine the power structures that advantaged them in the first place, are justifiable even when recipient states are fully legitimate. The same goes for state-led extra-institutional interventions where the interveners are not more powerful than the recipients.

What, then, about extra-institutional interventions led by nonstate actors? Do they treat recipient states as legitimate states? We've already established that (as long as they don't use force), they don't deny recipient states any policymaking authority. So, according to the account of how outsiders ought to treat legitimate states stipulated at the beginning of this chapter, what's left to do is determine whether extra-institutional interventions led by nonstate actors deny recipient states good standing in the international community. If they don't, they will be justifiable even when recipient states are fully legitimate.

As I've been conceiving of "good standing in the international community" so far, only *states* are capable of granting or denying it to other states. Therefore, it seems nonstate interveners can't deny recipient states good standing in the international community. If this is right, extra-institutional interventions led by nonstate actors are indeed justifiable even when recipient states are fully legitimate.

One might object to this conclusion by arguing that the account of how outsiders ought to treat legitimate states stipulated at the beginning of this chapter is mistaken. Objectors may argue that in order to treat a state as legitimate, outsiders must not only (1) grant it policymaking authority and (2) grant (or at least not deny) it "good standing" in the international

140   PROMOTING JUSTICE ACROSS BORDERS

community, but they must *also* (3) grant (or at least not deny) it "good standing" in another, more inclusive, global community—say a "global civil society" collective, containing states, INGOs, transnational activist networks, and multinational corporations. The objection continues: it may be true that only states can grant or deny other states good standing in the *international community*. But surely nonstate actors can grant or deny states good standing in this *global community*.

It's certainly right that there are other communities on the global stage besides the international community conceived of as a society of states. And the actions of these communities' nonstate members may have significant consequences for states. After all, nonstate actors are increasingly important in global politics—and much of the present work has been devoted to guiding our ethical judgments about their geopolitical activities. Often, nonstate actors' political choices will have significant consequences for the states they interact with. The decision of a large corporation to withdraw its operations from a given state, for example, may prove much more debilitating to that state's economy (and therefore to its geopolitical power) than would the decision of another, smaller state to end diplomatic relations with it.[46]

However, this doesn't mean that outsiders to a given state must grant (or at least not deny) it good standing in the global community in order to treat it as a legitimate state. It may mean (to put it in the language of my typology) that being denied good standing in the global community can expose a state to serious costs, just as being denied good standing in the international community can. But not everything that exposes a state to significant costs amounts to a denial of its legitimacy. And we have little reason to think denying a state good standing in the global community amounts to denying its legitimacy in the same way denying it good standing in the international community would. After all, membership (and therefore good standing) in the global community is not obviously connected to political legitimacy in the way membership in the international community conceptualized as a society of states is. The global community contains many members in good standing (NGOs, transnational activist movements, and corporations) not even claiming (let alone recognized as having) political legitimacy. Membership in good standing in this global community is not premised on legitimacy, so it's unclear why revoking a member's good standing should be interpreted as a denial of its legitimacy. Hence the specific formulation of condition (2): in

---

[46] I thank Anna Stilz for bringing this issue to my attention.

DEGREES OF LEGITIMACY 141

order to treat a state as legitimate, outsiders must grant, or at least not deny, it good standing in the *international* community—and good standing in the international community is something that can be denied only by other states.

The upshot is that, even if nonstate interveners could deny recipient states good standing in some global community (though not in the *international* community conceived of as a society of states), doing so wouldn't contravene a requirement for how outsiders ought to treat legitimate states. This is because states' good standing in the sort of community whose membership nonstate actors could police (the global community) isn't premised on their legitimacy in the first place. Thus, our original conclusion still stands: (non-forceful) non-state-led extra-institutional interventions are justifiable even when recipient states are fully legitimate.

Intra-Systemic Interventions

The final type of reform intervention I'll discuss here is what I've called *intra-systemic* intervention. Recall that intra-systemic interveners engage in political contestation *through* (rather than against or outside) recipients' established institutions, and only in ways *allowed by the rules of those institutions*. Consider the Latin American countries that submitted amicus briefs opposing Arizona's SB 1070. They attempted to produce political and legal change in the US (the invalidation of SB 1070). Their attempt, however, didn't in any way discredit US political institutions, as the rules of these very institutions provided that the courts should review the law in question, that they should consider amicus briefs, and that foreign countries were allowed to submit briefs. Far from denying their legitimacy, if anything, the act of submitting amicus briefs signaled an acknowledgment that US institutions *were* legitimate. When opponents to the political status quo direct their opposition through the official channels of the powers they seek to oppose, they implicitly grant that these institutions have legitimate authority over the political arena in which they seek to engage.[47]

---

[47] In reality, this may not be the interveners' goal at all. Interveners may choose to work within the constraints of recipients' established institutions simply because it is good strategy. This possibility, though, doesn't pose a problem for the account I offer here. My main points are that (i) intra-systemic interventions are justifiable even when recipient institutions are fully legitimate, and (ii) insofar as engaging in reform intervention via recipients' established political institutions lends them credibility or enables them to more easily exercise their power, it may reinforce their legitimacy. For one account of the relationship between "intra-systemic" opposition to a state's laws and that state's

142   PROMOTING JUSTICE ACROSS BORDERS

Certainly, one could justify an intra-systemic intervention like this one while still maintaining the recipient state had a claim to exclusive policy-making authority within its jurisdiction. And intra-systemic interventions do nothing to deny recipient states good standing in the international community. Thus, intra-systemic interveners treat recipient states as fully legitimate, and intra-systemic interventions are justifiable even when recipient states are fully legitimate.

On a Scalar Notion of Legitimacy

I'd now like to bring our attention to one important consequence of understanding the relationship between legitimacy and reform intervention as I've presented it. Namely, recognizing that some reform interventions are justifiable when recipient states are fully legitimate, some when they are partially legitimate, and some only when they are totally illegitimate, requires us to conceive of legitimacy as a trait that states can possess in degrees rather than a binary quality that they either have or don't.

Just as Chapter 2's discussion of toleration and reform intervention yielded a novel account of toleration, so the present discussion of legitimacy and reform intervention has yielded a novel, scalar notion of legitimacy. Note, in using the word "scalar," I don't mean to imply that how well a state does at fulfilling the various criteria of legitimacy (whatever they are) could be translated into an entry on a single, continuous, numerical scale. For that to be true, the different criteria of legitimacy (which might include, for example, protecting a number of different human rights) would, for one thing, have to be commensurable.[48] I make no such claim here. Rather, when I say legitimacy is scalar, I simply mean it is a property states can have in degrees. "More legitimate" states are those outsiders ought to grant more policymaking

---

legitimacy—albeit one specifically meant to apply to the domestic context—see Pettit, *On the People's Terms*, 137–8.

[48] For example, if a state had to protect a slate of basic human rights to be legitimate, evaluating its legitimacy on a single, continuous, numerical scale would require "scoring" how well it did at protecting each right and somehow combining those scores to yield an overall legitimacy score. This would require that we be able to express the quality of a state's performance at protecting each right in terms of the same "units." We'd have to be able to answer questions like "How many violations of the right to subsistence equals one violation of the right against torture?" Some may argue that rights violations are commensurable in this way, but I won't take a position on this controversial meta-ethical question here.

DEGREES OF LEGITIMACY 143

authority and/or grant good standing in the international community. In other words, more legitimate states are those in which it's harder (all else equal) to justify intervening in more (and more intrusive) ways. Conversely, "less legitimate" states are those to which outsiders owe more limited grants of policymaking authority and/or which they needn't grant good standing in the international community. That is, less legitimate states are those in which it's easier (all else equal) to justify intervening in more (and more intrusive) ways.[49]

This scalar notion of legitimacy is preferable to its binary alternative. Adopting a scalar notion of legitimacy allows us a more nuanced understanding of how legitimacy, and the normative obligations it brings with it, manifests in the real world. A scalar notion is truer to the ways in which actual states do and don't instantiate the criteria of legitimacy (whatever they are). After all, almost whatever values a state must instantiate or qualities it must exemplify in order to count as legitimate, it can instantiate or exemplify to greater or lesser degrees. For example, representativeness and procedural fairness, both commonly invoked metrics of legitimacy, can be possessed in degrees.[50] State institutions can be more or less responsive to citizens' input.[51] They can more or less perfectly instantiate values like freedom and equality.[52] And they can do better or worse jobs at fulfilling functional standards for legitimacy, such as ability and willingness to protect human rights.[53]

Moreover, I started with the assumption that outsiders to a legitimate state ought to (1) grant it policymaking authority and (2) grant (or at least not deny) it "good standing" in the international community. But my examination of different types of reform intervention—and whether they are

---

[49] I thank Aaron James and Michael Blake for pushing me to clarify these points.

[50] For an example of a view that takes representativeness as a criterion of legitimacy, see Walzer's discussion of the "fit" between a people and their government in "The Moral Standing of States." For a review of "purely procedural" views on the criteria of democratic authority, see Thomas Christiano's discussion in "The Authority of Democracy," *Journal of Political Philosophy* 12, no. 3 (2004): 266–90, 266–7.

[51] As explained in note 14 of this chapter, Rawls presents responsiveness to citizens' input as a criterion of legitimacy when he sets out the consultation procedure non-liberal societies must adopt in order to qualify as "decent" and therefore as members in good standing of the international community (*The Law of Peoples*, 62–78). So does Stilz, in *Liberal Loyalty*, 88–96. See also her discussion of "maker" interests in "Against Democratic Interventionism."

[52] Pettit makes sufficient realization of freedom-as-non-domination the criterion of legitimacy in *On the People's Terms*, especially ch. 3. Thomas Christiano argues that democratic authority depends on institutions' ability to publicly instantiate citizens' equality; see "The Authority of Democracy."

[53] Altman and Wellman offer a theory of legitimacy based on states' ability to fulfill human rights requirements in *A Liberal Theory of International Justice*. David Luban offers another based on states' ability to protect what he calls "socially basic human rights" in "Just War and Human Rights."

144 PROMOTING JUSTICE ACROSS BORDERS

co-realizable with conditions (1) and (2)—has revealed that outsiders can also fulfill these two conditions to greater or lesser degrees. Specifically, they can fulfill condition (1) fully by granting a state *exclusive* domestic policy-making authority; they can fulfill it partially by granting a state *some non-exclusive* domestic policymaking authority; or they can fulfill it not at all by granting a state *no* domestic policymaking authority. Moreover, an intervention might fully realize condition (1) but fail to realize condition (2), thus fulfilling the conjunction of conditions (1) and (2) only partially.

So both the criteria of legitimacy (basically whatever they are) and the requirements as to how outsiders ought to behave toward legitimate states (conditions (1) and (2) above) can be achieved in degrees. We should, then, prefer a conception of legitimacy that recognizes this (a scalar conception) to one that occludes it (as a binary conception would). In other words, a scalar understanding of legitimacy better reflects moral reality—that states can fulfill the criteria of legitimacy more or less well, and that outsiders can fulfill the moral requirements regarding how they should treat legitimate states more or less fully.

A scalar notion of legitimacy also better reflects political reality—that, arguably, real states often occupy a middle ground between unambiguous legitimacy and unambiguous illegitimacy, and that global political actors often treat states in ways that reflect this ambiguity. Adopting a scalar conception of legitimacy allows us to form moral judgments (e.g., about the moral status of particular states and the ways in which outsiders are permitted or obligated to treat them) more responsive to the actual conditions of global politics. With respect to reform intervention specifically, it allows us to identify and evaluate a class of interventions—those justifiable when recipient states are at least partially, but not necessarily fully, illegitimate—that we would be forced to ignore if we adopted a binary notion instead. As the foregoing discussion suggests, these kinds of interventions really do happen, so it's a significant disadvantage of binary accounts of legitimacy that they can't guide our judgments in these cases.

Some might object that, though my scalar notion of legitimacy has the distinct advantage of better reflecting both moral and political reality compared to its binary alternative, it has significant disadvantages as well. For example, some might argue that adopting a scalar notion of legitimacy risks obscuring the fact that, in some cases, all-or-nothing judgments about a state's legitimacy are appropriate. Sometimes states really are fully legitimate or fully illegitimate, and we should have the resources to judge them as such. Surely this is true, but it is no reason against adopting a scalar notion of legitimacy. Understanding legitimacy as scalar doesn't preclude judging a given state to be fully or not at all legitimate; it only adds the additional possibility of judging it to be somewhat but not fully legitimate.

Others might oppose adding this third possibility, arguing that doing so would make it harder for large and diverse pools of people to use standards of legitimacy to coordinate their judgments and behavior. Legitimacy is often presented as a standard that allows people to coordinate in these ways even in the face of widespread disagreement—especially about justice.[54] And some might say understanding legitimacy as a binary would make this coordination easier.[55] After all, with a binary understanding, there are fewer points at which people may disagree: they need agree only about whether a state is legitimate or not, not about what precise degree of legitimacy it possesses and what that means for how outsiders ought to treat it.

However, there is little reason to think a binary understanding of legitimacy would *as a general rule* facilitate coordination better than my scalar understanding—especially if, as suggested above, we live in a world where many states occupy a middle ground between unambiguous legitimacy and unambiguous illegitimacy. If people are faced with a state whose legitimacy is ambiguous or contestable—one that is neither obviously fully legitimate nor obviously totally illegitimate—and are forced to choose whether it is "legitimate" or "illegitimate," it's reasonable to expect significant disagreement about the right choice. The introduction of a third option—that the state is partly legitimate, and therefore deserves some but not all the deference owed to fully legitimate states—may actually facilitate coordination by providing an option that those who would disagree about which binary category the state fits best could agree upon.

Overall, then, my scalar notion of legitimacy seems preferable to its binary alternative: it better reflects moral and political reality; it doesn't preclude making all-or-nothing judgments about legitimacy when appropriate; and it won't necessarily hinder—and may even help—standards of legitimacy performing their distinctive coordination function.

---

[54] See, e.g., Buchanan, "Institutional Legitimacy"; Allen Buchanan and Robert O. Keohane, "The Legitimacy of Global Governance Institutions," *Ethics and International Affairs* 20, no. 4 (2006): 405–37; Stilz, *Liberal Loyalty*, especially ch. 4.

[55] Michael Blake suggests such a view (though here he discusses legitimacy as a legal, not a moral, concept) in *Justice and Foreign Policy* (Oxford: Oxford University Press, 2013), 68–9.

146   PROMOTING JUSTICE ACROSS BORDERS

Adopting this scalar notion of legitimacy marks a significant departure from the existing literature. Even those who acknowledge that, in reality, legitimacy is a property that states can possess to a greater or lesser degree, seldom discuss the normative significance of this finding. Certainly, they don't tell us what it means for how we ought to evaluate a given case of reform intervention. But, more generally, they don't tell us what it means for how anyone ought to act, engage in politics, or design institutions.

Pettit, for example, acknowledges that states can be more or less legitimate, in proportion to how good or bad a job they do at guaranteeing that people enjoy freedom as non-domination in their relationships to the state.[56] However, he then explicitly specifies that his own discussions of legitimacy and its normative significance will treat legitimacy *as if* it were a binary quality, employing an on/off heuristic test to distinguish legitimate from illegitimate regimes.[57]

Similarly, Buchanan at times seems open to granting that states can possess legitimacy to different degrees, as when he suggests we adopt Keohane's notion of "unbundling" the elements of sovereignty.[58] But Buchanan seems disposed to grant this (and to discuss its normative implications) only in a narrow range of cases: either when granting intrastate autonomy to minority groups or when a secessionist group that isn't yet able to adequately perform all the functions of a state seeks independence from a state that has badly mistreated them.[59] In the latter set of cases, Buchanan argues, the secessionists can't be expected to continue as subjects of their oppressors, but they also don't meet the normal standards for legitimate statehood. Thus, their group deserves partial recognition as a member of the international community but doesn't qualify as a fully legitimate state.[60] This seems to mean the secessionists deserve some, but not all, of the privileges typically granted to sovereign states. Here, though, I've moved beyond this narrow focus to give a more detailed account of the normative significance of scalar legitimacy in a wide variety of cases.

---

[56] Pettit, *On the People's Terms*, 139.
[57] Ibid.
[58] Buchanan, *Justice, Legitimacy, and Self-Determination*, 281; citing Robert Keohane, "Political Authority after Intervention: Gradations in Sovereignty," in *Humanitarian Intervention: Ethical, Legal, and Political Dilemmas*, ed. Jeffrey Holzgrefe and Robert Keohane (Cambridge: Cambridge University Press, 2003), 275–98.
[59] Buchanan, *Justice, Legitimacy, and Self-Determination*, 56–7, 280–1.
[60] Ibid.

DEGREES OF LEGITIMACY   147

Elsewhere, Buchanan defends what he calls a "variable and dynamic" account of legitimacy.[61] However, the variability and dynamism he highlights don't reflect the view that states can have greater or lesser degrees of legitimacy. Rather, they reflect the view that the criteria a state (or other institution) must fulfill in order to be legitimate may change depending on context—for example, depending on the importance of the benefits the state can offer to those governed by it, relative to available alternatives.[62] (As I take no position on what criteria a state must fulfill in order to be legitimate, I also take no position on whether they might change according to context.) Thus, Buchanan says an institution can be "seriously deficient" but still be legitimate—if the conditions are such that even deficient institutions fulfill the criteria of legitimacy.[63] Outsiders to a "seriously deficient" state may therefore be obligated to treat it as a legitimate state—because it may in fact be legitimate despite its deficiencies. This may be right—again, I take no position on the criteria of legitimacy—but it does not amount to a scalar view of legitimacy. (Though, it's worth noting, this move poses at least as big a challenge to legitimacy's ability to coordinate people's judgments and behavior as does characterizing legitimacy as scalar—since people who agree about whether a state meets a certain standard of legitimacy may still disagree about which standard is most appropriate in their context.) Buchanan does not say these deficient states enjoy legitimacy to a lesser degree than less deficient states—only that they enjoy legitimacy because the standards a state must meet to be legitimate are lower in their context than they would be if conditions were more favorable. Presumably, on Buchanan's view, whatever outsiders owe to (fully) legitimate states, they owe to these legitimate but otherwise deficient states.

My view, in contrast, is that states sometimes enjoy a degree of legitimacy (but not full legitimacy), such that outsiders who interact with them should practice *some* of the behaviors they should practice when interacting with a fully legitimate state—but need not practice *all* the behaviors they should practice when interacting with a fully legitimate state. For example, if a state is partially legitimate, it may be appropriate for outsiders to allow it exclusive domestic policymaking authority but deny it good standing in the international community. This is compatible with but neither entails nor is

---

[61] Buchanan, "Institutional Legitimacy," 77.
[62] Ibid., 60, 62, 67, 77.
[63] Ibid., 62.

148   PROMOTING JUSTICE ACROSS BORDERS

entailed by Buchanan's view that the criteria of legitimacy are contextually determined.

One might also think Buchanan endorses a scalar notion of legitimacy when he sketches several criteria of legitimacy, saying, "None of them is strictly necessary for legitimacy, but the more of them that are satisfied, and the greater the extent to which they are satisfied, the stronger the case for concluding that the institution is legitimate."[64] However, saying there can be a stronger or weaker case for concluding a state is legitimate is not the same as saying a state can possess legitimacy to a greater or lesser degree. Moreover, Buchanan gives no indication of how—or even if—people should behave differently toward some state when the case for its legitimacy is relatively weaker or stronger. My foregoing analysis, by contrast, illustrated how outsiders to a given state should adjust their behavior toward it based on whether it is fully, partially, or not at all legitimate. My analysis therefore goes beyond Buchanan's, giving additional guidance regarding how global political actors should behave.

Altman and Wellman are in principle open to the existence of partially legitimate states, but in their work, as in Buchanan's, the discussion of this possibility's normative implications is limited.[65] Moreover, though they hold that states may be legitimate to a greater or lesser degree, Altman and Wellman defend this position by arguing that a state can have or lack legitimacy—conceived of as a binary quality—in a variety of different arenas of governance, thus rendering the state as a whole "legitimate" in some areas and "illegitimate" in others.[66] Thus, they don't challenge the underlying conception of legitimacy as a binary in the way I have here.

Altman and Wellman's account still can't make sense of the phenomenon—exemplified by some of the interventions discussed here—in which a state has only partial legitimacy (read, a claim, but not an exclusive claim, to policymaking authority) *within a single policymaking arena.* Take the case of the trade deal between the US and Oman. Let's imagine that Oman accuses the US of violating the terms of the agreement by weakening its domestic labor laws, that a tribunal is assembled (as per the terms of the agreement), and that the US is found guilty and sanctioned. As I've described the case, we should think of this sanction as an oppositional intervention that would be justifiable only on the stipulation that the US government was partially

---

[64] Ibid., 59.
[65] See Altman and Wellman, *A Liberal Theory of International Justice.*
[66] Ibid., 151–3.

illegitimate. The justification might go like this: in weakening its labor laws, the US has forfeited some of its legitimacy, thereby forfeiting its claim (if ever it had one) to exclusive policymaking authority within its jurisdiction. The agents of the tribunal are therefore justified in stepping in to sanction the US government in an attempt to get it to strengthen its domestic labor laws again. Notice that on this account, the current US government is only partially legitimate. But it's *not* that the US is fully legitimate in some arenas and not at all legitimate in the arena of labor law, for example. It would be more fitting to say that the US is partially legitimate even within the arena of labor law. It still has *some* claim to domestic policymaking authority *in this arena* (perhaps it still has a claim to authoritatively pass various laws about working hours, conditions, and wages that don't contravene the terms of its trade agreement), but this isn't an *exclusive* claim to domestic policymaking authority *in this arena*. That Altman and Wellman's view of legitimacy can't account for this phenomenon is a point against it.

We might raise a similar objection to consent-based theories of legitimacy like Simmons'. On his view, a state is legitimate if and only if its subjects have consented to its rule.[67] A state may therefore be legitimate for some people subject to its rule and not for others; some may have consented, and others may not have.[68] In a way, this means Simmons adopts a radically individualized version of Altman and Wellman's claim that a state can be legitimate in some arenas and illegitimate in others. Instead of being a legitimate authority in some areas of lawmaking and not others, on Simmons' view, a state may constitute a legitimate authority for some persons (those who have consented to its rule) and not for others (those who haven't). Thus, we could say Simmons acknowledges that a state can be partially legitimate. The consent that gives rise to legitimacy, though, occurs as a binary: it either happens or it doesn't. The "partially legitimate" state, then, is really a state that is fully legitimate for some and not at all legitimate for others. It cannot be "partially legitimate" in relation to any given subject because no one can partially consent to its rule. Thus, Simmons' view is compatible with the state as a whole being more or less legitimate, but not with legitimacy itself being a scalar property.

All this is to say that adopting a scalar notion of legitimacy and examining in relative detail what a state's greater or lesser degree of legitimacy means

---

[67] See Simmons, "Justification and Legitimacy."
[68] Ibid., 746.

150   PROMOTING JUSTICE ACROSS BORDERS

for how global political actors ought to treat it (a significant departure from prominent scholarship on the topic) allows us to identify, make sense of, and evaluate a class of morally and politically interesting cases that we'd miss if we adopted a binary notion instead.

Summary

As the previous section illustrates, this chapter has developed a new way of thinking about legitimacy—as a scalar quality—that allows us to better understand some morally and politically interesting phenomena in global politics. Adopting this scalar notion of legitimacy also nuances our understanding of the relationship between legitimacy and reform intervention. In particular, this chapter has found:

1. Regime-change interventions are justifiable only when recipient states are entirely illegitimate.
2. Oppositional interventions are justifiable only when recipient states are at least partially illegitimate.
3. Extra-institutional interventions that use force are justifiable only when recipient states are at least partially illegitimate.
4. Extra-institutional interventions that don't use force and that are led by nonstate actors are justifiable even when recipient states are fully legitimate.
5. State-led extra-institutional interventions that don't use force and where interveners are *not* more geopolitically powerful than recipients are justifiable even when recipient states are fully legitimate.
6. State-led extra-institutional interventions that don't use force and where interveners *are* more geopolitically powerful than recipients are justifiable only when recipient states are at least partially illegitimate, *unless* the interveners do something to undermine the power structures that advantaged them in the first place (in which case, their interventions are justifiable even when recipient states are fully legitimate). Interveners can help undermine the power structures that advantaged them in the first place by (a) opening themselves up to the same kinds of interventions they aim at others or (b) subjecting their operations to some kind of oversight from other, less powerful states or other actors in global civil society. (There may be other ways as well.)

7. Intra-systemic interventions are justifiable even when recipient states are fully legitimate.

These findings allow us to identify which kinds of reform intervention are more or less likely to be rendered impermissible by the legitimacy objection, which says reform intervention is impermissible because it often involves treating actually (or presumptively) legitimate recipient states as if they're illegitimate.

I've shown that this objection relies on an oversimplified account of the relationship between legitimacy and reform intervention. In reality, only the most invasive reform interventions—regime-change interventions— involve treating recipient states as if they're *entirely* illegitimate. Once we accept a scalar notion of legitimacy, we can see that other kinds of reform intervention—oppositional interventions and some extra-institutional interventions—involve treating recipient states as if they're *partially* but not *entirely* illegitimate.

Moreover, if we accept that states can suffer partial losses of legitimacy without becoming entirely illegitimate, it makes sense to think these partial losses can be triggered by injustices less severe than those necessary to render a state entirely illegitimate. In other words, even those inclined to agree with Walzer that states are rendered (entirely) illegitimate only when they commit extraordinarily grave injustices (like massacre, mass expulsion, mass starvation, and enslavement)[69] should accept that states can be rendered *partially* illegitimate when they commit less grave injustices (like failing to adequately protect workers' rights).

Thus, if *regime-change interventions* were our only concern, it would be right to say reform intervention is often impermissible because it would often target states that haven't committed sufficiently grave injustices so as to be rendered entirely illegitimate. However, regime-change interventions are *not* our only concern. Reform intervention does often target states that haven't committed sufficiently grave injustices so as to be rendered entirely illegitimate. But, arguably, these states have often committed sufficiently grave injustices so as to be rendered *partially* illegitimate. And reform intervention often takes forms that involve treating recipient states as partially—but not entirely—illegitimate. Reform intervention is therefore not impermissible as often as the legitimacy objection suggests.

---

[69] Walzer, "Moral Standing," 217–8; Walzer, "Beyond Humanitarian Intervention," 257–8.

152   PROMOTING JUSTICE ACROSS BORDERS

And, perhaps even more striking, I've shown that some kinds of reform intervention (select extra-institutional interventions and all intra-systemic interventions) are justifiable even when recipient states are fully legitimate. They don't involve treating recipient states as illegitimate (to any degree), and so are surely immune to the legitimacy objection.

Taking these findings together with those of Chapter 2, we can start to work out some all-things-considered judgments about different reform interventions' permissibility. In order to be all-things-considered permissible, an intervention must escape both the toleration objection and the legitimacy objection. (It must meet other criteria, too. It must escape the standard objection from collective self-determination, which I'll discuss in the next chapter, and adequately address some pragmatic concerns, which I'll discuss in Chapter 5.)

Of the reform interventions I've been focusing on, Tostan's work in western Africa, the Latin American opposition to Arizona's SB 1070, and the US conditional offer of a preferential trade agreement to Oman look so far like promising candidates for all-things-considered permissible interventions. Chapter 2 argued, given that interveners in these cases exercised little or no control over recipients, they treated recipients with toleration. These interventions therefore escape the toleration objection.

These three interventions also escape the legitimacy objection. Tostan's work qualifies as an extra-institutional intervention. Tostan doesn't interfere with the normal operation of established institutions in the communities where it works. It doesn't use force, and it is a nonstate actor, so its interventions are governed by the fourth principle listed above: they're justifiable even when recipient states are fully legitimate. The Latin American opposition to SB 1070 was clearly intra-systemic, and so also justifiable even if the recipient state (the US) was fully legitimate. The same is true of the US conditional offer of a preferential trade agreement to Oman. As discussed above, an attempt to enforce the terms of the agreement after it had been signed, in response to an alleged breach, would count as an oppositional intervention. But the conditional offer *itself* counts as an intra-systemic intervention.

The others of my central cases are a bit more complex. Take BDS. It's not immediately clear whether BDS participants treat Israeli recipients with toleration. I assume that BDS's aims, if achieved, wouldn't discourage tolerant treatment within Israel. So BDS participants don't fail to practice toleration toward Israelis simply by promoting the specific reforms they do. But do they treat Israelis intolerantly (and therefore fail to practice toleration toward them) because of the manner in which they advocate those reforms? Since, I'll assume, a representative segment of Israeli society doesn't already support BDS's stated objectives, according to the standards developed in Chapter 2, BDS participants would have to exert no more than *slight* control over Israelis in order to treat them tolerantly. That is, BDS would have to be either a persuasive or a slightly controlling intervention. While there are persuasive elements to BDS, its participants do (as is typical in boycott movements) attempt to leverage economic and social power to incentivize Israel's adopting the movement's desired policies (and to disincentivize the alternatives). Thus, BDS participants do exercise a degree of control over Israel.

This raises the question of *how* controlling BDS is. On this score, BDS participants have not forced Israelis to adopt BDS's desired policies (BDS isn't totally controlling), nor have they put Israelis in the position of being able to refuse BDS's desired policies only at the expense of their own vital interests (BDS isn't highly controlling). Despite its sizable ambitions, BDS arguably hasn't had the economic impact that would be necessary to put Israelis in this position—and this is unlikely to change anytime soon.[70] So BDS is only a slightly controlling intervention—in which case it does treat Israeli recipients tolerantly. Since BDS neither discourages tolerant treatment within Israel nor treats Israelis intolerantly, it is immune to the toleration objection.

The parts of the movement that involve consumer, cultural, and academic boycotts (as opposed to attempts to get other governments to sanction Israel's government) also escape the legitimacy objection. They constitute an extra-institutional intervention in Israeli politics. BDS is a civil society movement; its leaders and many of its participants are nonstate actors. When these non-state actors engage in consumer, cultural, and academic boycotts as part of BDS, they act in ways that are justifiable even under the assumption that the Israeli state is fully legitimate. They act in ways that are immune to the legitimacy objection. This I argued earlier.

---

[70] See Dany Bahar and Natan Sachs, "How Much Does BDS Threaten Israel's Economy?," Brookings. 26 January 2018, https://www.brookings.edu/blog/order-from-chaos/2018/01/26/how-much-does-bds-threaten-israels-economy/. Note especially the finding, "The data suggests that, economically, anything short of official sanctions by important economic partners such as the United States or European Union would be unlikely to produce anything near the kind of economic pressure BDS supporters envision."

154   PROMOTING JUSTICE ACROSS BORDERS

Note, though, that other aspects of BDS—those involving state sanctions that qualify as oppositional interventions and those involving foreign *states* boycotting or divesting from Israel and that therefore qualify as state-led extra-institutional interventions—are harder to justify. After all, oppositional interventions are justified only when recipient states are at least partially illegitimate. And the same goes for some state-led extra-institutional interventions (depending on the power relationship between interveners and recipients). Thus, to determine whether these aspects of BDS were permissible, we'd have to pass judgment on whether the Israeli state was fully legitimate. This is an extraordinarily complex question that I won't attempt to answer here. Suffice it to say that our answer to this question would decide whether or not these state-orchestrated aspects of BDS were rendered impermissible by the legitimacy objection.

Let me consider another of my central cases: the European refusal to export lethal injection drugs. The European intervention is also slightly controlling. It goes beyond mere persuasion; it disincentivizes the US administering lethal injections by making it more difficult (i.e., costly) to obtain the requisite drugs. However, the Europeans' actions haven't made it impossible (or possible only at the cost of their vital interests) for Americans to carry out executions.[71] Again, it's safe to assume that this intervention doesn't threaten to discourage tolerant treatment within the recipient society (the US). Given this, and the fact that European interveners exercise only *slight* control via their intervention, we can conclude that they practice toleration toward American recipients. The European export ban is thus immune from the toleration objection.

I've also characterized it as an oppositional intervention, which means it's justifiable only if the recipient state (the US) is at least partially illegitimate. Our judgments about its permissibility should therefore ride on our judgments about the legitimacy of the US government. Some will be willing to accept that the US's continued use of the death penalty renders it partially illegitimate (which, as indicated earlier, could simply mean that the particular laws calling for the death penalty are illegitimate—that the US has no authority to enforce these laws in particular). These people should not object to

---

[71] In fact, executions have continued. One negative side effect of the European export ban has been that some US states have resorted to less reliable and arguably less humane methods of execution. See Mark Berman, "The Recent History of States Scrambling to Keep Using Lethal Injections," *Washington Post*, 19 February 2014, Online. https://www.washingtonpost.com/news/post-nation/wp/2014/02/19/the-recent-history-of-states-scrambling-to-keep-using-lethal-injections/?tid=a_inl&utm_term=.c8a028e78164.

the European export ban on the grounds that it fails to treat a fully legitimate state as such. Those who think the US *is* fully legitimate, on the other hand, will object to the ban on these very grounds. As with Israel, I won't attempt to settle the question of whether or not the US is a fully legitimate state. For now, it's enough to identify the considerations we'd need to account for in order to decide whether the export ban were, all things considered, justified, and how the standards I've been developing here could help us navigate this question.

Only one of my central cases now remains: NATO's 2011 intervention in Libya. NATO's intervention was intolerant in that it imposed—via totally controlling means—an outcome (Qaddafi's ouster) not clearly endorsed by a representative segment of Libya's population.[72] So NATO's intervention was vulnerable to the toleration objection. Granted, as argued in Chapter 2, some interventions subject to this objection may still be justified—when circumstances are so dire that the value of toleration is overridden, making intolerant action, all things considered, morally permissible. But this doesn't seem to have been the case with Libya. Remember, in order for an intolerant intervention to be justifiable despite its intolerance, the urgency of the objectives it will predictably achieve must exceed the costs it will predictably impose on recipients. But, in retrospect, we have good reason to think the initial estimates of the threat Qaddafi posed to civilians (as opposed to armed rebels) were dramatically overstated, and there is evidence to show NATO's involvement significantly raised, rather than lowered, the civilian death toll.[73] Kuperman argues the intervention in Libya also spurred a host of devastating aftereffects: Libya itself was destabilized, as rival factions competed for control over land and natural resources after Qaddafi's ouster, resulting in a fractured government, economic turmoil, and a significantly worsened human rights record.[74] He further argues the conflict in Libya destabilized the surrounding region, encouraging the proliferation of terrorism.[75] And Qaddafi's overthrow resulted in the release of a significant

---

[72] See Liz Sly, "Many Libyans Appear to Back Gaddafi," *Washington Post,* 24 March 2011, https://www.washingtonpost.com/world/many-libyans-appear-to-back-gaddafi/2011/03/24/ABHShlRB_story.html?utm_term=.43f21d4d8c07.

[73] Alan J. Kuperman, "A Model Humanitarian Intervention? Reassessing NATO's Libya Campaign," *International Security* 38, no. 1 (2013): 105–36; Alan J. Kuperman, "Obama's Libya Debacle: How a Well-Meaning Intervention Ended in Failure," *Foreign Affairs* 94, no. 2 (2015): 66–77; Arif Saba and Shahram Akbarzadeh, "The Responsibility to Protect and the Use of Force: An Assessment of the Just Cause and Last Resort Criteria in the Case of Libya," *International Peacekeeping* 25, no. 2 (2018): 242–65, 249–56, 259–61.

[74] Kuperman, "A Model Humanitarian Intervention?"; Kuperman, "Obama's Libya Debacle."

[75] Kuperman, "A Model Humanitarian Intervention?"; Kuperman, "Obama's Libya Debacle."

156   PROMOTING JUSTICE ACROSS BORDERS

store of weapons previously held by the Libyan government onto the open market in the region and into unknown hands.[76]

Some might argue that the Libya intervention's architects couldn't have known, when they decided whether to intervene and when they decided how to shape the course of the intervention as it went on, that things would turn out this way. However, there were some known (or knowable) facts even then that should have indicated a military intervention could risk rights and interests at least as important as those it would end up protecting. For example, it was known—but not widely reported—at the time that an early account of Qaddafi's forces firing on unarmed protestors was fallacious.[77] Soliman Bouchuiguir, who told reporters Qaddafi was on the verge of committing a " 'real bloodbath, a massacre like we saw in Rwanda,' " was himself part of the Libyan opposition, and so may have had incentive to exaggerate the danger.[78] Moreover, during the intervention, NATO took steps any reasonable person should have known weren't needed to avert imminent threats to civilian lives, but would endanger them—such as attacking Libyan forces on the retreat and in areas where civilians supported Qaddafi.[79]

Additionally, Hobson argues evidence that ousting Qaddafi wouldn't necessarily protect human rights—because Libyan rebels were themselves prone to committing human rights violations—emerged during the course of the intervention "since both Amnesty International and Human Rights Watch raised concern during the conflict over human rights abuses by rebels, including revenge killings, torture, and attacks on civilians."[80] While Hobson concedes that not every consequence of the intervention in Libya could have been predicted in advance, he argues that some, such as the "considerable dangers from removing [Q]addafi without a clear idea of what would follow," especially given the decentralized and unreliable character of the rebels who might try to take his place, could have been.[81] Indeed, the prescient warning from President Idriss Déby Itno of Chad that Libya represented a " 'Pandora's box,' " (issued in March 2011) testifies to the fact that some at the time did foresee such dangers.[82] Similarly, the African Union's (AU's) June 2011

---

[76] Kuperman, "A Model Humanitarian Intervention?"

[77] Ibid., 108–9.

[78] Ibid., 134.

[79] Ibid., 113–4.

[80] Christopher Hobson, "Responding to Failure: The Responsibility to Protect after Libya," *Millennium: Journal of International Studies* 44, no. 3 (2016): 433–54, 448.

[81] Ibid., 450.

[82] Ibid.; Alex de Waal, "African Roles in the Libyan Conflict of 2011," *International Affairs* 89, no. 2 (2013): 365–79, 370.

diagnosis that military intervention in Libya would endanger civilians, undermine regional security, and promote terrorism shows these effects were foreseeable.[83]

Some have claimed the effects of *not* intervening militarily in Libya would have been even worse than the effects of the actual intervention.[84] If true, these claims might render the intervention permissible even if its negative effects were foreseeable at the outset. However, this is a thin defense of the military campaign NATO in fact conducted, as it appears other, potentially less damaging options were available but not fully pursued. These include the negotiated resolution (still ending with Qaddafi's removal) advocated by the AU; a conditional offer, made early on in the conflict by the Libyan regime, for Qaddafi to step down; and missed opportunities to promote negotiation between Qaddafi's regime and Libyan rebels.[85] Indeed, de Waal argues the AU proposal might have succeeded had it been supported rather than undermined by Britain, France, and the US, and that this could have mitigated some of the negative aftereffects of the intervention.[86] Thus, even without the benefit of hindsight, those who intervened in Libya shouldn't have been confident that their intervention would protect more important rights and interests than it would endanger.

That NATO's operation unreasonably endangered civilians may also mean it was impermissible according to the usual "just war theory" constraints, requiring that any war have a sufficient chance of success via proportionate means. I won't evaluate the Libya intervention's compliance with just war theory standards here.[87] Suffice it to say, if I found the intervention permissible on all other grounds, it would be appropriate to consult just war theory before rendering a final judgment on its permissibility. As things stand, though, my analysis shows the intervention was impermissible because objectionably intolerant.

---

[83] De Waal, "African Roles," 373.

[84] See Shadi Hamid, "Everyone Says the Libya Intervention Was a Failure; They're Wrong," *Brookings Markaz Blog*, 12 April 2016, https://www.brookings.edu/blog/markaz/2016/04/12/everyone-says-the-libya-intervention-was-a-failure-theyre-wrong/; James Pattison, "Perilous Nonintervention? The Counterfactual Assessment of Libya and the Need to Be a Responsible Power," *Global Responsibility to Protect* 9 (2017): 219–28, 221–5.

[85] De Waal, "African Roles," 367–75, 379; Saba and Akbarzadeh, "The Responsibility to Protect," 256–9.

[86] De Waal, "African Roles," 379.

[87] For such an analysis, with respect to the "just cause" and "last resort" conditions of just war theory, see Saba and Akbarzadeh, "The Responsibility to Protect."

158   PROMOTING JUSTICE ACROSS BORDERS

NATO's operation in Libya was also a regime-change intervention and so was justifiable only if Qaddafi's regime was entirely illegitimate. However, since I've already shown the intervention was impermissible because it unjustifiably treated recipients with intolerance, I won't spend time here assessing whether or not Qaddafi's regime was in fact entirely illegitimate.

Leaving Libya aside, my analysis does suggest that *some* reform interventions are immune from both the toleration and legitimacy objections. This finding takes us one step closer to being able to form all-things-considered judgments about different interventions' moral permissibility. (We can't fully form these judgments now because we've yet to consider the collective self-determination objection, which I'll address in the next chapter, or the various pragmatic considerations I'll address in Chapter 5.) It also means the skeptical view of the natural duty of justice now has two marks against it: I've shown that reform intervention need not involve two of the serious moral wrongs skeptics associate with it—namely, treating recipients with intolerance and objectionably denying or disregarding the legitimacy of recipients' established institutions.

It's looking more and more like we'll find there are some morally permissible ways to promote justice in foreign societies after all. And, as argued in the previous chapters, if there *are* morally permissible ways to engage in reform intervention, the natural duty of justice (assuming there is one) sometimes requires us to do so. Specifically, we're required to adopt a set of projects in which promoting justice, including via reform intervention, enjoys a sufficiently prominent place. As this formulation indicates, engaging in reform intervention is one way in which we may be morally required to promote justice, but it's not the only way.

This chapter's discussion of legitimacy and reform intervention illuminates another way in which we can—and are sometimes required to—promote justice. In particular, I propose that we are sometimes morally required to open up our own (formal, political) institutions to some kinds of reform intervention. After all, whatever societies we belong to, our domestic institutions are probably not perfectly just. Certainly, they're not perpetually secured against becoming unjust. Thus, one way in which we can promote justice is by exposing ourselves to influences likely to correct our missteps.

Since we are all fallible judges of what justice requires, we should be open to the possibility that others—including foreigners—could contribute something valuable to our own thinking (and public deliberation) about the requirements of justice. This is all the more true because people from

DEGREES OF LEGITIMACY   159

outside our own societies may not share our predictable biases—which skew our judgments, including judgments about what justice requires. We noted earlier that reform interveners are subject to predictable biases, which it's sometimes important for them to overcome by consultation with epistemically diverse global political actors. The same logic that applies to reform interveners applies to people and organizations engaged in domestic political contestation. We therefore have reason to think opening our own societies to at least some kinds of foreign influence could help us promote justice "at home."

Further, I assume that whenever we pursue a goal (including justice promotion), all else equal, we ought to pursue it in whatever way involves doing or risking the least moral wrong. The idea behind this assumption is an intuitive one: we shouldn't commit, or encourage the commitment of, gratuitous moral wrongs to achieve our aims. If we can accomplish some aim without committing, or encouraging the commitment of, a moral wrong, we should. Applying this general principle to the issue at hand yields the conclusion that if we can effectively pursue the goal of justice promotion without committing, or encouraging the commitment of, some moral wrong, we should. I expect this to be a resoundingly uncontroversial position. But, taken together with the findings of this chapter, it has some surprising implications.

This chapter has argued that whether a reform intervention risks objectionably denying or disregarding the legitimacy of recipients' institutions (a moral wrong) depends on its relationship to those institutions. Some kinds of intervention—specifically, intra-systemic interventions and select extra-institutional interventions—treat recipient institutions as fully legitimate, so they don't risk wrongly denying or disregarding those institutions' legitimacy. But which activities count as extra-institutional or intra-systemic interventions depends on which activities are compatible with the normal operation of or can be enacted through recipient institutions. And, clearly, that depends on what recipient institutions in fact allow (or don't disallow) and what kinds of political channels they make available to would-be interveners.

Before March 2017, for example, BDS supporters could travel to Israel and make their case from inside its borders; Israeli law allowed it. But in March 2017, the Knesset passed a law banning foreign nationals who have publicly supported boycotting Israel or the Israeli settlements from entering the country.[88] Thus, one particular avenue of activism that was once allowed by

---

[88] Jonathan Lis, "Israel's Travel Ban: Knesset Bars Entry to Foreigners Who Call for Boycott of Israel or Settlements," *Haaretz*, 7 March 2017, http://www.haaretz.com/israel-news/.premium-1.775614.

160 PROMOTING JUSTICE ACROSS BORDERS

Israeli institutions is no longer available. Whereas someone wishing to effectively advocate for the boycott from within Israel could once have done so without interfering with the normal operation of Israeli institutions, now they might have to resort to thwarting the enforcement of this travel ban (turning their intervention from an extra-institutional to an oppositional one). Similarly, the courts that reviewed Arizona's immigration law were part of a system that allowed foreign actors to submit amicus briefs for the courts to review. Had the rules of the US judicial system not allowed for amicus briefs, or not allowed foreign governments to author them, this particular intra-systemic intervention would have been impossible (an attempt to accomplish it wouldn't have counted as *intra-systemic* intervention).

In conclusion, we are at least sometimes morally required to promote justice in our own societies. The natural duty of justice requires us to adopt a set of projects in which this aim has a sufficiently prominent place. (This position should be acceptable to everyone who endorses the natural duty of justice, including those who deny it's global in scope—that is, to everyone who thinks we have a natural duty to promote justice in *our own* societies.) Opening our own societies to at least some kinds of foreign influence is one way to pursue this goal of domestic justice promotion. Whenever we pursue a goal—including domestic justice promotion—we ought to, all else equal, pursue it in whatever way involves doing or risking the least moral wrong. Moreover, if we design the rules of our formal political institutions such that these institutions are more open to reform intervention, more activities will count as intra-systemic or extra-institutional interventions. This, in turn, means that *fewer* activities will risk wrongly denying or disregarding our institutions' legitimacy (because intra-systemic interventions and select extra-institutional interventions don't risk denying or disregarding recipient institutions' legitimacy at all).

So, if we are to pursue the goal of (domestic) justice promotion in the way that involves doing or risking the least moral wrong, we must design the rules of our formal political institutions such that these institutions are more open to reform intervention. If we designed our formal institutions to be closed to reform intervention, we'd still have reason to receive such intervention (as a means to domestic justice promotion). But by "closing off" our formal institutions, we would put interveners in the position of having to risk wrongly denying or disregarding our institutions' legitimacy in order to promote justice in our society. This is because "closing off" our institutions would make certain actions that might otherwise count as intra-systemic or extra-institutional interventions (and that could therefore *avoid* the risk of wrongly denying or disregarding our institutions' legitimacy) count instead as oppositional interventions (which *would* risk wrongly denying or disregarding our institutions' legitimacy), if they were possible at all. If we "close off" our institutions, we unnecessarily risk encouraging a moral wrong—namely, the wrongful denial of our institutions' legitimacy in the course of a reform intervention—in our pursuit of domestic justice (a pursuit that, as I've argued above, should involve *receiving* reform intervention). But I also said that we oughtn't unnecessarily risk encouraging moral wrongs when pursuing our goals. We should therefore "open up" rather than "close off" our institutions to foreign influence.

Some might object that the natural duty of justice requires us to promote justice only when it's not inordinately costly for us, but that opening up our political institutions to foreign influence could be very costly indeed. What should count as an "inordinate cost" is a complex question that I can't answer fully here. For now, I'll say that there will often be some clearly not too costly ways to open our societies up to foreign influence—for example, allowing foreigners to author amicus briefs, allowing and encouraging judges to cite foreign courts' decisions in their own opinions, and perhaps guaranteeing foreigners the same free speech protections we grant our own citizens. (I'll discuss the last proposal in more detail in Chapter 5.) None of these courses of action would seem to involve very great material costs.

Some might worry they would involve significant nonmaterial costs, like losses to our collective self-determination. We shouldn't, however, simply assume that allowing reform intervention in our own societies would undermine our collective self-determination. We have yet to explore under what circumstances reform intervention poses a genuine threat to recipients' collective self-determination, and under what circumstances it doesn't. It is to this question that I now turn.

4

Collective Self-Determination without Isolation

Introduction

This chapter will argue that not all kinds of reform intervention threaten recipients' collective self-determination (I will sometimes say only "self-determination," for brevity's sake). Though one standard objection to reform intervention alleges that it undermines recipients' self-determination, this objection (like the others I've dealt with), doesn't apply to all kinds of reform intervention. In fact, some reform interventions can even *bolster* recipients' self-determination.

Realizing this should change our understanding of how claims to collective self-determination ought to function in global politics. These claims don't argue in favor of a world without reform intervention; they argue in favor of a world where it takes the forms most likely to empower rather than subordinate recipient communities. Shoring up collective self-determination doesn't require (as is often assumed) fortifying the boundaries between societies, ensuring that each is as isolated from the political influence of others as possible. Rather, self-determination is best protected when political actors around the world work together to dismantle the power relationships—both domestic and international—that threaten it.

There are, of course, many competing views on the nature of self-determination—both the source of its value and what a society's institutions must look like in order to be self-determining.[1] That said, the next section lays out a generic idea of self-determination that captures the elements even divergent views share (though the adherents of different views will interpret these shared elements differently).

---

[1] I will occasionally refer to "self-determining institutions." By this, I mean institutions that enable and channel their subjects' collective self-determination. It would be more precise (but less concise) to say *a society* subject to some institutions (rather than the institutions themselves) was or was not self-determining.

Promoting Justice Across Borders. Lucia M. Rafanelli, Oxford University Press. © Oxford University Press 2021.
DOI: 10.1093/oso/9780197568842.003.0005

164 PROMOTING JUSTICE ACROSS BORDERS

The following sections discuss three ways in which reform intervention could be thought to undermine recipients' collective self-determination: by dominating recipients, reinforcing colonial hierarchies that subordinate recipients, or making recipients' governments less responsive to recipients' own interests. Ultimately, I'll argue that not all types of reform intervention undermine self-determination in these ways.

The chapter's summary discussion brings together my findings about which kinds of reform intervention escape the self-determination objection with my findings about which kinds escape the other standard objections. I'll argue that some reform interventions escape all three standard objections. This brings me one step closer to formulating some all-things-considered judgments about when reform intervention is morally permissible and toward refuting the skeptical view of the natural duty of justice.

The Concept of Collective Self-Determination

So as to better understand the ways in which reform intervention might threaten it, we'll need a better idea of what self-determination requires. Intuitively, self-determination is a society's ability to determine the content of its own laws and how its institutions are organized. This is a fine starting point, but it's too vague to give us much concrete guidance. Here, I lay out a generic idea of self-determination that captures the elements even divergent views of what self-determination requires share (though, again, the adherents of different views will interpret these shared elements differently).

First, on virtually all existing views, collective self-determination requires that political institutions (perhaps in their form, in the prescriptions they issue, or both) reflect in some way the character of the population they govern. In *what* way institutions must reflect the character of the population differs from view to view. On some views, institutions must reflect the population's shared culture, on others their interests or preferences, on still others their widely shared beliefs and values.

Divergent views of collective self-determination agree, second, that it requires members of a society to have some kind of influence over what their institutions do. It can't simply be an accident that the institutions in place *happen* to reflect the character of the population they govern. Members must have done something to make it the case that their institutions look the way they do; their institutions must have taken on their present form in response

COLLECTIVE SELF-DETERMINATION WITHOUT ISOLATION   165

to (not simply concurrently with) the population taking on its present character. Importantly, some may hold that this requires members to have designed their institutions democratically, but others may not. For Walzer, for example, it's enough that citizens engage with each other in whatever activities and practices make up their shared history and define their public culture, and that their institutions take a corresponding form as a result.[2] Again, exactly how much and what kind of influence citizens must exercise over their institutions in order to be collectively self-determining varies from view to view.

Third, in order to enjoy collective self-determination, members of a society must *know* (or at least reasonably believe) that they have the requisite kind of influence over their institutions. It is this knowledge (or reasonable belief) that allows them to see their political institutions as in some sense "their own." For some theorists, this may simply mean members can identify their institutions as those their community has fashioned.[3] For others, it may mean members have good reason to be confident that their institutions reliably track their common good.[4]

So, we have our generic idea of collective self-determination. A society is self-determining only when (1) its political institutions reflect the character of those they govern, (2) its members have the right kind of influence over their institutions, and (3) they know (or at least reasonably believe) they have this influence.

Any given view of collective self-determination will come with its own account of what a society must do to meet these three conditions. Each view will fill out the meaning of the three conditions in its own way. On some

---

[2] See, for example, Walzer's discussion in "The Moral Standing of States: A Response to Four Critics," *Philosophy and Public Affairs* 9, no 3 (1980): 209–29. Discussing "the right of Nicaraguans as a group to shape their own political institutions and the right of individual Nicaraguans to live under institutions so shaped," he says the latter amounts to "the right to live in a civil society of a Nicaraguan sort" (220). See also in the same article Walzer's notion of "fit" between a government and the political community it governs. And see his discussion of the connection between a community's "common life" and the state that represents it in *Just and Unjust Wars: A Moral Argument with Historical Illustrations*, 5th edition (New York: Basic Books, 2015), 54.

[3] See, for example, Walzer, *Just and Unjust Wars*. He writes, "Over a long period of time, shared experiences and cooperative activity of many different kinds shape a common life. . . . The moral standing of any particular state depends upon the reality of the common life it protects and the extent to which the sacrifices required by that protection are willingly accepted and thought worthwhile" (54).

[4] For example, see Joshua Cohen, *Rousseau: A Free Community of Equals* (Oxford: Oxford University Press, 2010). Cohen interprets Rousseau as arguing that governance by the general will (Rousseau's version of collective self-determination) requires a society to meet what Cohen calls the "reasonable confidence condition," according to which political institutions must in fact reliably track the common good, and citizens must have good reason to be confident that they do so (58–9).

166 PROMOTING JUSTICE ACROSS BORDERS

views, a society's meeting one of the conditions may entail that it meets others. However, I've separated them here to be as ecumenical as possible.

With this generic idea of collective self-determination in mind, we'll be able to see more clearly the ways in which reform intervention might undermine it, and therefore to better understand when this danger is real.

Reform Intervention as Domination?

One way in which reform intervention could undermine recipients' collective self-determination is by subjecting them to domination.[5] Philip Pettit defines domination as "exposure to another's power of uncontrolled interference."[6] Note that Pettit has something specific in mind by the term "uncontrolled."[7] Elsewhere, he defines domination more colloquially, saying, "To the extent that I have a power of interfering without cost in your choice, I count as dominating you."[8] Here, I will simply take Pettit's understanding of domination for granted; defending it is beyond this book's scope.

Much like individuals can be subject to domination at each other's hands, or at the hands of their own states, they can be subject to "foreign domination" at the hands of other states (or, presumably, other global political actors).[9] Societies as a whole, considered as group agents, can also be subject to domination—in which case, their individual members will be dominated as well.[10] Pettit writes, with reference to someone inside a dominated society, that "foreign domination" is "a form of rule which, by definition—that is, in virtue of what it means to be foreign—is going to be uncontrolled by you and your fellow citizens, as you actually are."[11]

Thus, if reform intervention really did dominate recipients, the institutions ruling over a recipient society would be "uncontrolled" (in Pettit's sense) by that society's members, so members wouldn't enjoy the kind of influence over

---

[5] I also argue domination can undermine collective self-determination in Lucia M. Rafanelli, "Toward an Individualist Postcolonial Cosmopolitanism," *Millennium: Journal of International Studies* (2020): 1–12, doi:10.1177/0305829820935520. However, there, I don't adopt Pettit's definition of domination, as I do here.

[6] Phillip Pettit, *On the People's Terms: A Republican Theory and Model of Democracy* (Cambridge: Cambridge University Press, 2012), 28.

[7] See ibid., 160–79 for Pettit's conception of "popular control."

[8] Philip Pettit, "The Instability of Freedom as Noninterference: The Case of Isaiah Berlin," *Ethics* 121, no. 4 (2011): 693–716, 707.

[9] See Pettit, *On the People's Terms*, 163–4.

[10] I thank Philip Pettit for clarifying comments on this topic.

[11] Pettit, *On the People's Terms*, 164.

COLLECTIVE SELF-DETERMINATION WITHOUT ISOLATION   167

their institutions necessary for self-determination. (Their society wouldn't meet condition (2) from above). Members therefore wouldn't know or reasonably believe themselves to have this kind of influence. (Their society wouldn't meet condition (3) either.)

The question before us, then, is under what circumstances reform intervention subjects recipients (considered either as individuals or at the societal level as group agents) to "another's power of uncontrolled interference"[12] or to another's "power of interfering without cost"[13] in their choices. I assume it's uncontroversial that when the *goal* of an intervention is to establish a dominating relationship between interveners and recipients, the intervention would (if successful) dominate recipients. For example, imagine if, when the US pushed for its trade agreement with Oman, it didn't support the establishment of an independent tribunal to investigate both parties' alleged breaches but instead advocated an arrangement whereby the US could at any point sanction Oman for suspected breaches, without due process, and without granting Oman reciprocal power. Such a regime would be objectionable on the grounds that it dominated Oman. No one who believes domination is morally wrong would deny this. The more puzzling theoretical question is whether an intervention subjects recipients to domination even when its goal doesn't involve domination—as in the actual case of the US's intervention in Oman, where the goal was to promote workers' rights and to ensure their protection by vesting enforcement capabilities in an independent tribunal accessible to both the US and Oman.

I will focus the rest of my discussion on this more puzzling question. I will assume the reform interventions I deal with don't aim to establish dominating arrangements and will investigate whether the act of intervening itself subjects recipients to domination. This *won't* likely happen when interveners are less geopolitically powerful than recipients. I'll call interventions where this is the case *counter-hegemonic in the non-domination sense*. (The next section will explore another sense in which interventions can be counter-hegemonic.) These interventions won't generally be dominating because more geopolitically powerful actors are typically capable of (regardless of whether they are justified in) imposing costs on others who act against their interests or in ways they otherwise disapprove of; this is the nature of their geopolitical power advantage. Thus, less geopolitically powerful interveners

[12] Ibid., 28.
[13] Pettit, "Instability," 707.

won't generally "have a power of interfering without cost"[14] in the choices of the more powerful recipients of their interventions. Similarly, insofar as more powerful recipients can influence how less powerful interveners behave by imposing costs on them, the recipients won't be subject to "uncontrolled influence." Instead, they will retain some control over how interveners' influence is exercised.

Arguably, the same holds true for cases in which interveners and recipients are on a par with one another in terms of geopolitical power. Since roughly equally powerful interveners and recipients will presumably be equally able to impose costs on one another, it's unlikely that one would, as a general rule, have a power of costless interference in the affairs of the other, and, since they would presumably be able to influence each other's actions reciprocally, interveners wouldn't generally subject recipients to uncontrolled influence.

This analysis suggests we have reason to grant a kind of political priority to interventions that are counter-hegemonic in the non-domination sense. Namely, they won't involve dominating recipients. When I say we should give interventions that are counter-hegemonic in the non-domination sense *political priority*, I mean we should especially support and encourage these kinds of interventions.

I don't mean to say we should encourage and support *all* interventions where interveners are less powerful than recipients, regardless of their specific aims and chosen means. They should still be subject to the principled constraints developed in previous chapters, and they should (as reform interventions) actually work toward the achievement of justice in recipient societies. But assuming there will be multiple actual or proposed reform interventions that meet these requirements, we, as participants in global politics, should prioritize supporting those interventions in that set that are counter-hegemonic in the non-domination sense. For example, given two comparable cases of justified reform intervention—one counter-hegemonic in the non-domination sense, and one not—and faced with the choice of how to allocate scarce political resources, we should allocate them to support the former.[15]

What about reform interventions that aren't counter-hegemonic in the non-domination sense? Do they always dominate recipients? I think not. Persuasive interventions, for example, are straightforwardly non-dominating

---

[14] Ibid.
[15] I make a similar recommendation in "Toward an Individualist," 9–11.

COLLECTIVE SELF-DETERMINATION WITHOUT ISOLATION   169

regardless of the power relations between intervener and recipient. Interveners using only persuasion to accomplish their ends don't exert control[16] over recipients. Recipients retain the freedom to adopt interveners' preferred policies or not, entirely dependent on their own preferences. Interveners don't subject recipients' choices to costless interference (or, really, any interference); recipients are still free to choose as they like and to act as they choose. Put another way, persuasive interventions don't subject recipients to "uncontrolled interference"[17] because recipients retain control over whether they adopt interveners' preferred policies.

Note, though, that this characterization holds only when an intervention genuinely belongs in the category of *persuasive intervention*. That is, interveners must rely only on persuasion—not "persuasion" backed up by the implicit or explicit threat that interveners will impose costs on recipients if they don't comply with interveners' requests. Consider President Barack Obama's public statement (in the form of a tweet from the White House account), in September 2014, that he hoped the UK would remain "strong, robust and united," an apparent response to the possibility of Scotland's secession.[18] Obama seemed to publicly voice opposition to·Scottish independence, but he didn't try to incentivize Scotland to remain in the UK by threatening negative consequences should it leave. His statement should therefore count as a genuinely persuasive intervention.

Contrast this with Obama's public denouncement of the Brexit campaign in April 2016. He didn't only publicly discourage Brexit, offering reasons why he thought it would be a mistake. He also warned there would be material consequences for the UK if it withdrew from the EU, noting that Europe would be the US's priority in trade negotiations and that the UK would "'be in the back of the queue.'"[19] Insofar as Obama's threat was credible, we should arguably categorize it as a slightly controlling intervention, rather than a persuasive intervention, because Obama effectively made it the case that the UK could leave the EU only at the expense of its non-vital interests (interests in preferred status during trade negotiations with the US).[20]

---

[16] Here, I mean "control" in the sense in which I use the term in the typology of reform intervention set out in Chapter 1, which may not be identical to the sense in which Pettit uses it.

[17] Pettit, *On the People's Terms*, 28.

[18] Krishnadev Calamur, "Obama's 'Brexit' Plea," *Atlantic*, 22 April 2016, https://www.theatlantic.com/international/archive/2016/04/obamas-brexit-plea/479469/.

[19] Ibid.

[20] There's room for debate about whether Obama's threat was credible. After all, he wouldn't be president for long after the Brexit vote. Nonetheless, to the extent that many expected Hillary Clinton to win the 2016 election and to adopt a foreign policy agenda in the same vein as Obama's, his threat may have retained some credibility.

170   PROMOTING JUSTICE ACROSS BORDERS

What, then, of slightly controlling interventions like this one—and like the trade negotiations between the US and Oman discussed in previous chapters? Do they subject recipients to domination? Recall that slightly controlling interventions, by definition, leave recipients with multiple reasonable options as to how to act. Though interveners incentivize their preferred option (or disincentivize its alternatives), such that recipients must absorb *some* cost if they refuse to act in accordance with interveners' preferences, they need not absorb an *unreasonable* cost. The question, I suppose, is whether interveners imposing reasonable costs on recipients if they don't act in certain ways counts as "uncontrolled interference" in recipients' choices that interveners can exercise without cost to themselves.

I've already noted this won't be the case when interveners are less geopolitically powerful than recipients, since recipients' power advantage will enable them to impose costs on interveners if the latter's interference is unwelcome. And I've argued the same holds true when interveners' geopolitical power is on par with that of recipients.

Thus, the real risk of domination comes when interveners are decidedly more powerful than recipients. In such cases, are slightly controlling interventions dominating? When considered as single cases, I propose they're not, as they don't actually close off options to recipients. They make some options costlier, but not unreasonably costly. It seems that, in these cases, too, recipients retain control over their choices. After all, virtually anyone faced with virtually any choice must choose among different options offering different combinations of costs and benefits, some (perhaps deliberately) produced by others' actions. That is, every choice is a choice to accept a certain bundle of costs and benefits, the content of which is at least partly determined by other people. As long as interveners don't eliminate options by making them unreasonably costly, it's hard to see how their intervention differs from this everyday situation—and it's therefore hard to see how their intervention is dominating. To conclude otherwise would be to conclude that the everyday choice situation described above—which would be ubiquitous in any society (even an ideal one)—constitutes domination. Thus, slightly controlling interventions where interveners are more geopolitically powerful than recipients don't amount to domination.

Some may object, pointing out that slightly controlling interventions don't eliminate any of recipients' options doesn't show that they don't

COLLECTIVE SELF-DETERMINATION WITHOUT ISOLATION   171

dominate recipients. After all, domination happens when someone has the *power* to costlessly eliminate others' options, regardless of whether they actually exercise that power. It is therefore a structural feature of the geopolitical relationships between more and less powerful actors that makes it such that the former dominate the latter. However, if the thinking behind this objection is right, more powerful actors dominate less powerful ones regardless of whether they engage in intervention. On this account, more powerful actors, simply because of their outsized geopolitical power, can costlessly eliminate recipients' options whenever they so choose. If the US has this power over Oman, for example, it is not in virtue of the fact that it launched a slightly controlling intervention there in the mid-2000s. Adopting a norm allowing slightly controlling intervention also wouldn't establish a relationship between (would-be) interveners and recipients such that the former had the power to costlessly eliminate the latter's options—because slightly controlling intervention doesn't involve eliminating recipients' options. If anything, adopting clear ethical standards to govern reform intervention (like those I develop here) will tend to make intervention less dominating by making interveners' influence over recipients less arbitrary.

Finally, highly and totally controlling interventions remove all but one (reasonable) option from recipients' option set. If we assume, as argued above, that interveners won't generally have the power to *costlessly* and *in an uncontrolled manner* interfere with (and therefore dominate) recipients when they are less powerful than or roughly equally as powerful as recipients, we can again focus our scrutiny on whether highly and totally controlling interventions involve domination when interveners are *more* geopolitically powerful than recipients.

Arguably, the answer depends on to what extent other actors in global politics are able to (and do) reliably, and in accordance with some legible standard, monitor and regulate these kinds of interventions. I have already suggested at several points that some interventions should be subject to approval or oversight by epistemically diverse actors, unlikely to share interveners' narrow interests and therefore unlikely to share their predictable biases. If such a system could be effectively implemented, highly and totally controlling interventions could be subject to approval or oversight by a global community capable of imposing reputational or other costs on interveners who flouted its norms, thus ensuring interveners wouldn't have

172   PROMOTING JUSTICE ACROSS BORDERS

a power of costless interference over recipients. Further, recipients would be part of this global community, even if they didn't oversee the specific interventions to which they were subject. In this way, recipients could retain a sufficient amount of control (i.e., sufficient to avoid domination) over the practice of reform intervention in general, even if they didn't have control over a specific intervention of which they were the recipients—just as non-dominated citizens may have control, in general, over the ways in which their state exercises power, but may not have control over every single policy decision or courtroom judgment.

Moreover, a system of oversight like this will arguably become more effective as reform intervention is practiced more and more, especially if it is practiced in a principled way, in line with identifiable standards. As principled reform intervention becomes more and more common, global political actors may become more acquainted with it, and as it becomes a more prominent part of global politics, the global community may adopt its standards as norms, which it may then engage in "enforcing."[21] How, then, can we encourage this development without risking establishing dominating hierarchies in the meantime (before the suggested oversight mechanism is sufficiently established and effective)? The answer, again, is to give political priority to reform interventions that are counter-hegemonic in the non-domination sense (and reform interventions where interveners' and recipients' power is on a par). Since these interventions are unlikely to be dominating even in the absence of an established oversight mechanism, it makes sense to support them when they are justified as a way to build up this mechanism.

This recurring recommendation to support reform interventions where interveners are less powerful than recipients is a consequential political imperative of immediate practical import. It is a direct instruction to global political actors as to how to distribute their political resources and prioritize their political commitments that doesn't obviously rely for its importance on the existence of (as yet nonexistent) international or global governance institutions. Further, it flags a way in which reform intervention can be a potent mode of emancipatory politics.

In sum, this section has shown that reform interveners do *not* dominate recipients when

---

[21] I mean to use the term "enforcement" loosely here, not limiting it to coercive enforcement, but including other mechanisms such as "naming and shaming."

COLLECTIVE SELF-DETERMINATION WITHOUT ISOLATION   173

A. interveners are not more geopolitically powerful than recipients.

The real risk of domination comes when interveners are more geopolitically powerful than recipients. But even in these cases, interveners don't dominate recipients if

B. they use persuasive or slightly controlling means to accomplish their ends; or
C. they use highly or totally controlling means but their interventions are subject to approval or oversight by epistemically diverse global political actors.

Dominating recipients, though, is not the only way interveners might undermine recipients' collective self-determination.

Reform Intervention as Neocolonialism?

Interveners could also undermine recipients' self-determination by perpetuating colonial hierarchies that establish interveners as superior to recipients, subordinating and disempowering the latter. This may or may not manifest as "domination" in the way Pettit understands that concept. Nonetheless, perpetuating colonial hierarchies is one way interveners may deprive recipients of the power to decide on their own the content of their laws and how their institutions are organized. To see how, I'll now examine the view that reform intervention is an extension of colonialism—that is, part of a pattern of behavior, common in international relations and codified in international law, that constructs Western societies as the bearers of progress, development, and civilization, as contrasted with non-Western societies, which must be constrained, reformed, and civilized to live up to standards defined by the West.[22]

Describing the main goals of the Third World Approaches to International Law (TWAIL) movement, Mutua writes, "The first is to understand, deconstruct, and unpack the uses of international law as a medium for the creation and perpetuation of a racialized hierarchy of international norms and

---

[22] See, for example, Antony Anghie, "The Evolution of International Law: Colonial and Postcolonial Realities," *Third World Quarterly* 27, no. 5 (2006): 739–53.

174 PROMOTING JUSTICE ACROSS BORDERS

institutions that subordinate non-Europeans to Europeans."[23] (Note that, while the literature sometimes refers to "Europeans" and "non-Europeans," the former category typically denotes a larger group of imperial powers from the global North and West, including, for example, the US and the international organizations through which it exerts influence.)[24]

Anghie characterizes human rights law and the institutions (such as the World Trade Organization, the IMF, and the World Bank) that often invoke it as recently emerged vehicles for perpetuating this hierarchy.[25] Through these laws and institutions, Anghie argues, the West essentially recognized postcolonial, independent, Third World[26] states only in order to hold them accountable for internal atrocities, thereby justifying Western intervention in their affairs.[27] Though in theory, human rights law and advocacy have the potential to help emancipate people in the Third World from the oppression carried out by their own governments, this goal has often been sacrificed in practice to serve neoliberal interests. So, for example, international financial institutions invoked human rights and "good governance" standards to defend programs (such as structural adjustment) that forced Third World societies to reform their domestic institutions to conform to neoliberal standards rather than to better protect the rights of their citizens.[28]

One thing is worth clarifying here. Though I've talked about them together, I don't mean to suggest that "human rights" and "good governance" standards are equivalent. Nor do I mean, by highlighting the activities of international financial institutions, to dismiss the role other institutions (such as the UN, the EU, and the various human rights treaty bodies) play in promulgating and applying human rights law. I've talked about "human rights" and "good governance" together and have focused on the role of international financial institutions in promoting them, because this is what Anghie

---

[23] Makau Mutua, "What Is TWAIL?," *Proceedings of the Annual Meeting (American Society of International Law)* 94 (2000): 31–40, 31.

[24] See Anghie, "Evolution of International Law"; see also Mutua, "What Is TWAIL?"

[25] Anghie, "Evolution of International Law," 749.

[26] I recognize the use of the term "Third World" could be contested. However, I will often use it here for two sets of reasons. First, it is frequently used in the literature I draw from, in which scholars and practitioners identify themselves with "Third World" Approaches to International Law. Second, some other candidate terms, such as non-Western, non-European, and non-White, all risk "otherizing" people in the Third World, recognizing their identity only as it is contrasted with a Western, European, or White referent; while terms such as "developing" may obscure the racial nature of the divisions that have historically set the Third World apart from the West.

[27] Anghie, "Evolution of International Law," 749.

[28] Ibid.

does. In an effort to faithfully interpret his view and the criticism of reform intervention that it represents, I've followed suit.

Anghie doesn't actually deny that there's a distinction between "human rights" and "good governance" standards either. But he argues that the good governance standards invoked to justify the forced neoliberalization of the Third World (which took place primarily through international financial institutions as opposed to other institutions more directly connected to the official apparatus of human rights law) were constructed with reference to human rights law.[29] Thus, human rights standards helped determine the content of—and, presumably, lent perceived legitimacy to—good governance standards.

Therefore, the argument proceeds, human rights law has often been effectively used as a tool to continue the subordination of people in the Third World—appearing to recognize them as full members of the global community but in fact doing so only insofar as was necessary to justify subjecting them to constraints, and no further.[30] So they are recognized as full members insofar as this means they can be held accountable by the international community for their domestic injustices, but not as full members insofar as this means, for example, they will be adequately represented in the international organizations that wield the power of this community. In this way, human rights law is one of the institutions of international law that, according to Anghie, was constructed and has evolved around the central concepts and strategies of colonialism.[31]

Importantly, this may be true even if no one involved in the creation or application of international human rights law or "good governance" standards explicitly *intended* them to give new life to the central concepts and strategies of colonialism. It would be enough to vindicate Anghie's worry that these standards were developed and employed in a way that in fact perpetuated the racialized hierarchies at the heart of colonialism.

Moreover, observing that people from the Third World have themselves contributed to the development of international human rights law and the institutions charged with implementing it, or that these institutions have sometimes been leveraged to protect the interests of people in the Third World, is not enough to alleviate the concerns Anghie raises. Indeed,

[29] Ibid.
[30] Ibid.
[31] Ibid.

176   PROMOTING JUSTICE ACROSS BORDERS

Anghie himself notes Third World actors' active engagement in the international legal system, as well as some of their successes, such as passing UN General Assembly resolutions calling for a New International Economic Order that would reverse Third World countries' economic dependence.[32] Anghie writes that, far from being ever-victorious, "imperial ambitions and structures . . . have been continuously contested at every level by Third World peoples."[33] But this doesn't contradict his overarching claims that imperialism and its attendant systems of thought have dramatically influenced the trajectory of international institutions and that even the potentially emancipatory elements of those institutions have often reflected imperial power dynamics.

Similarly, Getachew's work deftly illustrates that the involvement, innovation, and sometime success of Third World actors in political and intellectual struggles to shape the international order is no guarantee that it won't take on a neocolonial form.[34] For example, Getachew shows how the anticolonial nationalists she discusses (many based in Africa and the Caribbean) developed distinctive ideas about the nature of collective self-determination explicitly attentive to the need to overcome imperial domination and sought to see these ideas embodied in international institutions like the UN; however, she *also* shows how their ambitions were frustrated by the institution of racialized hierarchy in the League of Nations, the abandonment of the New International Economic Order in favor of a more neoliberal economic order, and the marginalization of the international institutions in which anticolonial nationalists saw emancipatory potential.[35]

One may, of course, argue that the *general tendency* of international human rights law and international institutions, and the international order more generally, is, and has been for some time, to promote equality and protect individual rights—that their influence has overall been a positive and liberating one, even if they've sometimes been co-opted for nefarious neocolonial purposes. Even if this is true, though, the risk that reform intervention could, going forward, function to reinforce or perpetuate neocolonial hierarchies remains. Thus, an ethics of reform intervention must still address this

---

[32] Ibid., 748, 751.

[33] Ibid., 751.

[34] See Adom Getachew, *Worldmaking after Empire: The Rise and Fall of Self-Determination* (Princeton, NJ: Princeton University Press, 2019).

[35] Ibid. Getachew makes these arguments over the course of her book. For a general summary, see her introduction, 1–13.

COLLECTIVE SELF-DETERMINATION WITHOUT ISOLATION 177

possibility and give guidance as to how we (and would-be interveners) can avoid it.

Thus, the salient worry for us is that if reform intervention became an accepted part of global political practice, it would simply become another vehicle for the subordination of people in the Third World, making them subject to the will of Western interveners, and denying them equal status as moral persons.[36] Though it would operate in the service of supposedly universal principles of justice, on this view, reform intervention would in reality be another manifestation of the "civilizing mission" that has always animated colonial exploits. Anghie calls this the "dynamic of difference," in virtue of which "international law posits a gap, a difference between European and non-European cultures and peoples, the former being characterized, broadly, as civilized and the latter as uncivilized (and all this implies in terms of the related qualities of each of these labels)."[37]

This criticism, it is worth emphasizing, is not merely a caution against malicious or self-interested interveners who intentionally deceive others into thinking they seek justice promotion when in fact they seek to subjugate or exploit recipients. Nor is it merely a caution against misinformed interveners who genuinely seek to promote justice but unwittingly harm recipients. It is, instead, a criticism of what we might call a structural feature of reform intervention. Because of the way geopolitical power is distributed, the criticism states, it will be Western actors who are most able to effectively intervene, and they will be most able (and most likely) to effectively intervene in the Third World.[38] Moreover, insofar as reform intervention is undertaken in the service of principles and standards of Western construction—which it may often be, again because of the West's disproportionate power to influence the content of geopolitical norms—it may constitute, in much the way colonialism's "civilizing mission" did, the use of standards designed by (and to serve the interests of) Western actors to constrain (and therefore subordinate) people in the Third World.

If reform intervention did, in this sense, constitute a new form of colonialism, it would mean the organization and operation of recipients'

---

[36] I explore this issue as a potential problem with putting limits on states' sovereignty, which could be imposed asymmetrically on formerly colonized states, in "Toward an Individualist," 7–10.

[37] Anghie, "Evolution of International Law," 742.

[38] This concern is familiar from debates about the desirability of the "Responsibility to Protect" norm in international relations. See Michael Doyle, *The Question of Intervention: John Stuart Mill and the Responsibility to Protect* (New Haven, CT: Yale University Press, 2015), 120–1, 140.

178   PROMOTING JUSTICE ACROSS BORDERS

institutions would reflect the conceptual categories and policy priorities of interveners rather than those of recipients themselves—just as, on a view like Anghie's, other forms of colonialism made the organization and operation of colonies' institutions reflect the conceptual categories and policy priorities of their colonizers.[39] If this were the case, institutions in societies subject to reform intervention wouldn't reflect the character of the populations they governed. Instead, they would reflect the character of the interveners. Recipient societies would be unable to enjoy collective self-determination because they wouldn't meet condition (1) from above.

As Anghie characterizes colonialism, it arguably also prevented colonized people from having the kind of influence over their institutions necessary for collective self-determination (and therefore from knowing or reasonably believing themselves to have such influence). Instead, this influence (at least a significant amount of it) was held by the colonizers. Thus, if it constituted a new form of colonialism, reform intervention would have the same effect—preventing recipients from having, and knowing or reasonably believing themselves to have, the kind of influence necessary for collective self-determination. Instead, this influence would be held by interveners. Recipient societies then wouldn't be able to meet conditions (2) or (3) from above either.

Thus, if reform intervention were an extension of colonialism, engaging in reform intervention really would undermine recipient societies' collective self-determination. So, does reform intervention constitute a new form of colonialism, serving to perpetuate a racialized hierarchy like the one Anghie describes between the West and the Third World? I propose that not all reform interventions fit this description. Indeed, some of the cases I've discussed so far directly challenge such hierarchies: they consist of historically less geopolitically powerful, non-White, non-Western actors taking action against historically powerful, White, Western actors.

The Latin American countries that submitted amicus briefs to the US Supreme Court in opposition to Arizona's immigration law defied entrenched racial hierarchies.[40] On some interpretations, so do the members of Palestinian civil society behind the BDS campaign.

---

[39] This problem, as Anghie characterizes it, doesn't arise only when literal colonizers impose their own concepts and priorities on their actual colonies. It arises whenever those historically empowered by colonial hierarchies exert such influence over those historically disempowered by colonial hierarchies. See Anghie, "Evolution of International Law."

[40] I also make this argument in "Toward an Individualist," 9–10.

COLLECTIVE SELF-DETERMINATION WITHOUT ISOLATION 179

Abigail Bakan and Yasmeen Abu-Laban interpret BDS as an explicitly antiracist, anti-hegemonic movement that may "serve as an important step in forging global solidarity against racism, colonialism and oppression."[41] BDS, on their view, stands in opposition to "an international racial contract which, since 1948, has assigned a common interest between the state of Israel and powerful international political allies, while absenting the Palestinians as both 'non-white' and stateless."[42] They go on to say that BDS is especially significant in that it poses this antiracist and anti-hegemonic challenge precisely as the Islamophobia of the "war on terror"—which Anghie characterizes as the most recent incarnation of colonialism—plays an ever more prominent role in global politics.[43]

Interventions like these, in which those at the "bottom" of the racialized hierarchies associated with colonialism lead efforts to produce political change in societies at the "top" of the same hierarchies, challenge colonial power dynamics. Especially when they, as Bakan and Abu-Laban argue BDS does, also directly challenge hegemonic ideologies and discourses that are themselves raced, they represent a mode of political activity that may help to undermine or reverse the "racialized hierarchy of international norms and institutions that subordinate non-Europeans to Europeans"[44] rather than perpetuate it.

We can consider interventions like this to be *counter-hegemonic* in a slightly different sense than those discussed in the previous section. For an intervention to be counter-hegemonic in the sense necessary for it not to risk dominating recipients, interveners must be less (currently) geopolitically powerful than recipients. (As established in the previous section, interventions in which interveners' and recipients' current geopolitical power is on a par don't risk dominating recipients either.) The relevant point of comparison is interveners' and recipients' current levels of geopolitical power, because domination occurs when one party (currently) has the power to interfere costlessly in the acts of another.

However, it's possible that interventions where interveners aren't *currently* more powerful than recipients could perpetuate a (racialized) colonial hierarchy (even though these interventions don't risk domination as Pettit

---

[41] Abigail B. Bakan and Yasmeen Abu-Laban, "Palestinian Resistance and International Solidarity: The BDS Campaign," *Race and Class* 51, no. 1 (2009): 29–54, 49.

[42] Ibid., 32.

[43] Ibid., 48; Anghie, "Evolution of International Law," 750–1.

[44] Mutua, "What Is TWAIL?," 31.

180 PROMOTING JUSTICE ACROSS BORDERS

understands it). The concern that reform intervention is a continuation of colonialism is a concern that it will continue patterns of behavior that perpetuate, and perhaps reinforce, a variety of problematic hierarchies present in global political life and that we can trace back to colonialism. Some of these hierarchies have to do with differentials in current geopolitical power, but they more fundamentally have to do with race, region, and historical differentials in geopolitical power. An intervention could perpetuate a problematic colonial hierarchy, for example, if it involved a former colonizer interfering in its former colony. This would risk perpetuating the colonial hierarchy in which they were once involved *even if* the interveners were *currently* no more powerful than the recipients. Similarly, an intervention could perpetuate a problematic colonial hierarchy if interveners were of a race or regional origin historically empowered by colonialism and recipients were of a race or regional origin historically disempowered by it. And this could happen regardless of interveners' and recipients' *current* power levels relative to each other. Thus, for an intervention to be counter-hegemonic in the sense necessary for it not to risk subjecting recipients to neocolonialism, interveners must occupy a lower position in historically established colonial hierarchies than recipients (where the positions in these hierarchies could be defined with reference to, for example, race, region, or past colonization). I'll call these interventions "counter-hegemonic in the anti-colonial sense." (And interventions in which interveners and recipients occupy comparable positions in colonial hierarchies don't risk subjecting recipients to neocolonialism either.)

This raises the question of what we should think when the different determinants of whether an intervention is counter-hegemonic pull in different directions. They will often pull in the same direction: interventions that are counter-hegemonic in the non-domination sense will often also be counter-hegemonic in the anti-colonial sense. But this isn't *necessarily* the case. What should we think of an intervention that's counter-hegemonic in the non-domination sense but not in the anti-colonial sense, or vice versa?

We might imagine, for example, that a small Western European country's intervention in China would be counter-hegemonic in the non-domination sense but not in the anti-colonial sense, and that a Chinese intervention in a small Western European country would be counter-hegemonic in the anti-colonial sense but not in the non-domination sense.[45] Whether one thinks an

---

[45] I thank Anna Stilz for pointing out this issue.

COLLECTIVE SELF-DETERMINATION WITHOUT ISOLATION   181

intervention that's counter-hegemonic in one sense but not the other could be justified arguably depends on how one weights the severity of the two different kinds of threats to self-determination (domination and neocolonialism). Say one thinks (either in general or in a given case) that subjection to domination is the most salient threat to recipients' self-determination, and that the perpetuation of a colonial hierarchy is a less salient concern. Then one might not think an intervention that's counter-hegemonic in the non-domination sense threatens recipients' self-determination (or not enough to make it impermissible), even if it's not counter-hegemonic in the anti-colonial sense. Alternatively, one could think the perpetuation of colonial hierarchies (not subjection to domination) poses the real threat to recipients' self-determination. Or one could think both subjection to domination and the perpetuation of colonial hierarchies threaten recipients' self-determination.

Which of these views one takes will likely depend on one's particular account of what self-determination requires. While I don't argue here for any one such account, it's worth noting that the specific account one adopts will affect which criticisms of reform intervention seem most serious or salient. This, in turn, may affect the kinds of interventions one can in principle endorse. (For example, it may affect in what sense an intervention must be counter-hegemonic in order for one to think it doesn't threaten recipients' self-determination.)

From now on, I'll use the unmodified term "counter-hegemonic" to describe interventions that are both counter-hegemonic in the non-domination sense *and* counter-hegemonic in the anti-colonial sense. That is, I'll use it to describe interventions where interveners are currently less powerful than *and* occupy lower positions in colonial hierarchies than recipients. These interventions will be susceptible *neither* to the criticism that they undermine recipients' self-determination because they dominate recipients *nor* to the criticism that they undermine recipients' self-determination because they perpetuate colonial hierarchies. The Latin American countries' submission of amicus briefs against Arizona's SB 1070 meets these criteria; on Bakan and Abu-Laban's reading, so does BDS.

Does the foregoing analysis mean, then, that an intervention *must* be counter-hegemonic in the anti-colonial sense to avoid taking on a neocolonial form? Must we conclude, for example, that any intervention by a Western actor in a Third World society constitutes a continuation of colonial power relationships? I don't think we must.

182   PROMOTING JUSTICE ACROSS BORDERS

I take it that one central element of colonialism was its denial that colonial subjects were fully developed persons. Hence Fanon's claim that colonial societies are divided into two "'species' of mankind," with the colonizer—quintessentially a foreigner—representing the "ruling species."[46] As Anghie emphasizes, colonial powers routinely characterized colonial subjects as "uncivilized" and seem to have recognized them as persons only to the extent necessary to sanction them for their alleged deficiencies as compared with supposedly universal (but in fact distinctively Western) standards of genuinely "human" behavior.[47] Martti Koskenniemi also notes the importance of the ideas of civilization and development in justifying colonialism. He recounts the rise of the "Comparative Method" in nineteenth-century international law, which "viewed primitive peoples as earlier stages of human development in an overall law-like frame of progressive history."[48] He goes on to describe the ways in which international lawyers of the period invoked different (perceived) levels of "civilization" to justify differential grants of political and legal recognition to non-Europeans, sometimes explicitly comparing them to children.[49]

As I read Koskenniemi, this denial of fully developed personhood wasn't a denial that non-Europeans subject to colonial rule had *any* valid claims of their own. But it *was* a denial of their standing to bring *certain kinds* of claims—namely claims to full political and legal recognition and inclusion in the international community on terms of equality with Europeans.[50]

This brings us to the second central element of colonial rule as I understand it—namely, that colonizers unjustifiably deprived colonial subjects of the ability to exercise their own political authority (which denial was, as demonstrated above, premised on the view that they weren't fully developed persons).

I propose that reform interveners can avoid denying recipients are fully developed persons by acting according to the standards set out in Chapter 2 (on toleration) and can avoid unjustifiably depriving recipients of the ability to exercise their own political authority by paying sufficient attention to the considerations set out in Chapter 3 (on legitimacy).

[46] Frantz Fanon, *The Wretched of the Earth,* trans. Richard Philcox (New York: Grove Press, 2004), 1, 5.
[47] Anghie, "Evolution of International Law."
[48] Martti Koskenniemi, *The Gentle Civilizer of Nations: The Rise and Fall of International Law 1870–1960* (Cambridge: Cambridge University Press, 2001), 101.
[49] Ibid., 127–32.
[50] See his discussion of the colonial "discourse of exclusion-inclusion" (ibid., 130).

COLLECTIVE SELF-DETERMINATION WITHOUT ISOLATION 183

On the first point, when interveners practice toleration in their relations with recipients, they necessarily recognize recipients as sources of weighty claims of their own about how their lives should go and what rules should govern them—the same kinds of claims that any people interacting as political equals would recognize each other as having. In encouraging (or at least not discouraging) tolerant treatment within recipient societies, interveners seek to empower (or at least refuse to disempower) recipients to determine the courses of their own lives according to their own free choices and freely adopted (or freely retained) values. And in using only those means that treat recipients tolerantly, interveners seek to ensure whatever policies they promote to achieve this end are designed and implemented in a way that itself incorporates the presumption that recipients are entitled to live according to their own choices and values. This is another way of recognizing that recipients make weighty claims of their own, just as interveners do in their own societies, regarding how their lives should go, including what rules should govern them.

As discussed in Chapter 2, interveners may permissibly treat recipients with intolerance in some extraordinary circumstances (when the value of toleration is overridden). However, refraining from intolerance except in these circumstances is itself a way of recognizing recipients as fully developed persons with weighty (if not decisive in strictly every case) claims of their own about how their lives should go and what rules should govern them. And even in the extraordinary cases where toleration is overridden, if interveners adhere to the standards developed in Chapter 2, they'll treat recipients with intolerance only when they are justifiably confident that others unlikely to share their own predictable biases would share their judgment that this is the right thing to do. This means that when interveners behave according to my standards, even when they treat recipients with intolerance, they are unlikely to impose a parochial conception of fully developed personhood on recipients (as colonizers did on colonized people).

On the second point, if interveners engage in only the kinds of interventions that are compatible with recipients' institutions being fully legitimate (identified in Chapter 3), they don't deny recipients the ability to exercise their own political authority. That is, when interveners seek to promote some change in recipient institutions, if they do so in a way that would be justifiable even assuming those institutions were legitimate, their intervention does nothing to deny recipient institutions' authority. In such cases, interveners interact with recipient institutions as they would be justified

184   PROMOTING JUSTICE ACROSS BORDERS

interacting with any legitimate political authority, not as colonial powers that rule over recipients precisely because the latter's independent institutions are (allegedly) illegitimate.

On the other hand, if interveners launched interventions premised on a (full or partial) denial of recipient institutions' legitimacy—regime-change interventions, for example—they would be at risk of unjustifiably denying recipients the ability to exercise their own political authority. That is, if interveners claim recipient institutions are either fully or partially illegitimate, and that a particular kind of intervention is therefore justified, the interveners could be mistaken (in which case their intervention would amount to an unjustifiable interference with legitimate institutions, premised on a mistaken characterization of those institutions as illegitimate—and would therefore amount to an unjustifiable denial of recipients' ability to exercise their own political authority). Further, the very fact that interveners are, in such a case, positioned to judge the legitimacy of recipients' institutions might perpetuate problematic colonial hierarchies (especially if the interveners are Western and the recipients are in the Third World). After all, this would mirror the discretion colonial-era Europeans had to decide who was and wasn't included on equal terms in the international community. As Koskenniemi writes, "if there was no external standard for civilization, then everything depended on what Europeans approved."[51]

Both these problems can be mitigated by subjecting interventions premised on the denial of recipient institutions' legitimacy to the kinds of decision mechanisms suggested in previous chapters—through which interveners' claims are assessed by other global political actors who are unlikely to share their (moral and evidential) biases. This would make it less likely that interveners would act on mistaken claims about the legitimacy of recipient institutions—and would help disperse the power to judge their legitimacy, ensuring it wasn't left up to a single group of interveners, all with similar geopolitical standing and interests.

Thus, we can conclude, reform intervention need not constitute a continuation of the colonial project. There is a caveat to this finding, though. Namely, even if individual interventions meet the criteria laid out above, such that no one on its own counts as a perpetuation of colonial hierarchies, it is possible that a *practice* or a *pattern* of reform intervention, in which interveners were generally from the West and recipients were generally from the Third

---

[51] Ibid., 135.

COLLECTIVE SELF-DETERMINATION WITHOUT ISOLATION 185

World, could perpetuate them nonetheless. This is especially true if Western societies have disproportionate control over the content of norms governing reform intervention in global politics (if Western actors are, by and large, the ones who get to decide on the standards proposed interventions must meet for global political actors to accept them as justified, and the ones who get to decide when a particular intervention meets these standards).

To avoid these problems, we need not eliminate all Western reform interventions with recipients in the Third World, and we need not claim they are all unjustified. But when interveners occupy a privileged position in colonial hierarchies with respect to recipients, and when there's a general pattern of reform intervention establishing those historically marginalized by colonialism as recipients and those historically empowered by it as interveners, interveners' actions can help reinforce and perpetuate this pattern and the hierarchy it reflects (and is reflected in). In order to counteract this effect, interveners in cases like this should also take action to subvert the problematic pattern of reform intervention and the corresponding colonial hierarchy. This is one way in which interveners could do something Rubenstein argues international actors have moral reason to do: help enhance the "capacities, power, connections, etc." of people in "the global South."[52] There are many tactics interveners could employ to subvert (neo)colonial behavioral patterns and hierarchies, and which specific strategies an intervener should use will likely change with the nature of the intervention as well as the capabilities and resources of the intervener. (I'll discuss one such strategy in this chapter's concluding section, when I examine how the ethical standards developed here apply to my focal cases.)

We should also grant a kind of political priority to reform interventions that are counter-hegemonic in the anti-colonial sense. This will help ensure that, even if reform intervention, as a global practice, *includes* interventions in which interveners occupy a higher position in colonial hierarchies than recipients, the practice of reform intervention won't merely be a vehicle for extending, perpetuating, and reinforcing those hierarchies.

Moreover, making the support and encouragement of counter-hegemonic (in the anti-colonial sense) interventions our political priority will itself act as another, distinct challenge (in addition to the counter-hegemonic

---

[52] Jennifer Rubenstein, *Between Samaritans and States: The Political Ethics of Humanitarian INGOs* (Oxford: Oxford University Press, 2015), 119.

186 PROMOTING JUSTICE ACROSS BORDERS

interventions themselves) to the hierarchies and ideologies that may be vestiges (or simply continuations) of colonialism.[53]

Finally, prioritizing support for counter-hegemonic (in the anti-colonial sense) interventions will arguably help build faith in the practice of reform intervention among historically marginalized people who have often, understandably, been some of intervention's harshest critics. Prioritizing these interventions will demonstrate that the proponents and practitioners of reform intervention are not simply establishing a new mechanism by which to exercise and extend the power of historically dominant political actors. As a show of "good faith," it will lend credibility to the claims that reform intervention can serve the interests and protect the rights of all people, including—and perhaps especially—those who have often been neglected or actively oppressed by the workings of global politics as usual. This may, in turn, encourage historically marginalized people to participate in the practice of reform intervention, which would be good both for those people and for the practice of reform intervention.

That is, it would be good for historically marginalized people if they had a more substantial voice in the direction of global politics. It's in light of this that Anghie, for example, recommends the people of the Third World not turn away from the apparatus of international law, despite its history of excluding and subjugating them. He argues, rather than "leave open the field of international law to . . . imperial processes," the people of the Third World and their allies must find ways to *use* international law to overturn imperial power structures, thereby promoting global justice.[54]

Further, global political institutions and practices like reform intervention will be fairer and more justifiable if people subject to their rules—and their effects—but who have historically been largely excluded from determining the direction of their operation play a greater role within them.

In sum, reform intervention does *not* reinforce or perpetuate colonial hierarchies when

D. interveners don't occupy a privileged position in colonial hierarchies compared to recipients.

---

[53] See also my discussion in "Toward an Individualist," 9–11.
[54] Anghie, "The Evolution of International Law," 752.

COLLECTIVE SELF-DETERMINATION WITHOUT ISOLATION   187

The real risk of neocolonial subordination comes when interveners occupy more privileged positions in the (historical, regional, racial, etc.) hierarchies associated with colonialism than recipients. In these cases, reform intervention won't constitute neocolonialism as long as

E. interveners practice toleration toward recipients, unless it's a case in which the value of toleration is overridden;

F. interveners treat recipients' institutions as legitimate institutions, unless the decision to treat them as illegitimate is authorized by epistemically diverse global political actors; *and*

G. there's no general pattern of reform intervention establishing those historically marginalized by colonialism as recipients and those historically empowered by it as interveners; or, if there is such a pattern, interveners work to undermine it.

Having identified which kinds of reform intervention avoid dominating recipients and which avoid subjecting them to neocolonial subordination, I'll now examine another way in which reform intervention might undermine recipients' collective self-determination.

Reform Intervention and Responsiveness to the Public Interest

Reform intervention could undermine recipients' self-determination by making their governments more responsive to interveners ("outsiders") and correspondingly less responsive to the "insiders" who are, after all, the ones routinely subject to the government's power. This problem could be exacerbated if, for example, interveners were financially dependent on (and therefore accountable to) other "outsiders" or if interveners "crowded out" local political actors in a recipient society.[55]

Several people endorse (in one form or another) the "all-subjected principle," which says that governments should be responsive to those routinely subject to their power.[56] For adherents of the all-subjected principle, if reform

---

[55] See Rubenstein's discussion of INGOs as "second-best actors" in *Between Samaritans and States*, 74–81.

[56] See Robert A. Dahl, *Democracy and Its Critics* (New Haven, CT: Yale University Press, 1989), 120; Claudio Lopez-Guerra, "Should Expatriates Vote?," *Journal of Political Philosophy* 13, no. 2 (2005): 216–34. Nancy Fraser endorses a version of the principle in "Abnormal Justice," *Critical*

188 PROMOTING JUSTICE ACROSS BORDERS

intervention made recipient governments more responsive to outsiders and less responsive to insiders, it could undermine recipients' collective self-determination. First, one might think those subject to a government's power must be able to translate their preferences or interests into changes in government policy. This is one view of the kind of influence members of a society must have (and must know or reasonably believe themselves to have) over their institutions in order to enjoy self-determination. If reform intervention undermined insiders' ability to exercise this influence by making their government more responsive to outsiders' interests or preferences than insiders', it would undermine recipients' self-determination (by preventing them from fulfilling conditions (2) and (3) of the generic idea of self-determination with which I began).

Moreover, if interveners' exertion of influence was effective, and if their preferences or interests were at odds with those of the recipient society's members, recipient institutions would *actually reflect* outsiders' interests and preferences *instead of* insiders'. This would, on some views, preclude recipient institutions from fulfilling condition (1) of the generic idea of self-determination (that they reflect in the relevant sense the character of the population they govern), thereby undermining recipients' self-determination in another way.

It's worth pausing here to recognize the distinction between interests and preferences, which, above, I talked about together. Though interests and preferences are often related, they aren't necessarily identical. Thus, we can consider there to be two versions of the present criticism of reform intervention. One says governments should be responsive to the preferences of those they govern, whereas reform intervention makes recipient governments responsive to interveners' preferences (at the expense of recipients' preferences). The other says governments should be responsive to the interests of those they govern, whereas reform intervention makes recipient governments responsive to interveners' interests (at the expense of recipients' interests). Here, I'll focus on the interest-based version of this criticism, because I take it that conducting a reform intervention such that it meets the conditions laid out in Chapter 2 (on toleration) would ensure it

---

Inquiry 34 (2008): 393–422, 411–3, but she doesn't endorse the interpretation on which it picks out citizens of states in particular as those "subjected" in the relevant way. For an overview of prominent expressions of the all-subjected principle, see Sofia Näsström, "The Challenge of the All-Affected Principle," *Political Studies* 59 (2011): 116–34, 118–22.

COLLECTIVE SELF-DETERMINATION WITHOUT ISOLATION 189

was sufficiently responsive to recipients' preferences so as to avoid most, if not all, of the preference-based criticism's force.

With that in mind, I ask, does reform intervention in fact make recipient governments responsive to interveners' interests (at the expense of recipients' interests)? The history of intervention suggests this is a valid worry. When interveners exercise control over recipients' institutions, it makes sense to think those institutions will become responsive (to some degree, at least) to interveners' particular interests. In the case of totally or highly controlling interventions, officials within recipient institutions have no reasonable option but to do as the interveners demand. This gives us reason to think they'll respond more reliably to interveners' interests than to the interests of those they actually govern. Developing countries seeking urgently needed loans from the IMF or the World Bank in the 1980s, for example, had no choice but to adopt austerity, trade liberalization, and privatization as part of the "structural adjustment" programs lenders demanded.[57] Recipient societies were denied the opportunity to decide which policies to adopt based on their assessment of their members' interests. (And, in fact, the programs were often vigorously opposed within recipient societies, with about half of countries forced to adopt them experiencing protest riots as a result.)[58] In such cases, recipients societies' laws arguably reflected the interests of their governments' foreign creditors rather than those of their own citizens.

Even in the case of slightly controlling intervention, we might wonder whether interveners' incentivizing recipients to act in certain ways undercuts recipients' self-determination. After all, in such cases, those within recipient institutions must *react to* and *take account of* the interests interveners advance, even if they aren't forced to ultimately adopt policies catering to them. So Oman, when faced with the prospect of either adopting certain workers' rights protections or losing the chance for a preferential trade agreement with the US, had either to adopt the US's desired policies or suffer the cost of losing the trade deal.[59] And at least on some readings of the situation, the US insistence on these particular policies reflected certain US interests (e.g., American workers' interests in not competing on an open market with Omani imports produced comparatively cheaply in the absence of

---

[57] See Richard W. Miller, *Globalizing Justice: The Ethics of Poverty and Power* (Oxford: Oxford University Press, 2010), 136–41.

[58] Ibid., 139.

[59] See Emilie Hafner-Burton, *Forced to Be Good: Why Trade Agreements Boost Human Rights* (Ithaca, NY: Cornell University Press, 2009), 144–9.

190   PROMOTING JUSTICE ACROSS BORDERS

significant labor regulations, and American politicians' interests in making American workers think they were responding to workers' interests).[60] As discussed earlier, the cost of Oman's refusal to adopt the US's desired policies wouldn't have been devastating, but it would have been significant.[61] Though officials in Oman still had a choice regarding whether or not to update national worker protections, when the US attached a significant cost to one of their options, it effectively added weight to one side of the scale. If Oman were to agree to the US's terms—which it did—it would be responding in part to the interests the US advanced in specifying those terms rather than its own citizens' interests.

Persuasive intervention, too, though it leaves the choice of which policies to adopt entirely up to recipient populations (at least as much as it was up to them before the intervention), may serve to make recipient institutions more responsive to foreign rather than domestic interests. Imagine, for example, that interveners (for whatever reason) use persuasion much more effectively than do recipients, and so are more able than recipients to advance their interests in the recipient society.

Each of these examples illustrates ways reform intervention may make recipient institutions answerable to interveners' interests—potentially at the expense of being answerable to those of their own constituents. For each of these examples, though, there is also one that illustrates how reform intervention may in fact make recipient institutions *more* responsive to those subject to their power. Indeed, sometimes reform intervention serves the interests of people in recipient societies currently marginalized, ignored, or victimized by their own institutions.

Consider, for instance, the US intervention in Haiti in the early 1990s, which restored popularly elected president Jean-Bertrand Aristide to power after he had been deposed by a military coup.[62] This was arguably a totally controlling intervention, as the US threatened the Haitian regime with military force, and had in fact deployed troops to the area—though the regime acquiesced in time to prevent actual armed conflict.[63] We could interpret Haitians' decision to elect Aristide as a declaration that an Aristide presidency would be in their interest. If a military coup sought to make

[60] See ibid., 147–8.
[61] See ibid., 147.
[62] For a brief description of the case, see Andrew Altman and Christopher Heath Wellman, *A Liberal Theory of International Justice* (Oxford: Oxford University Press, 2009), 102.
[63] Ibid.

COLLECTIVE SELF-DETERMINATION WITHOUT ISOLATION   191

government responsive to the interests of a small but powerful faction (who opposed Aristide), irrespective of the rest of the citizenry's interests, it would reduce the government's responsiveness to those it ruled—thereby undermining Haiti's self-determination. Consequently, an intervention that sought to reverse the coup and return Aristide to power would be a boon to self-determination.

Allen Buchanan makes a related point when he argues, more generally, that "genuine" self-determination may count in favor of some foreign interventions—namely, some armed interventions in support of revolutionary forces in non-democratic states—if the interventions are unlikely to be "predatory" or "blundering."[64]

Similarly, the Oman case effectively illustrates how foreign intervention can make recipient institutions more responsive (compared to the pre-intervention status quo) to some within the recipient society, even as it makes them less responsive to others. There were, presumably, some in Oman (perhaps factory owners and manufacturing companies) whose interests would be set back by adopting stricter protections for workers' rights. The US intervention arguably had the effect of making Oman's government less responsive to these parties. But it also made the government more responsive to the interests of workers who benefited from improved legal protections.[65] Here was a group of Oman's citizens whose needs were persistently unmet by their own institutions, and an intervention that encouraged those institutions to meet their needs.

When several Latin American countries submitted amicus briefs to the US Supreme Court opposing Arizona's immigration enforcement law SB 1070, they (self-consciously) aimed to make US institutions more responsive to the interests of Latin American immigrants and other Latin Americans in the US—people routinely subject to US power but whose interests were seriously threatened by the new law, and at least some of whom were systematically excluded from political decision-making (because not enfranchised). As noted earlier, Mexico's brief (which several other countries signed onto)

---

[64] Allen Buchanan, "Self-Determination, Revolution, and Intervention," *Ethics* 126 (2016): 447–73, 450–3. On the possible permissibility (and compatibility with self-determination) of interventions aiding revolutionary struggles within recipient societies, to encourage democratic transition, see also Christopher J. Finlay, "Reform Intervention and Democratic Revolution," *European Journal of International Relations* 13, no. 4 (2007): 555–81.

[65] See Emilie Hafner-Burton's discussion in *Forced to Be Good*, 144–9.

192 PROMOTING JUSTICE ACROSS BORDERS

invokes the rights and interests of Mexico's own citizens and those of other Latin Americans in the US.[66]

Thus, it is possible, at least, for reform intervention to encourage recipient institutions to be *more* responsive to the needs of those within their jurisdictions that they currently ignore (or worse). If self-determination requires institutions to be responsive to those subject to their power, and reform intervention serves to bring some of those people, who are currently marginalized, back into the political fold, inducing their own institutions to be more responsive to their interests, reform intervention may increase the degree to which recipient societies enjoy self-determination.

Noting that it's *possible* for reform intervention to make recipients' institutions more responsive to their own people doesn't tell us much in the way of normative principle, however. After all, the opposite is also possible, and has often been the case. Let's say we have shown there is nothing about reform intervention *as such* that means it must, *in principle,* make recipients' institutions less responsive to their own people, and that sometimes reform intervention may even improve recipient institutions' responsiveness. This is an interesting finding on its own, but the question remains what, if any, normative implications it has. Some may argue that, even if reform intervention doesn't *necessarily* make recipients' institutions less responsive to their own people, it has historically done so very often—so often, in fact, that we should adopt a general principle barring reform intervention, for the sake of safeguarding collective self-determination. After all, we should adopt normative principles that make sense when applied to a wide variety of cases, even if this means they will sometimes overlook or disregard the nuances of particular, atypical cases. Thus, the argument continues, we should refrain from reform intervention because, though it may be unobjectionable in some individual cases, it will *typically* undermine recipients' collective self-determination by making their institutions less responsive to them (and responsive instead to foreign interveners).

This argument would be convincing if the cases in which reform intervention would or wouldn't threaten recipient institutions' responsiveness to their own people were random or otherwise unpredictable—if there was no good way to tell ex ante if a proposed intervention was likely to undermine recipients' self-determination by making their institutions less responsive to

---

[66] See, for example, Amicus Curiae Brief of the United Mexican States in Support of Respondent, Arizona v. US, 567 US 387 (2012), at 1–4.

COLLECTIVE SELF-DETERMINATION WITHOUT ISOLATION   193

their own people. The question before us, then, is not simply whether reform intervention *can* make recipient institutions more responsive to the interests of people subject to their power, but whether there is some identifiable set of conditions under which this is likely to be the case. Can we identify certain *kinds* of interventions most likely to increase recipient institutions' responsiveness to their domestic constituencies, and/or develop guidelines for determining whether a given intervention will be one of these kinds? I believe we can.

An intervention is most likely to increase recipient institutions' responsiveness to their domestic constituencies if it is narrowly targeted to advance the interests of those who are formally disenfranchised—or otherwise clearly disempowered—compared with others in their own societies, even if their institutions are on the whole relatively representative. This point is important because, while there is wide disagreement on what institutions must look like if outsiders are to be justified in presuming those institutions (on the whole) represent the people they govern,[67] there may be less disagreement about when certain people therein are clearly underrepresented compared to others. That is, it may be easier to identify societies in which some members are significantly disempowered *compared* to others than to identify societies whose institutions fail to meet a generalizable standard of representativeness (because it may be more difficult to identify the correct generalizable standard).

As suggested above, we can read the anti–SB 1070 amicus briefs as one example of an intervention on behalf of the clearly disempowered—specifically, undocumented immigrants who are subject to state power but not enfranchised. We can say the same about Europe's refusal to sell lethal injection drugs; this intervention served the interests of people with felony convictions who are formally disenfranchised by the American political system.

Moreover, on some views about who counts as "routinely subject" to a state's power, there are certain policy areas in which even the *most* representative existing governments systematically exclude people routinely subject to their power from political decision-making and therefore can be said to be unresponsive to those people's interests.

---

[67] Compare Walzer, "Moral Standing"; John Rawls, *The Law of Peoples with "The Idea of Public Reason Revisited"* (Cambridge, MA: Harvard University Press, 1999), part II; Charles R. Beitz, "Rawls's Law of Peoples," *Ethics* 110, no. 4 (2000): 669–96, 686–7; Fernando Tesón, "The Rawlsian Theory of International Law," *Ethics and International Affairs* 9 (1995): 79–99, 87–90.

194 PROMOTING JUSTICE ACROSS BORDERS

In particular, I have in mind policy relating to migrants, refugees, and other stateless persons. These people are routinely subject to the institutions of societies they seek to enter. Whether they are allowed to enter is effectively up to the institutions of the receiving societies, and if they're denied, their exclusion is coercively enforced. As Arash Abizadeh argues, those seeking entry are therefore subject to the coercive power of receiving institutions in a way that theories of self-determination should recognize as relevant.[68] Despite being subjected to it, though, migrants, refugees, and other stateless persons aren't represented in the exercise of this power—they aren't, for example, enfranchised or consulted in the design of receiving institutions' border policy. Of course, Abizadeh's view that migrants are "subject" to the power of states they try to enter such that they deserve to have their interests represented in the making of those states' border policies is a controversial one. I can't defend it here. For now, I will simply note that, if you do endorse Abizadeh's view, you should think that interventions advancing the interests of migrants, refugees, and other stateless persons regarding border policy will generally increase rather than decrease the degree to which recipient institutions cater to the interests of people routinely subject to their power.

We can contrast these cases with those in which interveners act to cement the power of recipient societies' political elites, further insulating them from the influence of their own people (thereby making recipient governments less likely to serve their own people's interests and perhaps more likely to serve the interests of the interveners that have helped secure their power). Consider, for example, the consulting firm McKinsey & Co., which has recently been accused of helping prop up authoritarian political elites around the world.[69]

---

[68] See Arash Abizadeh, "Democratic Theory and Border Coercion: No Right to Unilaterally Control Your Own Borders," *Political Theory* 36, no. 1 (2008): 37–65.

[69] See Katie Benner, Mark Mazzetti, Ben Hubbard, and Mike Isaac, "Saudis' Image Makers: A Troll Army and a Twitter Insider," *New York Times,* 20 October 2018, https://www.nytimes.com/2018/10/20/us/politics/saudi-image-campaign-twitter.html?module=inline; Walt Bogdanich and Michael Forsythe, "How McKinsey Has Helped Raise the Stature of Authoritarian Governments," *New York Times,* 15 December 2018, https://www.nytimes.com/2018/12/15/world/asia/mckinsey-china-russia.html; Michael Forsythe, Mark Mazzetti, Ben Hubbard, and Walt Bogdanich, "Consulting Firm Keeps Lucrative Saudi Alliance, Shaping Crown Prince's Vision," *New York Times,* 4 November 2018, https://www.nytimes.com/2018/11/04/world/middleeast/mckinsey-bcg-booz-allen-saudi-khashoggi.html?rref=collection%2Fbyline%2Fwalt-bogdanich; Michael Posner, "How McKinsey & Co. Fails as a Global Leader," *Forbes,* 18 December 2018, https://www.forbes.com/sites/michaelposner/2018/12/18/how-mckinsey-co-fails-as-a-global-leader/#6c060a90376d. For McKinsey's reply to (some of) these accusations, see McKinsey & Co., "Statement on *New York Times* Article *on McKinsey Work in Southeast Asia, China, Eastern Europe and the Middle East,*" 16 December 2018, https://www.mckinsey.com/about-us/media-center/statement-on-new-york-times-article.

COLLECTIVE SELF-DETERMINATION WITHOUT ISOLATION 195

Among McKinsey's most alarming projects is a report it authored on those expressing opposition to the Saudi regime on Twitter.[70] The report identified three Twitter accounts in particular and identified the individuals behind two of them; one account's owner was later arrested, another account's owner said his brothers were imprisoned, and the third account (whose owner was unknown) was shut down.[71] If McKinsey's report did bring about these events, it could be rightly criticized for undermining Saudis' collective self-determination by enabling their government to silence its internal political opponents, arguably making it less responsive to its own citizens' interests.

McKinsey has also aided the development of China's Smart Cities program, which collects data on Chinese citizens from (for example) outdoor cameras, and which human rights activists characterize as a dangerous boost to the Chinese government's surveillance efforts.[72] In a June 2018 report, McKinsey writes, ominously, "Police patrols cannot be everywhere, for instance, but predictive analytics can deploy them in the right place at the right time."[73] If China's government deploys the Smart Cities program to stifle dissent and stymie political opposition, McKinsey could, again, be rightly criticized for helping make the Chinese government less responsive to the interests of its own people.

Though we should oppose interventions like McKinsey's, which shore up existing elites' power at the expense of their responsiveness to their own citizens, the other cases examined above show that it's possible for reform intervention to make recipient institutions *more* rather than less responsive to those routinely subject to their power. Moreover, I've identified guidelines for picking out cases in which the latter outcome is comparatively likely—in which recipient institutions persistently and manifestly fail to represent certain of their subjects, and in which foreign intervention on these subjects' behalf may therefore be expected to make recipient institutions more responsive to those they govern. Namely, we can suppose these conditions are met when

---

[70] Benner et al., "Saudis' Image Makers"; Bogdanich and Forsythe, "How McKinsey Has Helped"; Forsythe et al., "Consulting Firm Keeps Lucrative Saudi Alliance"; Posner, "How McKinsey & Co. Fails."

[71] Benner et al., "Saudis' Image Makers"; Bogdanich and Forsythe, "How McKinsey Has Helped"; Forsythe et al., "Consulting Firm Keeps Lucrative Saudi Alliance"; Posner, "How McKinsey & Co. Fails."

[72] Bogdanich and Forsythe, "How McKinsey Has Helped."

[73] Ibid.

196 PROMOTING JUSTICE ACROSS BORDERS

H. reform intervention is undertaken on behalf of people manifestly disempowered (e.g., formally disenfranchised) with respect to others in their societies.

If we endorse a view like Abizadeh's and affirm that migrants, refugees, and other stateless persons are manifestly disempowered in this way, we should also think reform interventions tailored to advance their interests regarding border policy will tend to make recipient institutions more rather than less responsive to a group of people routinely subject to those institutions' power.

Summary

Over the course of this chapter, I've explored several ways in which reform intervention might undermine recipients' collective self-determination by subjecting recipients to domination or neocolonial subordination or by making recipient governments more responsive to foreign interveners' interests and correspondingly less responsive to their own constituents' interests. However, I've also shown that not all interventions involve undermining recipients' collective self-determination in these ways: some interventions escape the collective self-determination objection.

Taking the findings of this chapter's different sections together, we can identify which kinds of reform intervention don't undermine recipients' self-determination in *any* of the ways described above (and that therefore escape the collective self-determination objection).

Reform intervention escapes the collective self-determination objection—and therefore has a chance at being, all things considered, permissible—only if it is justifiable according to the standards laid out in *all three* of the following categories.

Category 1: Interventions That Avoid Dominating Recipients
A reform intervention is justifiable only if *either*
A. interveners are not more geopolitically powerful than recipients *or* it meets *one* of the following two conditions:
B. it is persuasive or slightly controlling or
C. it is highly or totally controlling but is subject to approval or effective oversight by epistemically diverse global political actors.

COLLECTIVE SELF-DETERMINATION WITHOUT ISOLATION   197

Category 2: Interventions That Avoid Neocolonial Subordination
A reform intervention is justifiable only if *either*

D. interveners don't occupy a privileged position in colonial hierarchies compared to recipients
   or it meets *all* of the following three conditions:

E. interveners practice toleration toward recipients, unless it's a case
   in which the value of toleration is overridden;

F. interveners treat recipients' institutions as legitimate institutions,
   unless the decision to treat them as illegitimate is authorized by
   epistemically diverse global political actors; and

G. there's no general pattern of reform intervention establishing
   those historically marginalized by colonialism as recipients and
   those historically empowered by it as interveners; or, if there is
   such a pattern, interveners work to undermine it.

Category 3: Interventions That Make Recipient Governments More
Responsive to Their Constituents' Interests
A reform intervention is justifiable only if

H. it is undertaken on behalf of people manifestly disempowered
   (e.g., formally disenfranchised) with respect to others in their
   societies.

Moreover, several of these considerations argue in favor of giving political
priority to counter-hegemonic reform interventions, a recommendation I'll
discuss further in the next chapter.[74]

It isn't immediately obvious how this complex constellation of standards
should lead us to evaluate any given case. It is even less clear how these
standards *plus* the standards argued for in previous chapters should lead
us to evaluate any given case. To remedy this lack of clarity, and to give a
more concrete idea of how the ethical standards I've been defending require
us to act in the world, I'll consider here how these standards apply to my
focal cases.

At the end of Chapter 3, I identified four reform interventions that escape
both the toleration objection and the legitimacy objection: Tostan's work in
western Africa; the Latin American opposition to Arizona's SB 1070; the US's
conditional offer of a preferential trade agreement to Oman; and the parts
of the BDS movement that involve nonstate actors engaging in consumer,

---

[74] I make a similar recommendation in "Toward an Individualist," 9–11.

198 PROMOTING JUSTICE ACROSS BORDERS

cultural, and academic boycotts. I also argued that the European refusal to sell lethal injection drugs to the US escapes the toleration objection. If (and only if) the US's continued use of the death penalty renders it partially illegitimate, Europe's actions also escape the legitimacy objection.

If any of these five interventions *also* escape the collective self-determination objection, they stand a chance (subject to the pragmatic considerations I'll discuss in the next chapter) of being, all things considered, permissible. I'll now examine each case in turn.

Tostan's work in western Africa doesn't dominate recipients because it counts as a persuasive intervention. (It meets standard (B) above, so it's justifiable according to the standards laid out in Category 1.) However, Tostan does occupy a privileged position in colonial hierarchies compared to the recipients it works with. Though it is headquartered in Senegal, it is an INGO with major offices in "White" Western countries (the US, Sweden, Canada, and Denmark) and was founded by an American woman.[75] Even so, Tostan does not subject the recipients of its interventions to neocolonial subordination. As Chapters 2 and 3 established, Tostan practices toleration toward the recipients of its interventions and treats recipients' institutions as fully legitimate. (Its interventions meet standards (E) and (F) above.) Moreover, Tostan arguably works to undermine colonial hierarchies and corresponding patterns of intervention. (Its interventions meet standard (G) above.)

As I suggested earlier, what actions an intervener should take when working to undermine (neo)colonial hierarchies and patterns of behavior depends on the details of the case and the capabilities of that specific intervener. As an INGO, Tostan is especially well-placed to exercise what Rubenstein calls "discursive power," which is "the power to shape widely shared meanings."[76] Rubenstein identifies the exercise of discursive power as one of the main ways in which INGOs exercise political power.[77] (Though her work focuses specifically on "humanitarian" INGOs, a category that may or may not include Tostan, her analysis of discursive power seems equally applicable to INGOs like Tostan that take up more explicitly political tasks.) Rubenstein argues that INGOs' portrayals of recipients as helpless, alone, and disempowered victims of material deprivation (rather than of political malfeasance), who are in need of foreign saviors, is a nefarious exercise of

---

[75] Tostan, "Mission & History," accessed 9 October 2018, https://www.tostan.org/about-us/mission-history/.

[76] Rubenstein, *Between Samaritans and States*, 71.

[77] See ibid., esp. ch. 3.

COLLECTIVE SELF-DETERMINATION WITHOUT ISOLATION 199

discursive power.[78] Exercising discursive power in this way can reinforce colonial hierarchies by lending credence to the ideas used to justify them (e.g., ideas of people in the Third World as helpless victims in need of saving rather than autonomous agents subject to injustice and in need of empowerment). Indeed, Rubenstein says the misuse of discursive power can "contribute to people in donor countries developing (a) inaccurate perceptions about, (b) inappropriately patronizing attitudes toward, and/or (c) counterproductive ideas about how to 'help' severely poor and/or famine-affected people."[79] This, in turn, can reinforce the (geo)political marginalization of those already subordinated by colonial hierarchies.[80]

Thus, exercising discursive power to subvert these kinds of portrayals is one way to subvert colonial hierarchies and their associated patterns of intervention.[81] And Tostan does seem to exercise discursive power in this subversive way. For example, a brief review of its website will reveal many images of African people and few images of "White saviors." When White people are pictured, they are often presented as equals to the African people they accompany rather than as saviors providing services to the desperately needy. The Africans pictured are often engaged in activities that highlight their intelligence and agency—attending classes, speaking to community groups, engaging in political demonstrations, and doing labor. Moreover, the text on Tostan's website emphasizes community empowerment (rather than aiding helpless victims) as Tostan's main goal. Its mission statement reads, "We empower African communities to bring about sustainable development and positive social transformation based on respect for human rights."[82] Thus, Tostan does exercise discursive power to challenge colonial hierarchies, the ideas that underlie them, and the patterns of political behavior (including intervention) that typically go along with them. (We can conclude, then, that Tostan's work meets standards (E)–(G) above, so it's justifiable according to the standards laid out in Category 2.)

Tostan also works to empower people who are manifestly disempowered within their own societies, such as women and girls who aren't adequately represented in local governance institutions and who are subject to gender-based harms resulting from practices like child marriage and FGC. (Tostan's

[78] Ibid., esp. ch. 7.
[79] Ibid., 182.
[80] See ibid.
[81] Rubenstein discusses her own favored modes of exercising discursive power in ibid., ch. 7.
[82] Tostan, "Mission & History."

200 PROMOTING JUSTICE ACROSS BORDERS

work meets standard (H) above, so it's justifiable according to the standards laid out in Category 3.)

The Latin American opposition to SB 1070 didn't dominate recipients either, because it too was a persuasive intervention and because the interveners were less geopolitically powerful than the recipients. (It met standards (A) and (B) above, so it was justifiable according to the standards laid out in Category 1.) This intervention didn't subject recipients to neocolonial subordination because the Latin American signatories to the amicus briefs didn't occupy a privileged position in colonial hierarchies with respect to the American recipients of their intervention. (The intervention met standard (D) above, so it was justifiable according to the standards laid out in Category 2.) And the Latin American countries' intervention was undertaken on behalf of people manifestly disempowered within the US, such as undocumented immigrants who are subject to state power but not enfranchised. (The intervention met standard (H) above, so it was justifiable according to the standards laid out in Category 3.)

Next, consider the US's conditional offer of a preferential trade agreement to Oman. The US intervention didn't dominate Omani recipients, because it was slightly controlling. (It met standard (B) above, so it was justifiable according to the standards laid out in Category 1.) However, the US intervention in Oman did subject recipients to neocolonial subordination. Americans occupy a privileged position in colonial hierarchies compared to Omanis, since Oman is part of the Arab world and the US is a "White" Western country.[83] Given this, the US intervention would have to meet standards (E)–(G) in order to be justifiable according to the standards laid out in Category 2. I've argued in previous chapters that the intervention treated Omanis with toleration (standard (E)) and treated their institutions as fully legitimate (standard (F)). But since there arguably *is* a pattern of reform intervention establishing those historically marginalized by colonialism as recipients and

---

[83] Some might contest this claim, arguing that Oman's long history of political independence and the fact that it was once an empire itself (see "Oman Country Profile," *BBC News*, 25 April 2018, https://www.bbc.com/news/world-middle-east-14654150; "Oman Profile—Timeline," *BBC News*, 25 April 2018, https://www.bbc.com/news/world-middle-east-14654492) mean it doesn't in fact occupy a subordinate position in any colonial hierarchy as compared to the US. I think this view is mistaken because it overlooks the ways in which (neo)colonial patterns of thought and behavior can subjugate certain people simply because of their race or region of origin—regardless of whether they once wielded significant geopolitical power or once used that power to subjugate others. Nonetheless, it's worth noting, if the US *didn't* occupy a privileged position in colonial hierarchies compared to Oman, the US intervention would have met standard (D) above, and so would have been justifiable according to the standards laid out in Category 3.

COLLECTIVE SELF-DETERMINATION WITHOUT ISOLATION 201

those historically empowered by it as interveners, the US would have had to do something to undermine this pattern in order to fulfill standard (G). It would be hard to make the case that the US did so.

That said, the US intervention in Oman did serve the interests of people who were manifestly disempowered within Oman, such as workers who were denied rights to collective bargaining and subject to forced labor, and foreign workers within Oman who were denied the protections afforded to Omani citizens. (The intervention met standard (H) above, so it was justifiable according to the standards laid out in Category 3.)

Thus, the US intervention in Oman was impermissible because it undermined Omanis' collective self-determination by subjecting them to neocolonial subordination. However, it could have been made permissible if the US had acted to undermine the colonial hierarchies its intervention otherwise reinforced. This would have allowed the US to address workers' rights issues in Oman without objectionably reinforcing colonial hierarchies. So, if there's a general lesson to take from the US intervention in Oman, it's not that interventions like it can never be permissible but rather that, in order to be permissible, they must be accompanied by an effort to challenge colonial hierarchies.

Now consider the parts of the BDS movement that involve nonstate actors engaging in consumer, cultural, and academic boycotts. These parts of BDS are arguably undertaken by actors with less geopolitical power than Israeli recipients have. They therefore don't dominate recipients. (They meet standard (A) laid out above, so they're justifiable according to the standards laid out in Category 1.) The actors involved in these parts of BDS, such as the members of Palestinian civil society leading the movement, don't occupy a privileged position in colonial hierarchies compared to Israeli recipients. (These parts of BDS meet standard (D) above, so they're justifiable according to the standards laid out in Category 2.) Since one of its central goals is guaranteeing equal rights for Arab Palestinians within Israel, BDS is also undertaken on behalf of manifestly disempowered people within the recipient society. (BDS meets standard (H) above, so it's justifiable according to the standards laid out in Category 3.)

The final case I'll consider is the Europeans' refusal to export lethal injection drugs to the US. European interveners are arguably not more geopolitically powerful than American recipients and so don't dominate American recipients. (The export ban meets standard (A) above, so it's justifiable according to the standards laid out in Category 1.) Nor do European interveners occupy a privileged position in colonial hierarchies compared to American recipients. (The export ban meets standard (D) above, so it's justifiable according to the standards laid out in Category 2.) Finally, the export ban serves the interests of people within the US who are manifestly disempowered, such as people who are convicted of felonies and disenfranchised. (The export ban meets standard (H) above, so it's justifiable according to the standards laid out in Category 3.)

Taking all this together, it appears that Tostan's work in western Africa, the Latin American opposition to SB 1070, and the parts of the BDS movement that involve nonstate actors engaging in consumer, cultural, and academic boycotts escape all three standard objections to intervention—from toleration, legitimacy, and collective self-determination.

The US's offer of a preferential trade agreement to Oman, conditioned upon the latter's adopting labor rights reforms, escapes the standard objections from toleration and legitimacy, but not the standard objection from collective self-determination.

The European refusal to sell lethal injection drugs to the US certainly escapes the standard objections from toleration and collective self-determination. If one thinks the US's continued use of the death penalty diminishes its legitimacy, then—but only then—the European intervention also escapes the standard objection from legitimacy.

As the synthesis of this chapter's findings with the findings of the previous two chapters shows, we are one step closer to being able to form all-things-considered judgments about different reform interventions' permissibility. We are also one step closer to refuting the skeptical view of the natural duty of justice. I've now identified some types—and some actual cases—of reform intervention that escape all three standard objections to intervention. These cases don't involve the three serious moral wrongs skeptics typically associate with reform intervention—namely, treating recipients with intolerance, objectionably denying or disregarding the legitimacy of recipients' established institutions, and undermining recipients' collective self-determination.

What's left to do to form final all-things-considered judgments about different reform interventions' permissibility, and to fully refute the skeptical view, is to show that there are morally permissible ways to put the ethical standards developed in this and the previous two chapters into practice. To do this, we must address some pragmatic concerns associated with trying to implement these standards in our highly nonideal world. This is the topic of Chapter 5.

5

Chaos and Consequences

Promoting Justice in a Nonideal World

Introduction

I've spent Chapters 2 through 4 constructing ethical standards for the practice of reform intervention. I've argued that interventions living up to these standards escape the usual objections to intervention—from toleration, legitimacy, and collective self-determination. The ethical standards I've developed give us a model for how to engage in reform intervention in morally responsible ways. They can also serve as critical standards against which to evaluate actual interventions publicly justified in the name of justice promotion. In this chapter, I'll give an account of what it should look like to implement these standards for the ethical practice of reform intervention.

Any attempt to implement them will face two broad types of practical difficulties. The first is the absence of political institutions capable of enforcing (or even coordinating) compliance with the standards on a global scale. Coordinated compliance via global political institutions is perhaps the most obvious imaginable way of implementing such standards, but it's unlikely to be achieved in a world like ours. The usual mechanism for implementing behavioral standards in the domestic sphere (the state) is unavailable at the global level, and it will stay that way for the foreseeable future.

So we're left with the question of when (if ever) we should engage in or support reform intervention in the absence of global institutions capable of coordinating compliance with the appropriate ethical standards.[1] The lack of strong global institutions poses a problem because reform intervention undertaken in their absence—undertaken unilaterally or by "coalitions of the willing"—is likely to result in an uneven application of the standards I've proposed and an uneven distribution of intervention's costs. To put it more concretely, without strong global institutions to coordinate multiparty

---

[1] I thank Charles Beitz for suggesting this as a framing question.

Promoting Justice Across Borders. Lucia M. Rafanelli, Oxford University Press. © Oxford University Press 2021.
DOI: 10.1093/oso/9780197568842.003.0006

interventions and distribute the costs of participating in them, the only interventions likely to be undertaken are those that align with the self-interest of powerful geopolitical actors (those with enough resources to bear the costs of intervention alone).[2] In a society where public goods are provided by charity rather than a public system of taxation, the kind and distribution of public goods will mirror the interests of wealthy philanthropists. Similarly, in a world where interventions are undertaken by volunteers at their own discretion, the character of interventions that actually occur will mirror the interests of able volunteers. Indeed, this is one common criticism of the emergence of the "Responsibility to Protect" norm in international relations—that, in practice, it will only ever serve to justify powerful states' interventions in less powerful (usually non-Western) states, ensuring that whatever ethical standards it allegedly enacts will be unevenly applied across the globe.[3]

The lack of effective global institutions poses a further problem for those interventions my standards say are only justified *conditional* on some kind of multiparty approval or oversight. Can this condition ever be met in a world like ours, without formal global institutions able to carry out multiparty approval and oversight in a reliable, timely, and consistent manner?

The second practical difficulty with implementing my standards is that it may risk causing serious unintended consequences. Such unintended consequences could result from individual reform interventions or from the adoption of global norms or precedents approving of certain *kinds* of reform intervention. The risk of unintended consequences may even be greater in global, as opposed to domestic, politics, as reliable information gathering may be more difficult and the lack of strong global institutions capable of holding geopolitical actors accountable for the consequences of their actions may encourage reckless behavior.[4] So how should the risk of unintended consequences affect our decisions about when to engage in reform intervention? Presumably, even reform interventions compatible with my standards could have negative unintended consequences. Acting to establish certain norms or precedents governing the resort to reform intervention in global politics—again, even norms or precedents that reflect the ethical standards

---

[2] I don't mean to suggest interveners are the only ones who bear the costs of intervention. Clearly, recipients do (or at least may) bear costs as well, and that a proposed intervention would require recipients to bear inappropriate costs would count as a reason against it.

[3] See Michael W. Doyle, *The Question of Intervention: John Stuart Mill and the Responsibility to Protect* (New Haven, CT: Yale University Press, 2015), 140.

[4] I thank Ingrid Creppell for helpful discussion on this point.

I've developed—could also have unintended consequences. (And, depending on the political context, engaging in a single reform intervention could help establish a certain norm or precedent governing the resort to reform intervention in global politics.)

One significant risk is that these norms or precedents may be co-opted by inept or malicious actors who would use them to lend a veneer of legitimacy to their poorly executed or ill-intentioned interventions. Another risk is that a norm or precedent one helped establish may be used by other actors to pursue policy goals one doesn't endorse. This could happen even if these other actors are neither inept nor malicious. Since disagreement about justice is pervasive on the global stage, once a norm or precedent is established, even well-intentioned, competent actors may use it for purposes contrary to those the progenitors of the norm or precedent intended.[5] For instance, one actor may help establish a norm or precedent allowing reform intervention under certain circumstances. Another actor may later utilize this norm or precedent to justify engaging in a reform intervention intended to promote a conception of justice the first actor doesn't endorse. Just as a domestic free speech law will allow both me and those I disagree with to contribute to public discourse, a norm allowing people to, for example, submit briefs or testimony to foreign courts will allow both me and those I disagree with to advocate for our preferred judicial decisions there.

So far, I've given only a generalized account of the practical problems we'd face if we tried to implement my principles. I'll now try to make this account more concrete by exploring how the two kinds of problems outlined above could arise with reference to the specific standards developed in the previous three chapters.

The Perils of Implementation

Standards Relating to Toleration

In Chapter 2, we concluded the following:

1. Commitment to toleration generates a reason in favor of an intervention when it (A) encourages tolerant treatment in the recipient society;

---

[5] I thank Anna Stilz for this characterization of the problem.

206 PROMOTING JUSTICE ACROSS BORDERS

(B) does so by either trying to persuade or incentivizing a representative segment of the recipient society to adopt some reform, by trying to persuade or incentivizing an elite to adopt a reform favored by a representative segment of the society, or by directly implementing a reform favored by a representative segment of the society; and (C) it does not manipulate the recipient population.

2. If an intervention neither encourages nor discourages tolerant treatment but still meets conditions (B) and (C), commitment to toleration doesn't generate a reason for or against the intervention, but interveners do treat recipients with toleration. (They accomplish this by adhering to conditions (B) and (C).)

3. Commitment to toleration does generate a reason against some interventions, either because they discourage tolerant treatment among recipients or because they fail to meet either condition (B) or (C). Such an intervention may nonetheless be morally permissible if (i) it protects either basic rights or vital interests; (ii) the urgency of the objectives it will predictably achieve exceeds the costs it will predictably impose on recipients; and (iii) interveners are justifiably confident that their judgments that the intervention meets conditions (i) and (ii) would hold even for those who don't share their predictable biases. In other words, a commitment to toleration doesn't generate *decisive* reasons against intolerant interventions if they meet conditions (i)–(iii) (though it of course generates reasons against them).

Assuming we generally ought to treat others with toleration, one (necessary but insufficient) condition of an intervention's permissibility is that it either isn't intolerant or conditions (i)–(iii) are met.

However, the absence of strong global institutions poses a clear problem for implementing these standards, most obviously because it makes it harder to determine if condition (iii) is met in any given case. As I've suggested, one way to ensure condition (iii) is met is to subject proposed intolerant interventions to multiparty approval or oversight by actors unlikely to share interveners' predictable biases. However, it's (at best) unclear whether the world as it is could sustain an institution capable of performing this function consistently, reliably, and in a timely manner. Even if such an institution were established, it's far from given that would-be interveners would take its decisions as authoritative. And if they didn't, the original problem would re-emerge. After all, implementing the standards outlined above requires making it such that reform interveners act intolerantly only when conditions (i)–(iii) are met. Having an institution capable of reliably deciding if condition (iii) is met goes some way toward achieving that goal, but going the rest of the way requires would-be interveners to regulate their behavior based on that institution's findings.

Attempts to implement the above standards will also run into another practical difficulty: the possibility that an intervention (even if it meets the standards) will bring about unintended consequences. If the risk of unintended consequences is high enough, and the consequences themselves are grave enough, this possibility may be enough to render even an intervention that lives up to the standards, all things considered, impermissible. Here, I'll discuss one case in which a tolerant reform intervention risked serious unintended consequences that ultimately outweighed the reasons in favor of intervening and one in which a tolerant reform intervention risked unintended consequences but the risk wasn't so grave as to outweigh the reasons in favor of intervening.

The first case, which Sally Engle Merry details in *Human Rights and Gender Violence*,[6] involves a persuasive intervention in India in the 1990s and 2000s— though the story starts much earlier. When Britain colonized India, in order to discourage resistance to its rule, it allowed individual religious communities to adopt their own rules governing women's place in the family (rules governing, among other things, marriage, divorce, and inheritance). Rather than being determined by the civil code that would otherwise govern the whole of India, women's place in the family would be decided by the authorities in their respective religious communities.

In 2000, this became of interest to the Convention for the Elimination of All Forms of Discrimination Against Women (CEDAW) treaty body. The body urged India to adopt reforms mandating that women's status be governed by the civil code, in an attempt to guarantee equal treatment for women across the country rather than leaving them vulnerable to the preferences of the powerful actors in their religious communities.[7] Previously (pre-1990,

---

[6] This and the following paragraph reconstruct Sally Engle Merry's description of the case in *Human Rights and Gender Violence: Translating International Law into Local Justice* (Chicago: University of Chicago Press, 2006), 104–13.

[7] I've characterized the actions of the CEDAW treaty body as a persuasive intervention. One might argue that the treaty body was in fact positioned to impose costs on India should it refuse to comply with the body's recommendations (perhaps via public shaming meant to harm India's reputation in the international community). On this reading, the treaty body exerted control over Indian actors; it did not merely try to persuade them. However, at most the treaty body would have exerted *slight* control. Thus, its intervention still would have qualified as tolerant. This is what's important for

208 PROMOTING JUSTICE ACROSS BORDERS

before India had even ratified CEDAW), women's activists within India had also taken up this cause. However, by the 1990s, the "Hindu right"[8] (including the Bharatiya Janata Party) had effectively co-opted the issue, using it to demonize and marginalize Indian Muslims. The BJP and its allies claimed the desired reforms were needed because Muslim communities in particular oppressed their women members, thus reframing what had been a nonsectarian struggle for women's equality so as to blame Muslims for women's subjugation. (The claim that Muslim communities were especially blameworthy was implausible both because Hindu communities also subjected women to inequality and because of British colonizers' role in creating the situation in the first place.) After the Hindu right involved itself, women's activists in India shifted their focus away from their efforts to bring women's status under the jurisdiction of the civil code and toward other issues. However, in its 2000 meeting, the CEDAW treaty body urged the adoption of a universal civil code as part of what Merry calls "a secular universalism," seemingly ignorant of the implications for India's domestic politics.[9]

Given the grave consequences of the Hindu right's increasing prominence, including rioting and ethnic violence against Muslims,[10] CEDAW's insistence that India bring women's status under the uniform civil code's jurisdiction—with one expert at the 2000 hearing even suggesting that a failure to do so would risk negating "'the many specific advances in India's policies on education, health, and other areas'"[11]—was arguably irresponsible. In encouraging Indians to focus their energies on the expanding uniform civil code to cover women's status, CEDAW encouraged activity that would escalate a political conflict already deepening ethnic and religious divides and putting people's lives at risk—and all this when women's equality could have been pursued (as the activists within India realized) in other ways.

We can contrast this with another case, in which the risk of intervention's unintended consequences seems not to outweigh the reasons in favor of intervening. To do this, I'll examine in more detail the case of Tostan, already familiar from earlier chapters.

---

present purposes, since the present discussion is meant to illustrate that even a tolerant intervention can risk negative unintended consequences such that it is, all things considered, impermissible.

[8] This is a term Merry uses in *Human Rights and Gender Violence*, 104–13.
[9] Ibid., 112.
[10] Ibid., 105.
[11] Ibid., 111.

CHAOS AND CONSEQUENCES 209

A 2008 study funded by the US Agency for International Development (USAID), focusing on Tostan's work in Senegal, does note some negative side effects of the NGO's involvement there. Though most villagers interviewed had positive perceptions of the program, some criticized its inability to address the most pressing needs of host communities, its relatively short-term involvement in community life, and the degree to which it demanded support activities from host communities.[12]

Some villagers also felt resentment or thought they were treated unfairly by Tostan, which seemed to attract financial and material investments to some villages and not to others.[13]

Tostan's ongoing work, then, arguably risks bringing about these negative side effects: a degree of dissatisfaction in recipient communities, the imposition of costs on recipients who are called upon to support Tostan's program in a variety of ways (such as providing living quarters for Tostan's teachers), and an unequal distribution of economic resources across communities.

It would be hard to argue, though, that these risks outweigh the potential for significant benefits that Tostan's work seems to bring. For example, a 2003 study funded by USAID reports that Tostan collaborated with another NGO (Mwangaza Action) in Burkina Faso to replicate Tostan's program there.[14] The program successfully educated participants; changed their attitudes toward women's role in society; effectively eliminated the taboo against discussing violence against women and girls; and encouraged them to better utilize health services and family planning and to promote public hygiene, human rights, and reproductive health.[15] One participant said, "'There is new respect for women. More and more, women are consulted in the decision-making process and allowed to propose solutions. Before only the men did this.'"[16] Further, all twenty-three villages in which the program operated publicly declared they would abandon FGC.[17]

---

[12] Nafissatou J. Diop, Amadou Moreau, and Helene Benga, "Evaluation of the Long-Term Impact of the TOSTAN Programme on the Abandonment of FGM/C and Early Marriage: Results from a Qualitative Study in Senegal" (Washington, DC: US Agency for International Development, 2008), 10–11.

[13] Ibid., 27–8.

[14] Nafissatou J. Diop et al., "Replication of the TOSTAN Programme in Burkina Faso: How 23 Villages Participated in a Human Rights–Based Education Programme and Abandoned the Practice of Female Genital Cutting in Burkina Faso," (Washington, DC: US Agency for International Development, 2003), "Summary."

[15] Ibid., "Summary," 14–5.

[16] Ibid., 15.

[17] Ibid., "Summary," 15–6.

Monkman, Miles, and Easton argue that the Tostan program's bottom-up design gives it a distinctive advantage over other prominent approaches to ending FGC and makes it particularly promising as a tool to promote long-term social change, including changes to gender relations.[18] Though Monkman, Miles, and Easton examine an implementation of Tostan's program in Mali run by a local NGO (not by Tostan itself),[19] their study is still a useful commentary on Tostan's model, designed around interactive education, community empowerment, and grassroots change.

Another (2008) USAID-funded study of Tostan's work in Senegal reports that the program increased participating and nonparticipating women's knowledge of rights and responsibilities, especially regarding women's role in society.[20] (Rather than being an indication that the program made no difference, the parallel increase in knowledge in both participating and non-participating women is arguably a sign of the success of Tostan's model of "organized diffusion," through which each program participant "adopts" a nonparticipant with whom to share what they learn.)[21] The program increased knowledge of the dangers of FGC.[22] Several communities made public declarations and appear to have abandoned, or at least significantly curtailed, FGC.[23] Attitudes about early marriage also seemed to shift after the program, but this may be attributable to other causes, such as greater intercultural contact, increased school attendance among girls, media awareness-raising campaigns, and legal sanctions, as well as to Tostan's involvement.[24]

Though selection bias (both among villages chosen to partake in Tostan's program and among individual villagers who chose to attend the program for its full duration) may have contributed to these positive results,[25] even this wouldn't discredit Tostan's approach wholesale. Instead, it might suggest some necessary preconditions for the method's success, including a

---

[18] Karen Monkman, Rebecca Miles, and Peter Easton, "The Transformatory Potential of a Village Empowerment Program: The Tostan Replication in Mali," *Women's Studies International Forum* 30 (2007): 451–64.

[19] Ibid., 452.

[20] Diop, Moreau, and Benga, "Evaluation of the Long-Term Impact," ii.

[21] Ibid., 27; Tostan, "Today. Tomorrow. Together: Tostan Annual Report 2014," https://tostan.org/wp-content/uploads/2014_annual_report_final.pdf, 7; Beniamino Cislaghi, Diane Gillespie, and Gerry Mackie, "Expanding the Aspirational Map: Interactive Learning and Human Rights in Tostan's Community Empowerment Program," in *Human Rights Education: Theory, Research, Praxis*, ed. Monisha Bajaj (Philadelphia: University of Pennsylvania Press, 2017), 198–209, 207.

[22] Diop, Moreau, and Benga, "Evaluation of the Long-Term Impact," ii.

[23] Ibid., ii, 24–6.

[24] Ibid., ii, 23–4.

[25] Ibid., 26–7.

strong leader and the means to support program facilitators in the host community.[26]

Further, as noted above, though some were dissatisfied, most villagers USAID interviewed in its 2008 study had positive perceptions of the Tostan program,[27] and their testimony highlights Tostan's role in empowering local communities to make their own judgments and collective decisions about pressing issues of justice. The 2008 study I've been discussing notes, "Respondents indicate that it was the collective determination on the part of the communities to honour their commitments, along with the support of leaders, committees and especially women, that determined the effectiveness of a declaration [against FGC]."[28] One village chief reported that the women in his community organized discussions on the topic and that the community opted to end FGC because they themselves were convinced it was the right thing to do.[29]

Moreover, it seems the main disadvantages of Tostan's program could be addressed with more careful attention to the uneven economic effects its presence may have on different villages and to the possibility of providing longer-term support for participant villages. And Tostan has already adopted some measures that may help facilitate such progress. Namely, in 2006, Tostan started its Empowered Communities Network, which connects the community governance committees Tostan helps set up with outside institutions (such as governments, NGOs, financers, and businesses) in an effort to enable them to continue their community development projects after the Tostan program itself ends.[30] (Note, though the study in Senegal discussed above was published in 2008, its subject was villages who underwent the Tostan program in 1998–9, before the Empowered Communities Network was established.)[31] Additionally, in 2014, Tostan began partnering with the Gates Foundation and a consulting firm (ITAD) to update its monitoring, evaluation, and research systems.[32]

The preceding analysis shows the significant benefits Tostan seems to have brought recipients, recipients' generally positive reaction to its work, and that Tostan has already started taking steps to avert some of its work's

---

[26] Ibid.
[27] Ibid., 10–11.
[28] Ibid., 21.
[29] Ibid.
[30] Tostan, "Today. Tomorrow. Together," 23.
[31] Diop, Moreau, and Benga, "Evaluation of the Long-Term Impact," i–ii.
[32] Tostan, "Today. Tomorrow. Together," 17.

212 PROMOTING JUSTICE ACROSS BORDERS

worst unintended consequences. (A more recently published study, from 2016, which incorporates the findings of several other studies, including the 2008 USAID report, does also suggest some medium- to long-term positive effects from Tostan programs; however, it doesn't discuss the Empowered Communities Network explicitly.)[33] Given this, we can reasonably conclude that the risk of unintended consequences doesn't generate an overriding reason against Tostan's continuing its (otherwise commendable) interventions.

The point of this reflection has been to show how attempts to implement the ethical standards developed in Chapter 2 could run into a second practical challenge (besides that associated with the absence of strong global institutions), associated with the possibility that reform intervention could bring about negative unintended consequences. Interveners should always evaluate this risk; sometimes it will be great enough to make otherwise permissible interventions, all things considered, impermissible, but sometimes it won't be.

Note also that it isn't only the unintended consequences of single interventions, considered in isolation, that might generate overriding reasons of this sort. Establishing certain norms or precedents governing the practice of reform intervention—a process to which engaging in a single intervention could contribute—may also have unintended consequences.

To take an earlier example, a norm allowing contributions (e.g., in the form of amicus briefs) to foreign courts would allow contributions from actors of diverse interests, preferences, and ideological persuasions. Such a norm allowed the Latin American states opposing Arizona's SB 1070 to submit briefs arguing the law should be stricken, but the same norm would also allow anyone to submit briefs in defense of the law. The potential problem, then, is that we might want to adopt a norm allowing the submission of amicus briefs to foreign courts, with an eye to enabling justice-promoting interventions like that of the countries opposing SB 1070. However, adopting the norm will not only enable justice-promoting interventions like these. It will also enable interveners who seek to promote their narrow self-interest rather than justice. It will enable interveners who may be well-intentioned, but who are so inept that their interventions end up doing more harm than good. And it will enable interveners who, though both well-intentioned and competent, are

---

[33] See Beniamino Cislaghi, Diane Gillespie, and Gerry Mackie, *Values Deliberation and Collective Action: Community Empowerment in Rural Senegal* (Cham: Palgrave Macmillan, 2016), 103–42.

mistaken about what justice requires and will therefore promote the realization of some unjust social arrangement. This is an instance of a more general phenomenon: any political channel made generally available could be used to accomplish a wide variety of ends, including those contrary to the ends for which it was designed. That said, this issue may be more exaggerated in the context of reform intervention than in other contexts, simply because of the diversity of actors on the global political stage.

So it's possible that our norms regarding intervention will be taken up and used by actors who don't care to promote justice, who don't know how, or who simply disagree with us about what that requires. How should this affect our willingness to engage in or support reform intervention, when this may contribute to the adoption of one norm or another?

Later, I'll offer some guidance interveners can follow to surmount the two practical challenges canvassed here (the absence of strong global institutions and the risk of unintended consequences). But for now, I'll examine how these practical challenges would manifest if we tried to implement the ethical standards developed in Chapter 3.

Standards Relating to Legitimacy

In Chapter 3, we found:

1. Regime-change interventions are justifiable only when recipient states are entirely illegitimate.
2. Oppositional interventions are justifiable only when recipient states are at least partially illegitimate.
3. Extra-institutional interventions that use force are justifiable only when recipient states are at least partially illegitimate.
4. Extra-institutional interventions that don't use force and that are led by nonstate actors are justifiable even when recipient states are fully legitimate.
5. State-led extra-institutional interventions that don't use force and where interveners are not more geopolitically powerful than recipients are justifiable even when recipient states are fully legitimate.
6. State-led extra-institutional interventions that don't use force and where interveners are more geopolitically powerful than recipients are justifiable only when recipient states are at least partially

214 PROMOTING JUSTICE ACROSS BORDERS

illegitimate, unless the interveners do something to undermine the power structures that advantaged them in the first place (in which case, their interventions are justifiable even when recipient states are fully legitimate). Interveners can help undermine the power structures that advantaged them in the first place by (a) opening themselves up to the same kinds of interventions they aim at others or (b) subjecting their operations to some kind of oversight from other, less powerful states or other actors in global civil society. (There may be other ways as well.)

7. Intra-systemic interventions are justifiable even when recipient states' are fully legitimate.

I assume we ought to recognize legitimate institutions as legitimate. That is, we shouldn't treat institutions as if they have less legitimacy than they actually have. Thus, one (necessary but insufficient) condition of an intervention's permissibility is that it treats recipient institutions as if they have (at least) the degree of legitimacy they actually have. These seven standards enable us to tell when this is the case.[34]

However, when we try to put these standards into practice—by using them to decide if particular interventions treat recipient institutions as if they have (at least) the degree of legitimacy they actually have—we'll once again run into two kinds of practical difficulties: the lack of strong global institutions to coordinate compliance and the risk of unintended consequences.

In the absence of strong global institutions to make authoritative judgments about recipient institutions' legitimacy, individual interveners will be left to make their own judgments on the matter. These judgments may not be consistent with each other; different interveners may disagree about whether different recipient institutions are legitimate. Perhaps some will think this isn't a problem in itself: perhaps they'll think there's nothing wrong with different actors on the global political stage advancing opposing views of legitimacy. (In fact, one might say that simply is the status quo, and so

---

[34] Some might argue that interveners are sometimes justified in treating recipients' institutions as less legitimate than they actually are if they can achieve sufficiently important ends by doing so. They may argue that, though we're generally morally required to treat legitimate institutions as legitimate, this is an overridable constraint, and it's overridden when disregarding recipient institutions' legitimacy will produce significant enough gains in terms of justice. I make no such argument. I take it that one novel contribution of this work is to show the (surprising) range of interventions that can be justified *even assuming* the legitimacy of recipients' institutions generates hard constraints on interveners, such that they're not justified in disregarding recipient institutions' legitimacy even if they could produce very good outcomes by doing so.

would be the reality regardless of whether we tried to implement the ethical standards laid out above.) However, it arguably does pose a problem because it exaggerates the probability of reform intervention bringing about certain unintended consequences.

Namely, engaging in reform interventions recommended by the standards above may help establish a norm or precedent indexing the political acceptability of reform intervention to the (perceived) legitimacy of recipient institutions. Interveners may be able to effectively justify their interventions to other actors on the world stage and/or to their own domestic (or otherwise internal) constituencies[35] by claiming recipient institutions are to some degree illegitimate. Indeed, that would be the point of establishing such a norm or precedent. The worry is that, unless there were some widely accepted, highly specified account of what makes institutions legitimate to one degree or another, this would effectively give interveners free rein: they would be able to offer plausible justifications for virtually any intervention they wanted to undertake, as long as they couched them in terms of some conception of legitimacy.

This should give us pause because self-interested interveners may co-opt the norm (of indexing intervention's acceptability to recipient institutions' legitimacy), disingenuously claiming some other society's institutions are illegitimate to justify an intervention in fact undertaken to serve their own interests.[36] But it should also give us pause even if interveners are genuinely committed to intervening only in ways compatible with recipient institutions' actual legitimacy. This is because, as with justice, even well-intentioned global political actors disagree significantly about what legitimacy requires. Thus, establishing a norm allowing intervention when recipient institutions are illegitimate may have the consequence of empowering others—those who disagree with us about what legitimacy requires—to intervene in cases in which we'd oppose intervention. That is, as a participant in global politics, I may think a given intervention, considered in isolation, is justified and that I therefore have reason to support it. However, I must consider the possibility

---

[35] When interveners are states, their domestic constituencies are their domestic populations. But interveners aren't always states, in which case their "domestic or internal" constituencies are their members or other publics they typically answer to (which may or may not belong to different political communities from the interveners themselves). For example, the internal constituency of an association like Human Rights Watch would include its board members, employees, and donors. The internal constituency of a corporation would include its board members, employees, and customers.

[36] This is a version of the old realist warning in, for example, E. H. Carr, *The Twenty Years' Crisis, 1919–1939: An Introduction to the Study of International Relations* (London: Macmillan, 1939).

216   PROMOTING JUSTICE ACROSS BORDERS

that my supporting this intervention now could help pave the way for future interventions I may not want to (or ought not to) support.

Individual interventions (as opposed to the adoption of certain norms or precedents governing intervention)—even those compatible with recipients' full legitimacy—may also have unintended consequences. As in the previous section, the risk of these unintended consequences could outweigh the reasons in favor of a given intervention, making it, all things considered, impermissible even if it would treat recipient institutions as (at least) as legitimate as they actually are.

Consider, for example, the Palestinian BDS movement. The parts of it that constitute a non-state-led extra-institutional intervention that doesn't use force are compatible with Israeli institutions being fully legitimate. They therefore must be compatible with Israeli institutions having at least the degree of legitimacy they actually have. One possible objection to the movement, though, is that it will have the unintended consequence of stifling progressive politics within Israel. After all, BDS calls not only for an economic boycott (of "companies that are involved in the violation of Palestinian human rights") but also for academic and cultural boycotts.[37] These could involve academics refusing to work or to attend conferences at Israeli universities and artists refusing to perform in Israel. The worry is that universities and cultural centers are exactly the kinds of places most likely to nurture progressive political movements; it is there that progressives within Israel (those most likely to be sympathetic with BDS's cause and to oppose the occupation and the construction of "the Wall") will find the support and resources necessary to develop their position and effectively advocate for it within Israeli society. Thus, there's a danger that BDS's academic and cultural boycotts will undermine some of the most credible and potentially effective efforts to achieve BDS's own ends. If this is true, it may very well be an overriding reason not to support these aspects of the BDS movement, even though doing so would be compatible with recognizing Israel's institutions as fully legitimate (and therefore, necessarily, recognizing them as at least as legitimate as they actually are).

Before moving on to give more guidance as to how we might address these practical difficulties, let's consider how they'd manifest themselves if we tried to implement the final set of ethical standards I've developed, those from Chapter 4.

---

[37] See BDS, "What Is BDS?," accessed 6 March 2018, https://bdsmovement.net/what-is-bds.

Standards Relating to Collective Self-Determination

In Chapter 4, I found that reform intervention escapes the standard objection from collective self-determination—and therefore has a chance at being, all things considered, permissible—only if it is justifiable according to the standards laid out in *all three* of the following categories:[38]

> Category 1: Interventions That Avoid Dominating Recipients
> A reform intervention is justifiable only if *either*
> A. interveners are not more geopolitically powerful than recipients
> *or* it meets *one* of the following two conditions:
> B. it is persuasive or slightly controlling or
> C. it is highly or totally controlling but is subject to approval or effective oversight by epistemically diverse global political actors.
>
> Category 2: Interventions That Avoid Neocolonial Subordination
> A reform intervention is justifiable only if *either*
> D. interveners don't occupy a privileged position in colonial hierarchies compared to recipients
> *or* it meets *all* of the following three conditions:
> E. interveners practice toleration toward recipients, unless it's a case in which the value of toleration is overridden;
> F. interveners treat recipients' institutions as legitimate institutions, unless the decision to treat them as illegitimate is authorized by epistemically diverse global political actors; and
> G. there's no general pattern of reform intervention establishing those historically marginalized by colonialism as recipients and those historically empowered by it as interveners; or, if there is such a pattern, interveners work to undermine it.

---

[38] As with the standards regarding legitimacy, some might argue that interveners are sometimes permitted to undermine recipients' collective self-determination—for example, because self-determination is less valuable or important than the ends interveners could achieve by undermining it or because self-determination is valuable only insofar as it facilitates the achievement of justice. Beitz suggested the latter view in his early work; see Charles R. Beitz, *Political Theory and International Relations* (Princeton, NJ: Princeton University Press, 1979), 92–105. But, again, I make no such argument. Even assuming it's always impermissible to undermine recipients' collective self-determination, we can justify a surprising range of interventions. This is a significant enough finding on its own.

218 PROMOTING JUSTICE ACROSS BORDERS

Category 3: Interventions That Make Recipient Governments More
Responsive to Their Constituents' Interests
A reform intervention is justifiable only if
H. it is undertaken on behalf of people manifestly disempowered
(e.g., formally disenfranchised) with respect to others in their
societies.

The first kind of practical difficulty I've been discussing—the lack of strong
global institutions—poses a similar problem for implementing Chapter 4's
standards as it does for implementing those from Chapter 2. Without strong
global institutions capable of conducting the right kind of multiparty approval or oversight consistently, reliably, and in a timely manner—and
without any guarantee that global political actors would even take the
resulting directives as authoritative—it may be impossible to fully implement
standards (C) and (F) above. If we were able to effectively conduct multiparty
approval or oversight, we could engage in a wider range of interventions
without threatening recipients' collective self-determination. This is because,
as standards (C) and (F) highlight, the threats some interventions pose to
recipients' self-determination could be neutralized if the interventions were
approved or overseen by the right kind of multiparty institution. But, again, a
world that houses such an institution seems quite far off.

Moreover, even interventions compatible with a commitment to collective self-determination may have unintended consequences. For instance,
adopting norms allowing interventions compatible with collective self-
determination may inadvertently empower interveners who will (intentionally or not) undermine recipients' collective self-determination—or, again,
who will (perhaps because we disagree about what justice requires) promote
ends we don't endorse (note the similarities to the problems discussed in
the earlier section on toleration). For example, since, as the standards above
suggest, persuasive intervention is comparatively unlikely to undermine
recipients' self-determination, we may want to establish a norm allowing
(or even encouraging) persuasive interventions. However, doing so may
also open the door to interventions that use manipulation to achieve their
ends—though these interventions may very well undermine recipients' self-
determination. The problem is that, though interventions that use manipulation don't qualify, according to my typology, as "persuasive interventions,"
they can *look* a lot like persuasive interventions. It may not always be obvious whether a particular communication—be it, for example, an ad, a

social media campaign, or a news article—uses genuine persuasion or manipulation. It may not be obvious whether it's genuine persuasive advocacy or propaganda.

Russia's apparent involvement in the run-up to the 2016 US presidential election is a good illustration of this danger. Russia's efforts were not just persuasive; they were covert and deceptive. Let's assume for the moment that they rose to the level of "manipulation." They involved a large-scale misinformation campaign. And they seem to have aimed, in addition to deceiving people, at undermining Americans' confidence in their democratic institutions.[39] Certainly, Russia's campaign reduced the quality of Americans' democratic deliberation; it was a threat to their collective self-determination. Contrast this with a counterfactual case in which Russia had openly declared support for Donald Trump, had disseminated only true information without concealing its source, and had tried to *engage* with other perspectives in various public fora rather than trying (for example) to incite fear and exaggerate existing social divisions in the US.[40] In such a case, Russia's intervention would have been genuinely persuasive. And, though this counterfactual is a far cry from what actually happened, this may not have been immediately obvious as it was happening, if Russia's involvement was concealed and misinformation was believed to be accurate information.

Some may think our general inability to reliably distinguish persuasion and manipulation ex ante gives us reason to restrict persuasive interventions—or, more precisely, things that *look like* persuasive interventions, which will in fact include both persuasive and manipulative interventions. Thus, any attempt to implement my standards regarding intervention and self-determination should take account of this danger. I'll say more about how below.

Surmounting the Perils of Implementation

Acting in the Absence of Strong Global Institutions

The previous sections have outlined the major practical difficulties we'd face if we tried to implement the ethical standards I've developed for reform

---

[39] See Clint Watts, "Clint Watts' Testimony: Russia's Info War on the US Started in 2014," *Daily Beast*, 30 March 2017, https://www.thedailybeast.com/clint-watts-testimony-russias-info-war-on-the-us-started-in-2014.

[40] Ibid.

220 PROMOTING JUSTICE ACROSS BORDERS

intervention. Now I'll offer some guidance as to how we could avoid (or at least mitigate) these problems. Let's begin with the first practical difficulty: the lack of strong global institutions capable of coordinating compliance with ethical standards. This creates clear problems for implementing the standards developed in Chapters 2 and 4 because doing so will sometimes require subjecting proposed interventions to multiparty approval or oversight. As suggested above, the lack of global institutions poses a problem for implementing the standards developed in Chapter 3 primarily because it amplifies the risk of interventions creating unintended consequences. Thus, I'll focus for now on how to mitigate the problems the absence of global institutions causes for the standards from Chapters 2 and 4. The next section, on unintended consequences, will be sufficient to address the main problems with implementing Chapter 3's standards.

Recall, Chapter 2's standards tell us that an intolerant intervention (one in which interveners treat recipients with intolerance) is permissible only if (i) it protects either basic rights or vital interests; (ii) the urgency of the objectives it will predictably achieve exceeds the costs it will predictably impose on recipients; and (iii) interveners are justifiably confident that their judgments that the intervention meets conditions (i) and (ii) would hold even for those who don't share their predictable biases. One obvious way of ensuring condition (iii) was met would be to subject proposed intolerant interventions to a multiparty approval or oversight procedure designed to incorporate the judgments of those unlikely to share interveners' predictable biases. The question we face now is whether intolerant interventions can ever be justified in the absence of institutions capable of reliably carrying out such a procedure. Can condition (iii) ever be met in a world like ours?

I think sometimes it *can* be, though how frequently it *will* be is another question. One way to attempt to meet condition (iii) in a world like ours is to look for other ways to "consult" with epistemically diverse global political actors, besides participating with them in a formally institutionalized multiparty approval or oversight procedure. For example, would-be interveners could look to the publicly taken positions of citizens, officials, or political groups unlikely to share the interveners' own biases. These positions—which might be communicated by public statements, reports (such as those produced by organizations like Human Rights Watch and Amnesty International), or articles or by signing onto human rights treaties, for example—could give an indication of whether others in global politics would agree with would-be interveners' judgments about a particular case. For instance, if epistemically diverse political actors have signed treaties or adopted norms that classify certain wrongs as grave violations of human rights, this could help establish that they would judge an intervention targeting similar wrongs to meet condition (i). If epistemically diverse political actors have taken public stances on the likely costs and benefits of an intervention like the one being proposed in a given case, this could help establish whether they'd judge it to meet condition (ii). And if sufficiently epistemically diverse actors judge conditions (i) and (ii) to be met, condition (iii) will also be met.

I don't mean to suggest that interveners will always be eager to consult the publicly endorsed positions of epistemically diverse political actors before intervening. But if they want to undertake intolerant interventions in the absence of the kind of multiparty institutions suggested above, this is what they ought to do—otherwise their interventions will not be justifiable. As individuals, we therefore shouldn't engage in or support intolerant reform interventions unless interveners have demonstrated that they've consulted sufficiently with (the public positions of) epistemically diverse political actors. As citizens, this is a standard to which we should hold our governments; as donors, it's a standard to which we should hold NGOs; as potential participants, it's a standard to which we should hold transnational movements, and so on. We should withhold our support from intolerant interventions that don't meet this standard.

Arguably, it would be best to also adopt as a long-term goal the development of stronger global institutions capable of carrying out more formalized multiparty approval and oversight procedures reliably, consistently, and in a timely manner.

This really would be a very long-term goal. It would require significant changes in the way we currently conduct global politics, which would be politically (and probably otherwise) difficult to bring about. It would, for example, require integrating nonstate actors into global governance practices more so than they have been at present. After all, one thing that's obvious from the foregoing discussion is that our future multiparty decision-making body should represent a wide range of actors in global politics—including global civil society. We might take as a starting point the idea that any kind of political actor who could, in principle, engage in reform intervention should also be (able to be) represented in the multiparty body.

In order to serve its central purposes (of counteracting bias, motivated reasoning, and narrow self-interest promotion on the part of interveners), the body—I'll call it the Assembly for now—would have to contain diverse global

222   PROMOTING JUSTICE ACROSS BORDERS

political actors with different (even contradictory) interests and values and (relatedly) different epistemic resources. Ideally, it would contain state representatives, regional representatives (perhaps chosen by major regional organizations such as NATO, the Organization of American States, the Association for East Asian Nations, the European Union, and the African Union), and interest group representatives (e.g., women's rights advocacy groups might send a delegation or choose a representative to participate in the Assembly). We may also think that some Assembly representatives should be individuals elected by a global popular vote. (After all, I've suggested that anyone who could engage in reform intervention should be able to be represented in the Assembly, and individuals certainly can engage in reform intervention, even when they're not organized into states, regional associations, or interest or advocacy groups.) However, if this proves too difficult to implement (e.g., because we lack the kind of global political coordination and institutional apparatus necessary for holding a free and fair global election), non-affiliated individuals could still be allowed to speak before the Assembly, and so could still contribute to its decision-making.

Though some scholars have begun to recommend that global governance include (and be designed around the goal of including) nonstate actors,[41] prominent global governance institutions are, as of now, largely state-centric. Nonstate actors are increasingly prominent in global politics, but their activity often takes place outside formal institutional structures. Thus, incorporating nonstate actors to the degree necessary to make the Assembly function as I've envisioned it would constitute a major shift.

And the international community has faced significant difficulty maintaining a commitment to new norms even when they don't so directly challenge the state-centric nature of global (really, international) institutions. The Responsibility to Protect (RtoP) norm is a case in point. Though RtoP poses a challenge to strict, uncompromising conceptions of state sovereignty, it does so in a way that accepts the basic premises of a state-governed world order (with states as the primary guarantors of protection for their own citizens, and states in the international community as the secondary guarantors, should citizens' own states fail to fulfill their responsibilities). RtoP is also

---

[41] See, for example, Richard Falk, *Power Shift: On the New Global Order* (London: Zed Books, 2016); Kate Macdonald and Terry Macdonald, "Democracy in a Pluralist World Order: Corporate Power and Stakeholder Representation," *Ethics and International Affairs* 24, no. 1 (2010): 19–43; Roland Paris, "Global Governance and Power Politics: Back to Basics," *Ethics and International Affairs* 29, no. 4 (2015): 407–18; Thomas G. Weiss and Rorden Wilkinson, "Change and Continuity in Global Governance," *Ethics and International Affairs* 29, no. 4 (2015): 397–406.

arguably congruent with moral commitments the international community had begun to accept in some form decades before its emergence, with the adoption of the Universal Declaration for Human Rights (namely, commitments that suggest at least the most serious individual rights violations could be legitimate matters of concern for the international community).

Even given this, though, it's proved very difficult for the international community to maintain an effective commitment to RtoP. It seemed for a time that RtoP was clearly on its way to being ever more widely adopted and relied on in global politics, but, especially after NATO's 2011 intervention in Libya, its status in international relations is highly dubious.[42] The Libyan intervention was originally lauded as an exemplar of RtoP's promise and a sign that the international community was well on its way to fully accepting the norm as a part of the typical conduct of foreign affairs.[43] However, its swift transition from a "civilian protection" to a "regime change" operation turned the Libyan intervention into an exemplar of how powerful actors could abuse RtoP by invoking it to justify geopolitical adventures that went well beyond averting humanitarian crises.[44] Similarly, the ensuing civilian deaths, instability, and terrorist activity turned the Libyan intervention into an exemplar of how adopting RtoP could enable an overly ambitious military interventionism that could have disastrous unintended consequences.[45]

All this is to say that a world unable to maintain a firm commitment to RtoP—which would have required a much less dramatic change in the way global politics is currently practiced than would establishing an institution like the Assembly—is unlikely to be able to effectively establish an institution

---

[42] See Doyle, *The Question of Intervention*, 127–41. For the dubious nature of the RtoP norm after the 2011 intervention in Libya in particular, see Alex de Waal, "African Roles in the Libyan Conflict of 2011," *International Affairs* 89, no. 2 (2013): 365–79, 379; Christopher Zambakari, "The Misguided and Mismanaged Intervention in Libya: Consequences for Peace," *African Security Review* 25, no. 1 (2016): 44–62, 50–1, 56.

[43] See Alex J. Bellamy, "Libya and the Responsibility to Protect: The Exception and the Norm," *Ethics and International Affairs* 25, no. 3 (2011): 263–9; Alex J. Bellamy and Paul D. Williams, "The New Politics of Protection? Cote d'Ivoire, Libya and the Responsibility to Protect," *International Affairs* 87, no. 4 (2011): 825–50; Simon Chesterman, "'Leading from Behind': The Responsibility to Protect, the Obama Doctrine, and Humanitarian Intervention after Libya," *Ethics and International Affairs* 25, no. 3 (2011): 279–85; Christopher Hobson, "Responding to Failure: The Responsibility to Protect after Libya," *Millennium: Journal of International Studies* 44, no. 3 (2016): 433–54, 435, 443–4; Thomas G. Weiss, "RtoP Alive and Well after Libya," *Ethics and International Affairs* 25, no. 3 (2011): 287–92.

[44] Doyle, *The Question of Intervention*, 140–1; Zambakari, "The Misguided," 50–1, 56.

[45] See Hobson, "Responding to Failure"; Alan J. Kuperman, "A Model Humanitarian Intervention? Reassessing NATO's Libya Campaign," *International Security* 38, no. 1 (2013): 105–36 and "Obama's Libya Debacle: How a Well-Meaning Intervention Ended in Failure," *Foreign Affairs* 94, no. 2 (2015): 66–77; Zambakari, "The Misguided."

224 PROMOTING JUSTICE ACROSS BORDERS

like the Assembly any time soon. So we need some normative guidance for the meantime: we need some idea of what we should do unless and until we have an institution like the Assembly. Hence the recommendations in the first part of this section. Unless and until we have a global institution capable of adequately carrying out multiparty approval and oversight, would-be interveners seeking to engage in intolerant intervention should seek more informal ways to consult with epistemically diverse actors in global politics. And those who might support or oppose proposed intolerant interventions should oppose them unless they're justifiably confident sufficient consultation has taken place. This is a standard to which we, as participants in global politics, should hold ourselves and other would-be interveners accountable.

In fact, even once a formal institution like the Assembly were established—depending on exactly how it was constituted and how smoothly and reliably it operated—these more informal methods could prove useful as a supplement or alternative to the formal institution if it became overly inflexible or gridlocked. The availability of a more informal decision-making process could help address some of the problems with current global governance institutions—namely, that they can be overly rigid and more state-centric than appropriate for an increasingly non-state-centric global politics.[46] (One need look no further than the frequently hamstrung UN Security Council for verification of this problem.)

We can use similar logic to guide us in applying the standards developed in Chapter 4. If we must subject a proposed intervention to multiparty approval or oversight in order to prevent it from undermining recipients' collective self-determination, we should do so (i.e., would-be interveners should do so, and others should condition their support of the intervention on its being done) via the informal modes of consultation suggested above, at least until there's a formal global institution sufficiently capable of coordinating multiparty approval or oversight.

Avoiding Unintended Consequences

As illustrated earlier, even interventions compatible with commitments to toleration, legitimacy, and collective self-determination risk bringing about

---

[46] See discussion in Falk, *Power Shift*; Macdonald and Macdonald, "Democracy in a Pluralist World Order"; Paris, "Global Governance and Power Politics"; Weiss and Wilkinson, "Change and Continuity in Global Governance."

unintended consequences, either in their particular context or by contributing to the establishment of a norm or precedent regarding reform intervention that itself has unintended consequences. This can happen for a variety of reasons.

First, actual interveners will often act (to some degree, at least) out of self-interest rather than a genuine concern for justice. This raises the legitimate worry that their self-interested motivation will lead them to pursue ends contrary to what justice requires—either because it biases their judgments about what justice requires or because it means they'll be motivated to pursue their own interests at the expense of justice *even if* they correctly judge what the latter requires. Thus, one might argue, if a lot of self-interested actors engaged in reform intervention (the predictable result of global political actors accepting my standards for when reform intervention is and isn't justified), the world would be a lot worse (and likely more unjust).

Second, if acted on, the ethical standards I've developed (or, rather, the practice of intervention they justify) could be used (or abused) by powerful geopolitical actors to objectionably subordinate others. In some cases, the risk of such subordination would be a subspecies of the risks posed by self-interested interveners, described in the previous paragraph. That is, self-interested actors may use the principles I've proposed to make their self-interested attempts to subordinate others palatable to the global public. This would enable interveners to intentionally pursue subordinating interventions with less risk of exposing themselves to public scrutiny or sanction—thereby making these interventions more attractive options for would-be interveners. But subordination need not involve mal-intent. Well-intentioned interveners may still behave toward recipients so as to establish dominating relationships with them, for example. Some may worry that acting on the standards I've proposed would make this more likely, since it would make reform intervention more likely, compared to acting on the principles commonly adopted in international relations today.[47]

---

[47] It's perhaps a contestable empirical claim that adopting the standards I've proposed would lead global political actors to engage in more reform intervention than they do now. It's true that one goal of the present project is to illustrate how reform intervention can be justifiably incorporated into quotidian global politics—and to show that reform intervention can be a morally acceptable response to global injustice, and not only, as is sometimes thought, during states of exception. However, another goal of the project is to provide ethical standards to guide (and guide our judgments about) activities that global political actors *already* engage in. Many such actors already try to effect political change in societies beyond their own (and they often invoke justice promotion as a justification). Thus, we might see the principles defended here as providing a critical standard according to which we can evaluate this *existing* practice rather than as providing a justification for expanding the

226   PROMOTING JUSTICE ACROSS BORDERS

Third, actual interveners will sometimes be mis- or under-informed. Even well-motivated interveners would be subject to the kinds of uncertainty outlined in Chapter 1: moral uncertainty (about what justice requires), factual uncertainty (about the conditions on the ground in recipient societies), and political uncertainty (about the likely effects of their interventions). One might also think that if lots of misinformed interveners engaged in reform intervention (supposedly the predictable result of putting my standards into practice), their interventions would likely go awry, bringing on unintended and often negative consequences and making the world worse. Arguably, this is what went wrong with the CEDAW treaty body's work with India, discussed above. The treaty body was ill-equipped to appreciate and respond to the emerging political conditions on the ground in India, and therefore unwittingly advocated that people in India take actions that would have aided the BJP's efforts to marginalize and endanger Indian Muslims.[48]

Fourth, even well-informed and well-motivated participants in global politics will often disagree about what justice requires. Thus, one intervener may help establish a precedent or norm that others can then use to pursue ends the first intervener doesn't endorse. Take the hypothetical case considered above, of political opponents utilizing a norm allowing the submission of briefs to foreign courts, each to advocate for their own (opposing) ends.

If these are the most salient risks of reform intervention—the standard ways in which reform intervention can bring about unintended consequences—we should take steps to mitigate them. We may need to decide when we, as individuals, should participate in, support, or oppose a given reform intervention. Or we may want to take a position on what standards the global public should adopt to govern reform intervention. In either case, we'll want

---

practice. On this interpretation, adopting my standards wouldn't so much encourage *more* reform intervention as it would encourage those already practicing reform intervention to align their behavior with the standards. One might even argue that if the standards I've proposed became a significant part of the practice of global politics, they could *constrain* would-be interveners by subjecting their interventions to more public scrutiny than they currently face. Ultimately, I don't think I'm equipped to predict the exact effects adopting my standards would have on the ubiquity of reform intervention. However, I suspect that taking them seriously would increase the occurrence of certain types of interventions (perhaps persuasive and counter-hegemonic interventions) and decrease the occurrence of others (perhaps some military interventions). In any case, assuming adopting my standards would increase rates of reform intervention makes the objection I'm currently considering more difficult for me to answer. So, I'll move forward with that assumption.

[48] See Merry, *Human Rights and Gender Violence*, 104–13, especially her discussion of CEDAW's inability to deal with intersectional political challenges (113).

to do so in a way that's designed to mitigate the negative consequences reform intervention is most likely to cause.

To decide whether an intervention (or adopting a certain norm or precedent about intervention) is, all things considered, justified, we can't evaluate it "in a vacuum." We must take into account its likely unintended consequences.

Doing so will help ensure that the justice-enhancing ends of proposed reform interventions are, to use Laura Valentini's phrase, "morally accessible;" in other words, "we have reason to hope [they] can be realized or approximated without excessive moral costs."[49] This, in turn, will help mitigate one common worry about the feasibility of justice promotion via intervention (and indeed justice promotion in general)—namely, that pursuing morally desirable but not clearly achievable ends in a way that risks serious (unintended) negative consequences might actually make the world worse than it is now: it might bring us further from our goal of creating a more just world.

The presence of this worry might seem to suggest that we should abandon the pursuit of reform intervention's ends altogether, unless we can conclusively demonstrate that they can be achieved without sufficiently serious negative consequences.[50] However, taking this course would also involve serious moral cost. As Valentini notes in her discussion of feasibility, there are many things worth pursuing such that we won't know in advance what precise sequence of actions could bring them about.[51] If this is right, it must also be true that there are many things worth pursuing such that we won't know in advance all the consequences even of a successful pursuit. (Without

---

[49] See Laura Valentini, "No Global Demos, No Global Democracy? A Systematization and Critique," *Perspectives on Politics* 12, no. 4 (2014): 789–807, 791. Valentini uses "morally accessible" to refer to ideals rather than states of the world, but the concept seems equally applicable to the ends interveners seek to achieve.

[50] David Wiens suggests we adopt an attitude like this toward the principles of forward-looking, ideal political theory in "Political Ideals and the Feasibility Frontier," *Economics and Philosophy* 31 (2015): 447–77. He recommends that political theorists reorient themselves away from forward-looking ideal or quasi-ideal theory that envisions how we could organize our politics in some distant future. Instead, he recommends a backward-looking political theory, centered around addressing "concrete *social failures*" (471, emphasis original) with obviously feasible solutions. At least, he recommends this unless and until political theorists are willing to do the hard work of showing their forward-looking ideals are feasible—and it is hard work, involving complex assessments and long-term predictions about what (perhaps distant) possible worlds we could bring about with our various resources (economic, political, psychological, etc.) or with stocks of resources we could acquire using our current resources (456–60). One might take a similar stance toward pursuing justice through reform intervention, arguing that we shouldn't do so unless we can conclusively show there's a path from our current world to a world in which our justice-enhancing ends are achieved without sufficiently serious negative consequences. (I argue taking such a stance would be a mistake.)

[51] See Valentini, "No Global Demos," 791.

228   PROMOTING JUSTICE ACROSS BORDERS

knowing the precise sequence of actions a successful pursuit would involve, how could we?)

This raises the question of how we could be justified in pursuing these valuable ends without being able to conclusively demonstrate their unintended consequences wouldn't make the world more unjust overall. After all, we wouldn't want to simply abandon these ends until such a conclusive demonstration was within our means (which, given the complexity of large-scale political processes and our limited predictive capabilities, would likely be never). This would involve giving up (prematurely) on morally very important goals that might very well be achievable.

Indeed, Keck and Sikkink note that achieving the *in fact feasible* but *not demonstrably feasible* is one main charge of reforming political struggles. They write, "One of the main tasks that social movements undertake . . . is to make possible the previously unimaginable, by framing problems in such a way that their solution comes to appear inevitable."[52] Moreover, if people throughout history had abandoned not demonstrably feasible ends, some of history's most impressive moral victories may never have even been fought for, let alone won. Abolition may have seemed impossible in the antebellum US, as with desegregation in the wake of *Plessy v. Ferguson*, the growth of an international human rights regime at the height of Nazi Germany's expansionism, and the nationally recognized right to same-sex marriage after its denial in California, one of America's most liberal states. But people did fight for these outcomes, improbable as they may have seemed, and they were successful in the end.[53] Had everyone refused to pursue them because they seemed unachievable, the world would be dramatically worse for it; we would have forgone significant achievable moral progress. Significant structural or systemic change will hardly ever (if ever) be demonstrably feasible, but it's also immensely important. It's arguably our only hope at eliminating the most pervasive and deep-seated forms of oppression.

So, below, I propose some guidelines specifically designed to mitigate the unintended consequences reform intervention is (for the reasons outlined above) distinctively likely to bring about. These guidelines show us a "middle way" between (on the one hand) recklessly pursuing reform intervention's

---

[52] Margaret E. Keck and Kathryn Sikkink, *Activists beyond Borders: Advocacy Networks in International Politics* (Ithaca, NY: Cornell University Press, 1998), 40–1.

[53] Thank you to Desmond Jagmohan for suggesting this point. See ibid., 41–51 for an account of international efforts to abolish slavery in the US. Valentini also mentions abolition as an example of a morally worthy goal that wasn't obviously feasible when first adopted ("No Global Demos," 791).

CHAOS AND CONSEQUENCES 229

ends without paying any attention to the negative consequences this might bring about and (on the other hand) refusing to pursue them unless we can conclusively demonstrate they can be accomplished without sufficiently serious side effects (which, realistically, we'll never be able to do).

First, we should adopt a presumption in favor of less controlling interventions. I've already argued that less controlling interventions will often be better able to avoid some moral problems—such as intolerance or objectionably undermining recipients' collective self-determination—than their more controlling counterparts. But we can go even further than this and say that, in a world full of self-interested and potentially misinformed political actors, it would be a good prudential rule to favor less over more controlling interventions. The more nonideal our world is—the more self-interested and misinformed political actors are—the stronger the presumption in favor of less controlling interventions should be. This is because concentrating political power in the hands of a few actors is especially dangerous when those actors are malicious or ill-informed. Thus, on the assumption that would-be interveners have one of these traits, we should want whatever power they exercise through their interventions to be contestable (and, if necessary, contested). This will be more likely if their interventions are less controlling. If the interveners themselves exercise less control over which courses of action recipients actually take, recipients (and others) will be more able to contest interveners' proposed courses of action.

Similarly, less controlling interventions will leave recipients and others freer to contest interveners' proposals when they disagree with interveners' accounts of what justice requires (even when interveners are neither malicious nor ill-informed). Under such conditions, the fact that norms allowing reform intervention might be used to justify interventions whose ends we wouldn't ourselves endorse shouldn't stop us from endorsing the norms. It would be one thing if these norms would empower interveners to *force, coerce,* or *otherwise control* us (or others) into adopting policies we didn't endorse. But the situation seems much more palatable if the norms governing reform intervention mainly empower interveners to *propose* or *incentivize* policies we don't endorse, leaving us (and others) relatively free to choose whether or not to adopt them and to counter interveners' political influence with our own.

Moreover, when interveners are malicious or ill-informed, their interventions will generally be riskier for recipients. Malicious or ill-informed interveners will be comparatively unlikely to reliably bring about

230   PROMOTING JUSTICE ACROSS BORDERS

just outcomes and comparatively likely to bring about unintended or otherwise bad consequences. Recipients will therefore be comparatively unlikely to reap the benefits of an actually justice-promoting intervention and comparatively likely to suffer the costs of a misguided or poorly executed one. Given this, recipients ought to have more rather than less of a say in whether or not to accept the risks of interveners' proposed courses of action. After all, we generally think that, while subjecting others to minor risks without their permission may be acceptable, subjecting them to more serious risks may be acceptable only if they opt in (when they had the opportunity to opt out). And if recipients ought to have more rather than less of a say in whether or not to accept the risks of interveners' proposed courses of action, then interveners ought to favor less rather than more controlling interventions. Again, consider the CEDAW case: the treaty body's inattention to the political conditions in India made even its persuasive intervention objectionable. But because it was persuasive, actors within India could freely choose not to take the treaty body's advice and to refrain from engaging in political activity that would arguably impose grave costs on Indian Muslims.[54]

One way to operationalize this presumption in favor of less controlling interventions would be to adopt something like a global free speech guarantee. I'm envisioning a norm that says everyone should be guaranteed a reasonable opportunity to speak in public fora, even beyond their own political communities. The bounds of "reasonable opportunity" may be, as is commonly thought in the domestic case, circumscribed by the need to restrict speech that puts others in immediate physical danger, incites violence, or runs afoul of independent principles of fairness (such as those that define a fair regime of campaign finance). We might imagine individual states signing onto a treaty requiring them to guarantee comparable protections for the free speech of foreign nationals as they do for their own citizens and/or an international body like the International Criminal Court taking such issues to be under its jurisdiction. (These reforms don't seem obviously infeasible; they're not exceptionally more ambitious than other protections already enshrined in international human rights law.)[55] A global free speech guarantee is also

---

[54] The same logic holds if we think of the CEDAW treaty body's intervention as slightly controlling. (But it wouldn't hold if the intervention were highly or totally controlling.)

[55] See, for example, United Nations, Office of the High Commissioner on Human Rights, *International Covenant on Civil and Political Rights*, 1966, Article 19, paragraph 2, http://www.ohchr.org/en/professionalinterest/pages/ccpr.aspx. It includes a right to free expression, encompassing "freedom to seek, receive and impart information and ideas of all kinds, regardless of frontiers, either orally, in writing or in print, in the form of art, or through any other media of [one's] choice."

"neutral" enough to be adopted as part of international law. That is, political actors need not agree on what justice requires (and therefore on the range of acceptable goals for reform intervention) in order to see value in adopting the guarantee. A global free speech guarantee (like its domestic analogue) might be accepted by people whose conceptions of justice vary widely, as they do on the global stage.

Such a guarantee could help operationalize a presumption in favor of less controlling interventions because, with more avenues open for persuasive intervention and more publics reliably available to be persuaded, would-be interveners may be more likely to try to achieve their aims via this rather than other, more controlling means. Adopting a global free speech guarantee would also be one way to discharge the duty (which Chapter 3 argued that we have) to open up our own societies to certain kinds of potentially justice-promoting foreign influence.

Additionally, a global free speech guarantee would likely improve the informal multiparty consultation scheme proposed in the previous subsection. More political actors would have more opportunity to go on the public record about more issues, thus making it easier for would-be interveners (and their would-be supporters and opponents) to gauge what epistemically diverse political actors would think about a proposed intervention. Global free speech would also likely encourage more cross-border intellectual exchange, heightening one effect of tolerant reform intervention highlighted in Chapter 2: its ability to create occasions for interveners and recipients to reflect, together, on what justice requires. As argued in Chapter 2, this would help alleviate the worry that reform intervention involves imposing on foreign others moral rules they couldn't possibly accept as their own—by facilitating the development of moral concepts and language, and a moral world, that interveners and recipients *share*. This could also serve to strengthen global civil society, helping to shift the standard focus of political activity from the domestic to the global stage. This may, in turn, help pave the way toward the long-term goal of establishing stronger, more reliable global institutions, like the Assembly.

Some may object that a global free speech guarantee would heighten the danger I highlighted earlier in discussing Russia's involvement in the 2016 US presidential election. Objectors may claim that such a guarantee would allow too many manipulative interventions masquerading as persuasive ones. To this, I'll just say briefly that the political contestation encouraged by global free speech may also work in the other direction, to mitigate this

232 PROMOTING JUSTICE ACROSS BORDERS

danger. Much as, in the domestic context, it's often thought that free speech encourages public debate that can be helpful in uncovering the truth, so we might think global free speech would help us root out deception and manipulation more reliably.

Of course, predicting the trajectory of global politics isn't my main task here. I offer the global free speech guarantee as one suggestion for how we might (begin to) operationalize a presumption in favor of less controlling interventions in international law. I don't mean this suggestion to provide a definitive account of the *only* or *right* way to operationalize the presumption in favor of less controlling interventions, but rather to illustrate how this presumption *could* be brought to bear on global politics in the real world.

Another guideline we should adopt aligns with a recommendation that's recurred several times in previous chapters. It says (all else equal) we should give political priority to supporting counter-hegemonic interventions.[56] As we saw in Chapter 4, adopting this priority rule would help ensure reform intervention doesn't undermine recipients' collective self-determination. It would, as argued in that chapter, protect against the establishment of dominating or other problematic hierarchical relationships among interveners and recipients and against the norms of such relationships setting behavioral precedents in international relations.

Adopting this priority rule would also provide some protection against the other dangers associated with reform intervention. I take it that, as a matter of fact, the geopolitically powerful are those most likely to have the resources (material and otherwise) to impose their preferred policies on other societies without sufficient justification or information. Less powerful interveners will often need to rely on others' cooperation (perhaps including recipients' cooperation) in order to implement their preferred policies, and will therefore be compelled to offer plausible justifications for their interventions—that is, justifications that interveners' potential cooperators will see as plausible. This will often require gathering reliable information about the conditions on the ground in recipient societies and reliable evidence about the likely effects of an intervention. More powerful interveners, however, will be comparatively more able to impose their desired policies without cooperation from others, and will therefore have less incentive to restrict their interventions to those for which they can furnish plausible justifications and convincing

---

[56] I make a similar recommendation in Lucia M. Rafanelli, "Toward an Individualist Postcolonial Cosmopolitanism," *Millennium: Journal of International Studies* (2020): 1–12, doi:10.1177/0305829820935520, 9–11.

intelligence. To take one example, perhaps the US wouldn't have invaded Iraq in 2003 had it not had the military might to achieve (some of) its objectives without a large international coalition. As it happened, the US was able to prosecute the war with only a modest coalition of allies. The Bush administration failed to convince much of the international community that the war was worth fighting, but, it turned out, the administration had no need to convince them.

Giving political priority to counter-hegemonic interventions would help avoid situations like this. Granted, it may not eliminate the problem. After all, insofar as geopolitically powerful interveners really can effectively intervene without others' cooperation, it may make little difference to them (at least in the immediate term) whether other participants in global politics support their interventions or forsake them to support counter-hegemonic interventions instead. However, even many powerful interveners may need to rely on *some* amount of cooperation from others, even if it's far less than what less powerful interveners would need. (Would the US have gone into Iraq had it literally been able to recruit no international allies? It's hard to judge what would have happened counterfactually, but the answer isn't obviously yes. At the very least, the political consequences of having to commit more US troops to the war effort may have given the Bush administration some pause.) In such cases, powerful interveners' would-be allies abandoning their alliance to support counter-hegemonic interventions instead may indeed have a constraining effect.

Summary

Here, I've identified the main practical difficulties someone trying to act on or otherwise implement my ethical standards for reform intervention in the real world would face. These include the challenge of acting in a world without strong global institutions to facilitate multiparty approval or oversight of reform interventions when such approval or oversight is a condition of their permissibility. The other main practical difficulty with trying to implement these ethical standards is that doing so may result in unintended consequences—sometimes grave ones. This difficulty is made worse by the lack of strong global institutions, which also means there are no such institutions capable of coordinating compliance with ethical standards.

234 PROMOTING JUSTICE ACROSS BORDERS

I've argued that, in the absence of strong global institutions,

1. when interveners are morally required (given that they've decided to intervene) to subject their intervention to multiparty approval or oversight, they should seek out more informal ways to "consult" with epistemically diverse political actors unlikely to share their own predictable biases. Correspondingly, others should hold would-be interveners to this standard, refusing to support their proposed interventions unless they meet it.

This informal consultation could involve looking to the publicly taken positions of citizens, officials, or political groups—those communicated by public statements, reports, or articles or by signing onto human rights treaties, for example.

In order to help us surmount the second practical difficulty—that of unintended consequences—I've suggested we adopt two guidelines. Of course, would-be interveners, and those deciding whether to support or oppose them, should first evaluate each proposed intervention using the ethical standards developed throughout this book. They should then evaluate the likely consequences of each proposed intervention directly, on a case-by-case basis. For the latter endeavor, the expertise of policy specialists, political practitioners, and theorists who emphasize moral assessments of intervention's effects[57] would be especially valuable. However, in the absence of a case-specific analysis, these two guidelines provide some more general directions. We should

2. adopt a presumption in favor of less controlling interventions and
3. give political priority to counter-hegemonic interventions.

With these general recommendations in mind, I can move on to evaluate my focal cases specifically. Taking into account the ethical standards developed in Chapters 2 through 4, and paying sufficient attention to the pragmatic difficulties associated with actually acting on them in the real world, are any of the interventions I've focused on, all things considered, morally permissible? Four of the focal cases remain candidates for all-things-considered permissibility: Tostan's work in western Africa, the Latin American amicus briefs, the civil-society-led aspects of BDS, and the European export ban on lethal injection drugs. I'll address them one by one.

---

[57] E.g., James Pattison's "pragmatic approach" in *The Alternatives to War: From Sanctions to Nonviolence* (Oxford: Oxford University Press, 2018), esp. 22, 53–6.

I've already argued that Tostan's work escapes all three standard objections—from toleration, legitimacy, and collective self-determination. Does it, in addition, adequately address the practical difficulties laid out here? Yes, it does. Tostan doesn't engage in the kinds of intervention that my ethical standards say must be vetted by a multiparty body in order to be morally permissible. So we need not determine whether Tostan has consulted with epistemically diverse political actors about its interventions in order to determine if they're justified. And the analysis at the beginning of this chapter has already shown that Tostan is justified in continuing its work despite the risk of some unintended consequences. These consequences are not serious enough to outweigh the great benefits Tostan seems to provide for recipient communities.

The Latin American opposition to SB 1070 also escaped all three standard objections to intervention and adequately addressed the practical difficulties described here. Like Tostan's work, the Latin American countries' submission of amicus briefs was not the kind of intervention that must be vetted by a multiparty body in order to be morally permissible. And it is hard to imagine what grievous consequences this intervention could have caused, even if it had totally failed in its objective to influence the Supreme Court. (Since this intervention was both non-controlling and counter-hegemonic, undertaking it was compatible with both guidelines recommended above, as well.)

The parts of the BDS movement that involve nonstate actors engaging in consumer, cultural, and academic boycotts escape all three standard objections to intervention. These parts of BDS need not be vetted by a multiparty body in order to be morally permissible, either. However, earlier in this chapter, I discussed a possibly serious unintended consequence of BDS— namely, that it could undercut progressive political movements within Israel, thereby frustrating BDS's own stated goals. As my earlier analysis indicates, though, this is at most a risk of the cultural and academic boycotts associated with BDS. Thus, the consumer boycott seems to escape this worry as well.

There is another serious unintended consequence critics of BDS accuse it of bringing about. Namely, some argue that BDS encourages anti-Semitism (perhaps because it is itself anti-Semitic).[58] However, others, including some Jewish groups, cast doubt on this claim, arguing that we shouldn't be

---

[58] See, e.g., Anti-Defamation League, "What Is . . . Anti-Israel, Anti-Semitic, Anti-Zionist," accessed 14 October 2018, https://www.adl.org/resources/tools-and-strategies/what-is-anti-israel-anti-semitic-anti-zionist; Adam Milstein, "BDS Is Continuing to Spread Hate and Anti-Semitism across the US," *HuffPost*, 30 May 2017, https://www.huffingtonpost.com/entry/bds-is-continuing-to-spread-hate-and-anti-semitism_us_592dab59e4b075342b52c080.

236 PROMOTING JUSTICE ACROSS BORDERS

too quick to equate legitimate criticism of Israel with anti-Semitism.[59] And surely one can oppose Israeli occupation, the Wall, and systematic discrimination against Arab Palestinian citizens of Israel without being anti-Semitic. Even taking the understandably more controversial position advocating the right of return for displaced Palestinians doesn't seem to necessitate anti-Semitism. And these positions encompass all of BDS's official goals: ending the occupation and dismantling the Wall, guaranteeing equality for Arab Palestinian Israelis, and securing the right of return.[60]

Some accuse BDS, despite its official agnosticism regarding a one- versus a two-state solution to the Israel-Palestine conflict,[61] of *really* aiming at the destruction of Israel (some add "as a Jewish state").[62] The progressive American pro-Israel group J Street criticizes BDS for not explicitly endorsing the two-state solution.[63] But this criticism is somewhat misplaced, both because, as indicated above, BDS officially takes no position on the choice between a one- or two-state solution[64] and because Israeli settlements (which BDS opposes and works to curtail) are at least as much of an obstacle to a two-state solution as any of BDS's activities. This is because the settlements (some say intentionally) partition contested territory in ways that would make the establishment of a viable, unified Palestinian state anywhere on that territory difficult, if not impossible.[65]

---

[59] See, e.g., Jewish Voice for Peace, "First-Ever: 40+ Jewish Groups Worldwide Oppose Equating Antisemitism with Criticism of Israel," *Jewish Voice for Peace*, 17 July 2018, https://jewishvoiceforpeace.org/first-ever-40-jewish-groups-worldwide-oppose-equating-antisemitism-with-criticism-of-israel/; David Rosenberg, "BDS Is a Lot of Things, but It's Not Anti-Semitic," *Haaretz*, 21 September 2016, https://www.haaretz.com/opinion/bds-is-a-lot-of-things-but-it-s-not-anti-semitic-1.5440228; Rebecca Vilkomerson and Richard Kuper, "As Jews, We Reject the Myth That It's Antisemitic to Call Israel Racist," *Independent*, 22 July 2018, https://www.independent.co.uk/voices/antisemitisim-jews-israel-labour-party-bds-jewish-coalition-palestine-a8458601.html. To be fair, the Anti-Defamation League also calls for a distinction between legitimate criticism of Israel and anti-Semitism, but it believes BDS falls into the latter category; see Anti-Defamation League, "What Is . . . Anti-Israel."

[60] BDS, "Palestinian Civil Society Call for BDS," 9 July 2005, accessed 23 August 2018, https://bdsmovement.net/call.

[61] BDS, "FAQs," accessed 14 October 2018, https://bdsmovement.net/faqs#collapse16233.

[62] See Anti-Defamation League, "What Is . . . Anti-Israel"; Milstein, "BDS Is Continuing to Spread Hate."

[63] J Street, "J Street Policy Principles on the Global BDS Movement and Boycotts, Divestment and Sanctions Efforts," accessed 14 October 2018, https://jstreet.org/policy/boycott-divestment-and-sanctions-bds/#.W8MAP7alRjU.

[64] BDS, "FAQs."

[65] See Adam Entous, "The Maps of Israeli Settlements That Shocked Barack Obama," *New Yorker*, 9 July 2018, https://www.newyorker.com/news/news-desk/the-map-of-israeli-settlements-that-shocked-barack-obama; Jonathan Ferziger, "Quick Take: Israeli Settlements," *Bloomberg*, 22 March 2018, https://www.bloomberg.com/quicktake/israeli-settlements; Greg Myre and Larry Kaplow, "7 Things to Know about Israeli Settlements," *National Public Radio*, 29 December 2016, https://www.npr.org/sections/parallels/2016/12/29/507377617/seven-things-to-know-about-israeli-settlements.

CHAOS AND CONSEQUENCES   237

And again, surely one could engage in the parts of BDS I've been defending—consumer boycotts targeting businesses that profit from Israeli occupation and settlement—without opposing the two-state solution or contributing in any significant way to the destruction of the Israeli state. Indeed, this kind of boycott comes quite close to the action J Street itself says it doesn't oppose (though it also doesn't support), when it writes, "We do not oppose boycott, divestment, or sanctions initiatives that explicitly support a two-state solution, recognize Israel's right to exist, and focus only on occupied territory beyond the Green Line."[66]

That said, it's perhaps hard to know if participating in BDS's consumer boycott could lend some unwitting encouragement to genuine anti-Semites. Arguably, this is a judgment participants in BDS must make individually, in a way that's sensitive to their particular political contexts. (This is not a problem unique to BDS; participants in social movements and other large-scale political campaigns will often have to judge the likely contribution of their involvement to phenomena in their wider political contexts.) Given all the considerations outlined here, though, it seems implausible that the possibility of unwittingly encouraging anti-Semitism would argue against participating in the boycott in *all* contexts. This is especially true given the severity of rights violations Palestinians suffer as a result of Israeli policy. The UN Human Rights Council finds Israeli settlement has significantly endangered Palestinians' rights, including rights to self-determination, free movement and expression, due process, access to important goods and services such as housing and water, and freedom from discrimination.[67]

Let's now consider the European refusal to sell lethal injection drugs to the US. This intervention escapes the standard objections from toleration and collective self-determination. If one thinks the US's continued use of the death penalty diminishes the country's legitimacy, then—but only then—it also escapes the standard objection from legitimacy. The question remains whether European interveners have done enough to address the practical challenges discussed in this chapter. Like the other focal cases discussed so

---

[66] J Street, "J Street Policy."

[67] United Nations General Assembly, Human Rights Council, "Report of the Independent International Fact-Finding Mission to Investigate the Implications of the Israeli Settlements on the Civil, Political, Economic, Social, and Cultural Rights of the Palestinian People throughout the Occupied Palestinian Territory, Including East Jerusalem," 7 February 2013, 21–22, https://digitallibrary.un.org/record/745109?ln=en.

238 PROMOTING JUSTICE ACROSS BORDERS

far, this intervention need not be vetted by a multiparty body in order to be permissible.

That said, the European export ban has had a significant negative side effect. Determined to continue enforcing the death penalty but unable to obtain the usual drug cocktail, some US states have resorted to less reliable and arguably less humane methods of execution.[68] Does this negative side effect render the Europeans' intervention impermissible? We can overlook the issue of whether European interveners could have predicted this side effect when they first instituted their export ban. Regardless of whether they could have predicted it then, they certainly should know about it now. Thus, the question becomes, does this negative side effect render the Europeans *continuing* their intervention impermissible?

I propose the answer is no; the European intervention is permissible despite its negative side effect (that some US states have adopted less humane methods of execution). I do not doubt that dying in a painful or drawn-out execution is worse for the person executed than dying in a quick and painless one. However, the question here is whether this outcome is *so much worse* that third parties ought to avoid making any contribution to bringing it about *even at the expense* of undertaking activism to abolish the death penalty altogether—and even if eliminating their contribution to the negative side effect would make the third parties themselves complicit in execution (as European actors would be if they resumed supplying lethal injection drugs). This seems implausible. Those set to be executed would be *much* better off if the death penalty were abolished. So it seems we shouldn't automatically reject an attempt to abolish the death penalty because one of its indirect and unintended side effects makes some of these people somewhat worse off in the meantime. Moreover, anti-death-penalty Europeans don't bear full moral responsibility for US states' inhumane executions. Their situation exemplifies what Rubenstein calls "the problem of spattered hands," whereby one party's action contributes to enabling another party, whose purposes the first opposes, to commit some wrong.[69] Rubenstein's treatment of this problem is highly contextualized to the situation of INGOs providing humanitarian

---

[68] See Mark Berman, "The Recent History of States Scrambling to Keep Using Lethal Injections," *Washington Post,* 19 February 2014, https://www.washingtonpost.com/news/post-nation/wp/2014/02/19/the-recent-history-of-states-scrambling-to-keep-using-lethal-injections/?tid=a_inl&utm_term=.c8a028e78164.

[69] Jennifer C. Rubenstein, *Between Samaritans and States: The Political Ethics of Humanitarian INGOs* (Oxford: Oxford University Press, 2015), esp. ch. 4.

CHAOS AND CONSEQUENCES 239

aid at or near sites of conflict, so it's not immediately clear how her overall findings would apply to the European export ban case. However, her insight that we are morally responsible for our contributions to others' unjust acts, but not for the entirety of the resulting injustice—which after all, was created mainly by someone else—does seem applicable.[70]

Similarly, to justify the European export ban, we must be able to claim that its contribution to bringing about US states' unjust cruelty was justifiable. However, the fact that the Europeans aren't morally responsible for the cruelty itself makes this a much less demanding standard than it would otherwise be. Arguably, the great moral value of the Europeans' contribution to efforts to abolish the death penalty (as outlined above, those on death row would benefit immeasurably if these efforts succeeded—presumably much more than they are harmed by being killed in more rather than less painful ways), combined with the Europeans' legitimate interest in not being complicit in executions, is enough to meet this less demanding standard.

Taking this all together, I've argued that Tostan's work in western Africa, the Latin American opposition to SB 1070, and (at least in certain political contexts) the consumer boycott element of BDS are, all things considered, permissible. They escape all three standard objections to intervention, and they adequately address the main practical challenges of acting in a highly nonideal world. The European export ban is also, all things considered, permissible if we believe that the US's continued use of the death penalty diminishes its legitimacy (otherwise the export ban is vulnerable to the legitimacy objection).

So I've identified some cases of reform intervention that escape all three standard objections *and* that deal adequately with the pragmatic challenges facing interveners who act in our highly nonideal world. We can therefore conclude that these interventions are, all things considered, morally permissible.

In addition to identifying specific cases of reform intervention that are, all things considered, morally permissible, I've developed a set of ethical standards we can use to morally evaluate other actual and proposed instances of reform intervention. The fact that I've found some cases these standards identify as permissible (and that we can imagine other cases like them, which

---

[70] See ibid., 113. James Pattison makes a similar point when he says "the wrongness of an agent *doing* harm can be mediated somewhat by the interceding agency of others" in *The Alternatives to War*, 24, emphasis original.

240 PROMOTING JUSTICE ACROSS BORDERS

would also live up to the standards I've developed) shows that attempting to promote justice in other societies *does not*, as a rule, involve committing serious moral wrongs. There are, of course, some ways of promoting justice abroad that involve committing serious moral wrongs, but the ethical standards constructed here pick out the set of reform interventions that *don't* involve committing such wrongs—and my examination of the book's focal cases has shown that this is not an empty set.

Thus, we should reject the skeptical view of the natural duty of justice. If you're persuaded that we have a natural duty of justice that is global in scope (a duty to do our part to ensure people everywhere live in just conditions), then you should also think this duty has significant normative implications for the conduct of everyday politics. Since there are ways to promote justice abroad without committing serious moral wrongs (or absorbing inordinate costs ourselves),[71] if there is a global duty of justice, it requires us to do just that. Readers who aren't persuaded that there is a global duty of justice need not accept the conclusion that engaging in reform intervention is sometimes morally required. However, they should still accept the ethical standards I've developed here as identifying the kinds of reform interventions that are morally permissible. (None of my arguments for these standards considered as standards of permissibility has relied upon the existence of a global duty of justice.) All readers should therefore accept that anyone who does in fact engage in reform intervention should adhere to these standards.

As I've said before, if there is a global duty of justice, it requires each of us to adopt a set of projects in which promoting justice, including via reform intervention, enjoys a sufficiently prominent place. This raises the question, what does it mean to adopt a set of projects in which promoting justice enjoys "a sufficiently prominent place"? In Chapter 1, I described the following scenario: I stand in a position to affect another person who suffers some injustice, and I'm able to help remedy this injustice *not only* without sacrificing anything comparable myself (i.e., without submitting myself to equally serious injustice), *but also* without even significantly disrupting the pursuit of

---

[71] Without launching into a detailed discussion of what counts as an inordinate cost, it seems clear that there will be ways to promote justice abroad without absorbing inordinate costs. For one thing, none of the interveners in the four cases we've been discussing (Tostan, the Latin American amici, Palestinian civil society, and European governments and drug companies) seems to have suffered inordinately because of their interventions. Moreover, there are clearly several ways even individuals may contribute to justice promotion abroad without suffering great costs—for example, by making small donations to NGOs, joining consumer boycotts, and voting for politicians who will help ethically promote justice around the world.

CHAOS AND CONSEQUENCES 241

any of the particular purposes I've actually adopted as central to my own life. I then argued that in this scenario, I am morally required to help remedy the injustice the other person faces. If I refuse to do so, I fail to treat them as my moral equal.

We can apply this logic here to understand what it means to give justice promotion "a sufficiently prominent place" in the projects we adopt. We each ought to adopt a set of projects that involves promoting justice whenever we can do so without significantly disrupting the pursuit of whatever *other* projects we think are central to our lives. Practically speaking, this means we're required to spend substantial effort to promote justice—to take justice-promoting actions in the real world. It probably means we're required to do more than a lot of us actually do. The exact actions any given person is required to take in the pursuit of justice will of course depend on what projects they see as central to their own life, as well as on their capacities, and perhaps on other things as well (such as whether they have contributed to or benefited from certain injustices in particular). But the bottom line is that the natural duty of justice requires us to make justice promotion a significant part of our lives. As individuals, this might mean (for example) donating to NGOs, joining transnational social movements, changing which corporations we patronize, and voting certain politicians in and others out of office.

Further, since the natural duty of justice is global in scope, we're required to adopt projects giving sufficiently prominent place not only to *domestic* justice promotion but also to justice promotion elsewhere. We're required to give the pursuit of a world in which everyone, everywhere lives under just conditions sufficiently prominent place in our life projects. This means we ought to take on a more "global" perspective when participating in politics than is typical. We should not think of political contestation as something we usually engage in with and for our fellow citizens, engaging in global political contestation only at the margins (in cases of supreme emergency or once domestic justice has been fully achieved) or at our own discretion (as an act of charity). Rather, we should think of global political contestation—contestation for the achievement of justice in societies beyond our own—as part and parcel of everyday politics.

Granted, some will still argue that we ought to give priority to the pursuit of domestic justice over the pursuit of justice abroad. I can't fully settle this issue here. However, the present elaboration of the natural duty of justice as a global duty with normative implications for our conduct of politics in the real world *at least* suggests that the burden of proof lies with those who would

242 PROMOTING JUSTICE ACROSS BORDERS

prioritize domestic justice in this way. And, more than that, the analysis in this and the foregoing chapters has discredited many of the arguments often offered in favor of prioritizing domestic justice (that doing so best respects the values of toleration, legitimacy, and collective self-determination, or that domestic justice alone is feasibly achievable in our nonideal world).

The view I've defended here requires that we work to pursue justice around the world not only in emergency conditions but also in the course of quotidian global politics. It is a cosmopolitan view of political contestation that requires all kinds of global political actors to commit in significant ways to pursuing justice everywhere, for everyone. But it doesn't require the kind of extreme self-sacrifice some cosmopolitans are criticized for demanding. It doesn't require devoting *all* one's energy or *all* one's resources to the pursuit of justice. It doesn't require giving to the poor until you yourself are on the brink of poverty.[72] It doesn't require forsaking all other projects in favor of the singular pursuit of justice. Nor does the view I've defended require the kind of interpersonal homogenization liberal cosmopolitanism (or perhaps liberalism in general) is sometimes thought to engender. Because what someone is required to do to promote justice is limited by what they take to be their most central life projects, this view leaves people room to develop and pursue diverse and distinctive projects of their own.

And, as noted earlier, the view I defend here avoids another common objection to cosmopolitanism: that it is supposedly premised upon or aimed at bringing about the end of politics.

The view I've proposed is a cosmopolitanism that requires neither subject-effacing self-sacrifice nor an overly idealistic withdrawal from politics. Rather, it requires us to rethink the ordinary boundaries of political activity. It calls upon us—upon all participants in global politics—to engage in political contestation to help ensure all persons live under just conditions. It calls upon us to make this political contestation a significant part of our lives. Because, after all, the promotion of justice *for everyone* ought to be everyone's (political) concern.

---

[72] For an example of a view that does require this, see Peter Singer, *The Life You Can Save* (New York: Random House, 2009).

6

Conclusion

The foregoing chapters have developed a set of ethical standards for reform intervention and, in so doing, have refuted the skeptical view of the natural duty of justice. I've found that some kinds of reform intervention are immune from all three standard objections to intervention: the objections from toleration, legitimacy, and collective self-determination. Moreover, some of these reform interventions also adequately address the main practical challenges facing interveners acting in our highly nonideal world. Those interventions that escape all three standard objections and surmount these practical challenges are, all things considered, morally permissible. I have developed theoretical standards for deciding whether a reform intervention is, all things considered, morally permissible and have used these standards to evaluate several real-world cases of intervention—yielding the conclusion that some of them are (or were) permissible.

Since I just rehearsed these standards in Chapter 5, I won't reproduce them here. I will, however, highlight that, having identified some actual reform interventions that escape all three standard objections, that deal adequately with the pragmatic challenges facing interveners who act in our highly nonideal world, and that are therefore, all things considered, permissible, I have effectively refuted the skeptical view of the natural duty of justice. The skeptical view says that, though there is a global duty of justice, the reasons we have to promote justice in foreign societies are typically swamped by other concerns. On the skeptical view, we have a duty to do our part to ensure all people live in just conditions, but "doing our part" oughtn't involve committing serious moral wrongs. And, so the argument goes, attempting to promote justice in other societies, as a rule, involves committing serious moral wrongs. Therefore, though we have a global duty of justice in some formal sense, the duty is not actionable for us in the real world: it isn't the case that we actually ought to pursue the achievement of justice in other societies.

But this view is mistaken. I've shown reform intervention need not involve committing the moral wrongs typically associated with it. (I've

Promoting Justice Across Borders. Lucia M. Rafanelli, Oxford University Press. © Oxford University Press 2021.
DOI: 10.1093/oso/9780197568842.003.0007

244 PROMOTING JUSTICE ACROSS BORDERS

shown that some kinds of reform intervention are immune from all three standard objections and adequately address the main practical challenges facing interveners acting in our highly nonideal world.) Indeed, I've shown that some reform interventions are, all things considered, permissible. And I haven't merely identified a few abnormal, one-off cases of reform intervention that happened to have been permissible. I've developed standards for deciding *in principle* which kinds of reform interventions are and aren't permissible. This suggests that the skeptical view of the natural duty of justice is wrong, and that if there *is* a global duty of justice (as argued in Chapter 1), it obligates us to actively pursue justice—including justice in other societies—as part of our everyday engagement in global politics.

More specifically, global political actors are morally required to adopt a set of projects in which promoting justice, including via reform intervention, enjoys a sufficiently prominent place. "Adopting a set of projects" may mean different things in different contexts and for different actors. For individuals, it may mean adopting certain life projects; for states, adopting certain policy priorities; for NGOs, undertaking certain missions; for corporations, holding themselves to certain standards (e.g., related to working conditions in their often global supply chains). For individuals at least, adopting a set of projects in which promoting justice enjoys "a sufficiently prominent place" means adopting a set of projects that involves promoting justice whenever we can do so without significantly disrupting the pursuit of whatever *other* projects we think are central to our lives.

And importantly, the general injunction to adopt a set of projects in which promoting justice, including via reform intervention, enjoys a sufficiently prominent place requires not only sometimes *engaging* in reform intervention but also *opening up our own societies* to certain kinds of reform intervention conducted by others. (All who accept we have a natural duty of justice, even if they think it requires us to help promote justice only *within our own societies*, should accept this conclusion.) We can do this by opening up official channels through which foreigners can engage in intra-systemic intervention and by leaving enough unregulated space in civil society for them to engage in extra-institutional intervention.

When done alongside another of this book's directives—to give political priority to counter-hegemonic interventions—opening up our own societies to reform intervention from outside could also help address the hermeneutical marginalization of those currently and historically disempowered in global

CONCLUSION 245

politics.[1] I don't have space to fully explore this issue here, though a fuller exploration would be an excellent avenue for future work. The basic idea is that when certain groups of people (often because of identity-based inequalities in social and political power) participate unequally in constructing the concepts we all use to interpret a significant area of social experience, they are "hermeneutically marginalized."[2] Dominant ways of interpreting important social phenomena don't reflect the input or experiences of the hermeneutically marginalized, and in turn leave them without the interpretive frames necessary to fully comprehend what they experience (as, for example, some women struggled to understand their experiences with predatory men in the workplace before the concept of "sexual harassment" was invented).[3] When it operates in this way, Fricker says, hermeneutical marginalization not only *harms* victims but also creates a kind of epistemic *injustice*.[4]

Arguably, something similar is at work in global politics, where the dominant interpretive frames (including dominant ideas about what justice requires) are overwhelmingly crafted by the (currently and historically) geopolitically powerful. This leaves the geopolitically disempowered (often people of color, Indigenous people, residents of the Third World, and citizens of "developing" countries) unable to participate on equal terms in the collective process of shaping the concepts used to interpret political experience on the world stage. Geopolitically powerful societies opening themselves up to counter-hegemonic reform intervention—to the influence of the geopolitically marginalized (including their ideas about what justice requires)—would go a long way to remedying this inequality.

Of course, the standards developed in this book can't, on their own, answer *all* the moral questions associated with reform intervention in any given case. For example, determining whether a given recipient society's institutions should be treated as fully legitimate, partially legitimate, or totally illegitimate (and therefore deciding which kinds of intervention could be morally permissible in that society) would require adopting a specific theory of legitimacy. In other words, though the standards developed in Chapter 3 should be acceptable to adherents of a wide range of theories of legitimacy, applying them to particular cases may sometimes require taking a position on what

---

[1] For a detailed analysis of hermeneutical injustice, on which I draw here, see Miranda Fricker, *Epistemic Injustice: Power and the Ethics of Knowing* (Oxford: Oxford University Press, 2007), ch. 7.
[2] Ibid., 153.
[3] Ibid., ch. 7.
[4] Ibid.

the requirements of legitimacy *actually are* (as evidenced by my analysis of the European export ban). More generally, theorists and practitioners alike will continue to argue about the costs and benefits of proposed interventions, how they compare to each other, and whether they're likely to be fairly distributed in each specific case. Even if theorists and practitioners all accept the ethical standards I've developed here, they will continue to argue about how exactly to apply them in different cases.

I can't hope to settle all these disagreements. I have, however, tried to give an account of what it would look like to take seriously both our natural duty of justice (considered as global in scope) and some of our most central political-moral commitments (to toleration, legitimacy, and collective self-determination). In so doing, I've moved beyond the overly abstract question of whether "we" owe justice to distant "others" that has often occupied and divided theorists of global justice. I have asked, instead, what specific kinds of political action different actors are morally justified in taking in order to promote justice in foreign societies. In a globalized world, where transnational interconnection is the norm and opportunities to engage in cross-border political contestation are ubiquitous, it's this question that cries out for an answer. If I've succeeded, though it doesn't give us all the answers, this book offers a vision of principled global political engagement in the pursuit of justice—and a set of ethical standards against which we can measure both the depths of many historical interveners' wrongs and the heights of our own aspirations.

References

Abizadeh, Arash. "Democratic Theory and Border Coercion: No Right to Unilaterally Control Your Own Borders." *Political Theory* 36, no. 1 (2008): 37–65.

Altman, Andrew, and Christopher Heath Wellman. *A Liberal Theory of International Justice.* Oxford: Oxford University Press, 2009.

Amicus Curiae Brief of the United Mexican States in Support of Respondent, Arizona v. US, 567 US 387 (2012).

Anghie, Antony. "The Evolution of International Law: Colonial and Postcolonial Realities." *Third World Quarterly* 27, no. 5 (2006): 739–53.

Anscombe, G. E. M. "War and Murder." In *Nuclear Weapons and Christian Conscience*, ed. Walter Stein, 47–62. London: Merlin Press, 1961.

Anti-Defamation League. "What Is … Anti-Israel, Anti-Semitic, Anti-Zionist?" Accessed 14 October 2018. https://www.adl.org/resources/tools-and-strategies/what-is-anti-israel-anti-semitic-anti-zionist.

Baetz, Jeurgen. "EU's Stance Forces US Executioners to Improvise." *Seattle Times*, 18 February 2014. http://www.seattletimes.com/nation-world/eus-stance-forces-us-executioners-to-improvise/.

Bahar, Dany, and Natan Sachs. "How Much Does BDS Threaten Israel's Economy?" Brookings, 26 January 2018. https://www.brookings.edu/blog/order-from-chaos/2018/01/26/how-much-does-bds-threaten-israels-economy/.

Bakan, Abigail B., and Yasmeen Abu-Laban. "Palestinian Resistance and International Solidarity: The BDS Campaign." *Race and Class* 51, no. 1 (2009): 29–54.

BDS, "FAQs." Accessed 14 October 2018. https://bdsmovement.net/faqs#collapse16233.

BDS, "Get Involved: Know What to Boycott." Accessed 26 July 2017. https://bdsmovement.net/get-involved/what-to-boycott.

BDS, "What Is BDS?" Accessed 26 July 2017. https://bdsmovement.net/what-is-bds.

BDS, "What Is BDS?" Accessed 6 March 2018. https://bdsmovement.net/what-is-bds.

Beitz, Charles R. *The Idea of Human Rights.* Oxford: Oxford University Press, 2009.

Beitz, Charles R. "Nonintervention and Communal Integrity." *Philosophy and Public Affairs* 9, no. 4 (1980): 385–91.

Beitz, Charles R. *Political Theory and International Relations.* Princeton, NJ: Princeton University Press, 1979.

Beitz, Charles R. "Rawls's Law of Peoples." *Ethics* 110, no. 4 (2000): 669–96.

Bellamy, Alex J. "Libya and the Responsibility to Protect: The Exception and the Norm." *Ethics and International Affairs* 25, no. 3 (2011): 263–9.

Bellamy, Alex J., and Paul D. Williams. "The New Politics of Protection? Cote d'Ivoire, Libya and the Responsibility to Protect." *International Affairs* 87, no. 4 (2011): 825–50.

Benhabib, Seyla. "*The Law of Peoples*, Distributive Justice, and Migrations." *Fordham Law Review* 72, no. 5 (2004): 1761–87.

Benner, Katie, Mark Mazzetti, Ben Hubbard, and Mike Isaac. "Saudis' Image Makers: A Troll Army and a Twitter Insider." *New York Times*, 20 October 2018.

248 REFERENCES

https://www.nytimes.com/2018/10/20/us/politics/saudi-image-campaign-twitter. html?module=inline.

Berman, Mark. "The Recent History of States Scrambling to Keep Using Lethal Injections." *Washington Post,* 19 February 2014. https://www.washingtonpost.com/news/post-nation/wp/2014/02/19/the-recent-history-of-states-scrambling-to-keep-using-lethal-injections/?tid=a_inl&utm_term=.c8a028e78164.

Bicchieri, Cristina. *Norms in the Wild: How to Diagnose, Measure, and Change Social Norms.* Oxford: Oxford University Press, 2017.

Bicchieri, Cristina, and Peter McNally. "Shrieking Sirens: Schemata, Script, and Social Norms. How Change Occurs." *Social Philosophy and Policy* 35, no. 1 (2018): 23–53.

Blake, Michael. *Justice and Foreign Policy.* Oxford: Oxford University Press, 2013.

Blake, Michael. "Justice and Foreign Policy: A Reply to My Critics." *Ethics & International Affairs* 29, no. 3 (2015): 301–14.

Blake, Michael. "Tolerance and Theocracy: How Liberal States Should Think about Religious States." *Journal of International Affairs* 61 (2007): 1–17.

Bogdanich, Walt, and Michael Forsythe. "How McKinsey Has Helped Raise the Stature of Authoritarian Governments." *New York Times,* 15 December 2018. https://www.nytimes.com/2018/12/15/world/asia/mckinsey-china-russia.html.

Buchanan, Allen. "Institutional Legitimacy." In *Oxford Studies in Political Philosophy,* vol. 4, ed. David Sobel, Peter Vallentyne, and Steven Wall, 53–78. Oxford: Oxford University Press, 2018.

Buchanan, Allen. *Justice, Legitimacy, and Self-Determination: Moral Foundations for International Law.* Oxford: Oxford University Press, 2004.

Buchanan, Allen. "Self-Determination, Revolution, and Intervention." *Ethics* 126 (2016): 447–73.

Buchanan, Allen, and Robert O. Keohane. "The Legitimacy of Global Governance Institutions." *Ethics and International Affairs* 20, no. 4 (2006): 405–37.

Calamur, Krishnadev. "Obama's 'Brexit' Plea." *Atlantic,* 22 April 2016. https://www.theatlantic.com/international/archive/2016/04/obamas-brexit-plea/479469/.

Caney, Simon. *Justice beyond Borders: A Global Political Theory.* Oxford: Oxford University Press, 2005.

Carr, E. H. *The Twenty Years' Crisis, 1919–1939: An Introduction to the Study of International Relations.* London: Macmillan, 1939.

Chesterman, Simon. "'Leading from Behind': The Responsibility to Protect, the Obama Doctrine, and Humanitarian Intervention after Libya." *Ethics and International Affairs* 25, no. 3 (2011): 279–85.

Christiano, Thomas. "The Authority of Democracy." *Journal of Political Philosophy* 12, no. 3 (2004): 266–90.

Cislaghi, Beniamino, Diane Gillespie, and Gerry Mackie. "Expanding the Aspirational Map: Interactive Learning and Human Rights in Tostan's Community Empowerment Program." In *Human Rights Education: Theory, Research, Praxis,* ed. Monisha Bajaj, 198–209. Philadelphia: University of Pennsylvania Press, 2017.

Cislaghi, Beniamino, Diane Gillespie, and Gerry Mackie. *Values Deliberation and Collective Action: Community Empowerment in Rural Senegal.* Cham: Palgrave Macmillan, 2016.

Cohen, Andrew Jason. "What Toleration Is." *Ethics* 115, no. 1 (2004): 68–95.

Cohen, Joshua. *Rousseau: A Free Community of Equals.* Oxford: Oxford University Press, 2010.

Creppell, Ingrid. *Toleration and Identity: Foundations in Early Modern Thought.* New York: Routledge, 2003.

Dahl, Robert A. *Democracy and Its Critics.* New Haven, CT: Yale University Press, 1989.

de Waal, Alex. "African Roles in the Libyan Conflict of 2011." *International Affairs* 89, no. 2 (2013): 365–79.

Diop, Nafissatou J., et al. "Replication of the TOSTAN Programme in Burkina Faso: How 23 Villages Participated in a Human Rights–Based Education Programme and Abandoned the Practice of Female Genital Cutting in Burkina Faso." Washington, DC: US Agency for International Development, 2003.

Diop, Nafissatou J., et al. "The TOSTAN Program: Evaluation of a Community Based Education Program in Senegal." Washington, DC: US Agency for International Development, 2004.

Diop, Nafissatou J., Amadou Moreau, and Helene Benga. "Evaluation of the Long-Term Impact of the TOSTAN Programme on the Abandonment of FGM/C and Early Marriage: Results from a Qualitative Study in Senegal." Washington, DC: US Agency for International Development, 2008.

Doyle, Michael. *The Question of Intervention: John Stuart Mill and the Responsibility to Protect.* New Haven, CT: Yale University Press, 2015.

Dworkin, Ronald. *Taking Rights Seriously.* Cambridge, MA: Harvard University Press, 1977.

Easterly, William. "Human Rights Are the Wrong Basis for Healthcare." *Financial Times,* 12 October 2009. https://www.ft.com/content/89bbbda2-b763-11de-9812-00144feab49a.

Entous, Adam. "The Maps of Israeli Settlements That Shocked Barack Obama." *New Yorker,* 9 July 2018. https://www.newyorker.com/news/news-desk/the-map-of-israeli-settlements-that-shocked-barack-obama.

Fabre, Cécile. "The Case for Foreign Electoral Subversion." *Ethics and International Affairs* 32, no. 3 (2018): 283–92.

Fabre, Cécile. *Cosmopolitan War.* Oxford: Oxford University Press, 2012.

Fabre, Cécile. *Economic Statecraft: Human Rights, Sanctions, and Conditionality.* Cambridge, MA: Harvard University Press, 2018.

Falk, Richard. *Power Shift: On the New Global Order.* London: Zed Books, 2016.

Fanon, Frantz. *The Wretched of the Earth.* Trans. Richard Philcox. New York: Grove Press, 2004.

Ferziger, Jonathan. "Quick Take: Israeli Settlements." *Bloomberg.* 22 March 2018. https://www.bloomberg.com/quicktake/israeli-settlements.

Finlay, Christopher J. "Reform Intervention and Democratic Revolution." *European Journal of International Relations* 13, no. 4 (2007): 555–81.

Forsythe, Michael, Mark Mazzetti, Ben Hubbard, and Walt Bogdanich. "Consulting Firm Keeps Lucrative Saudi Alliance, Shaping Crown Prince's Vision." *New York Times,* 4 November 2018. https://www.nytimes.com/2018/11/04/world/middleeast/mckinsey-bcg-booz-allen-saudi-khashoggi.html?rref=collection%2Fbyline%2Fwalt-bogdanich.

Fraser, Nancy. "Abnormal Justice." *Critical Inquiry* 34 (2008): 393–422.

Fricker, Miranda. *Epistemic Injustice: Power and the Ethics of Knowing.* Oxford: Oxford University Press, 2007.

Getachew, Adom. *Worldmaking after Empire: The Rise and Fall of Self-Determination.* Princeton, NJ: Princeton University Press, 2019.

250 REFERENCES

Gillespie, Diane, and Molly Melching. "The Transformative Power of Democracy and Human Rights in Nonformal Education: The Case of Tostan." *Adult Education Quarterly* 60, no. 5 (2010): 477–98.

Godfrey-Smith, Peter, and Benjamin Kerr. "Tolerance: A Hierarchical Analysis." *Journal of Political Philosophy* 27, no. 4 (2019): 403–21.

Hafner-Burton, Emilie. *Forced to Be Good: Why Trade Agreements Boost Human Rights.* Ithaca, NY: Cornell University Press, 2009.

Hamid, Shadi. "Everyone Says the Libya Intervention Was a Failure. They're Wrong." *Brookings Markaz Blog*, 12 April 2016. https://www.brookings.edu/blog/markaz/2016/04/12/everyone-says-the-libya-intervention-was-a-failure-theyre-wrong/.

Hobson, Christopher. "Responding to Failure: The Responsibility to Protect after Libya." *Millennium: Journal of International Studies* 44, no. 3 (2016): 433–54.

Human Rights Watch. "China: Events of 2015." *World Report 2016.* https://www.hrw.org/world-report/2016/country-chapters/china-and-tibet.

Human Rights Watch. "United States: Events of 2016." *World Report 2017.* https://www.hrw.org/world-report/2017/country-chapters/united-states#e81181.

International Development Research Centre. *The Responsibility to Protect: Report of the International Committee on Intervention and State Sovereignty.* Ottawa: International Development Research Centre, 2001.

J Street. "J Street Policy Principles on the Global BDS Movement and Boycotts, Divestment and Sanctions Efforts." Accessed 6 February 2021. https://jstreet.org/policy/boycott-divestment-and-sanctions-bds/#.W8MAP7alRjU.

Jewish Voice for Peace, "First-Ever: 40+ Jewish Groups Worldwide Oppose Equating Antisemitism with Criticism of Israel," *Jewish Voice for Peace*, 17 July 2018, https://jewishvoiceforpeace.org/first-ever-40-jewish-groups-worldwide-oppose-equating-antisemitism-with-criticism-of-israel/.

Julius, A. J. "Nagel's Atlas." *Philosophy and Public Affairs* 34, no. 2 (2006): 176–92.

Keck, Margaret E., and Kathryn Sikkink. *Activists beyond Borders: Advocacy Networks in International Politics.* Ithaca, NY: Cornell University Press, 1998.

Keohane, Robert. "Political Authority after Intervention: Gradations in Sovereignty." In *Humanitarian Intervention: Ethical, Legal, and Political Dilemmas,* ed. Jeffrey Holzgrefe and Robert Keohane, 275–98. Cambridge: Cambridge University Press, 2003.

Koskenniemi, Martti. *The Gentle Civilizer of Nations: The Rise and Fall of International Law 1870–1960.* Cambridge: Cambridge University Press, 2001.

Kuperman, Alan J. "A Model Humanitarian Intervention? Reassessing NATO's Libya Campaign." *International Security* 38, no. 1 (2013): 105–36.

Kuperman, Alan J. "Obama's Libya Debacle: How a Well-Meaning Intervention Ended in Failure." *Foreign Affairs* 94, no. 2 (2015): 66–77.

Lefever, Ernest W. "The Perils of Reform Intervention." *Worldview* 13, no. 2 (1970): 7–10.

Lis, Jonathan. "Israel's Travel Ban: Knesset Bars Entry to Foreigners Who Call for Boycott of Israel or Settlements." *Haaretz*, 7 March 2017. http://www.haaretz.com/israel-news/.premium-1.775614.

Lopez-Guerra, Claudio. "Should Expatriates Vote?" *Journal of Political Philosophy* 13, no. 2 (2005): 216–34.

Luban, David. "Just War and Human Rights." *Philosophy and Public Affairs* 9, no. 2 (1980): 160–81.

Luban, David. "The Romance of the Nation-State." *Philosophy and Public Affairs* 9, no. 4 (1980): 392–7.

REFERENCES   251

Macdonald, Kate, and Terry Macdonald. "Democracy in a Pluralist World Order: Corporate Power and Stakeholder Representation." *Ethics and International Affairs* 24, no. 1 (2010): 19–43.

Macedo, Stephen. "What Self-Governing Peoples Owe to One Another: Universalism, Diversity, and the Law of Peoples." *Fordham Law Review* 72, no. 5 (2004): 1721–38.

Mackie, Gerry. "Social Norms Change: Believing Makes It So." *Social Research: An International Quarterly* 85, no. 1 (2018): 141–66.

McKinsey & Co. "Statement on *New York Times* Article on McKinsey Work in Southeast Asia, China, Eastern Europe and the Middle East." 16 December 2018. https://www.mckinsey.com/about-us/media-center/statement-on-new-york-times-article.

Merry, Sally Engle. *Human Rights and Gender Violence: Translating International Law into Local Justice.* Chicago: University of Chicago Press, 2006.

Mill, John Stuart. "A Few Words on Non-Intervention." In Michael Doyle, *The Question of Intervention: John Stuart Mill and the Responsibility to Protect.* New Haven, CT: Yale University Press, 2015: 205-26.

Miller, David. "Defending Political Autonomy: A Discussion of Charles Beitz." *Review of International Studies* 31, no. 2 (2005): 381–8.

Miller, David. *National Responsibility and Global Justice.* Oxford: Oxford University Press, 2007.

Miller, Richard W. *Globalizing Justice: The Ethics of Poverty and Power.* Oxford: Oxford University Press, 2010.

Milstein, Adam. "BDS Is Continuing to Spread Hate and Anti-Semitism across the US." *HuffPost,* 30 May 2017. https://www.huffingtonpost.com/entry/bds-is-continuing-to-spread-hate-and-anti-semitism_us_592dab59e4b075342b52c080.

Monkman, Karen, Rebecca Miles, and Peter Easton. "The Transformatory Potential of a Village Empowerment Program: The Tostan Replication in Mali." *Women's Studies International Forum* 30 (2007): 451–64.

Moser-Puangsuwan, Yeshua, and Thomas Weber. "Nonviolent Humanitarian Intervention: A Framework for the Future." In *Nonviolent Intervention across Borders: A Recurrent Vision,* ed. Yeshua Moser-Puangsuwan and Thomas Weber, 319–37. Honolulu: Spark M. Matsunuaga Institute for Peace, University of Hawaii Press, 2000.

Motion of Argentina, Bolivia, Brazil, Chile, Colombia, Costa Rica, Dominican Republic, Ecuador, El Salvador, Guatemala, Honduras, Nicaragua, Panama, Paraguay, Peru, and Uruguay for Leave to Join the United Mexican States as Amici Curiae in Support of Respondent, Arizona v. US, 567 US 387 (2012).

Motion of the Republic of Haiti for Leave to join the United Mexican States as Amicus Curiae in Support of Respondent, Arizona v. US, 567 US 387 (2012).

Mutua, Makau. "What Is TWAIL?" *Proceedings of the Annual Meeting (American Society of International Law)* 94 (2000): 31–40.

Myre, Greg, and Larry Kaplow. "7 Things to Know about Israeli Settlements." *National Public Radio,* 29 December 2016. https://www.npr.org/sections/parallels/2016/12/29/507377617/seven-things-to-know-about-israeli-settlements.

Näsström, Sofia. "The Challenge of the All-Affected Principle." *Political Studies* 59 (2011): 116–34.

Nicholson, Peter P. "Toleration as a Moral Ideal." In *Aspects of Toleration: Philosophical Studies,* ed. John Horton and Susan Mendus, 158–73. London: Routledge Taylor & Francis, 1985.

252 REFERENCES

Nozick, Robert. "Coercion." In *Philosophy, Science, and Method: Essays in Honor of Ernest Nagel,* ed. Sidney Morgenbesser et al., 440–72. New York: St. Martin's Press, 1969.

Oberdiek, Hans. *Tolerance: Between Forbearance and Acceptance.* Lanham, MD: Rowman & Littlefield, 2001.

"Oman Country Profile." *BBC News.* 25 April 2018. https://www.bbc.com/news/world-middle-east-14654150.

"Oman Profile—Timeline." *BBC News.* 25 April 2018. https://www.bbc.com/news/world-middle-east-14654492.

Palestinian Civil Society, "Palestinian Civil Society Call for BDS," BDS. 9 July 2005. https://bdsmovement.net/call.

Paris, Roland. "Global Governance and Power Politics: Back to Basics." *Ethics and International Affairs* 29, no. 4 (2015): 407–18.

Pattison, James. *The Alternatives to War: From Sanctions to Nonviolence.* Oxford: Oxford University Press, 2018.

Pattison, James. "Covert Positive Incentives as an Alternative to War." *Ethics and International Affairs* 32, no. 3 (2018): 293–303.

Pattison, James. "Perilous Noninterventions? The Counterfactual Assessment of Libya and the Need to Be a Responsible Power." *Global Responsibility to Protect* 9 (2017): 219–28.

Pettit, Phillip. *On the People's Terms: A Republican Theory and Model of Democracy.* Cambridge: Cambridge University Press, 2012.

Pettit, Philip. "The Instability of Freedom as Noninterference: The Case of Isaiah Berlin." *Ethics* 121, no. 4 (2011): 693–716.

Posner, Michael. "How McKinsey & Co. Fails as a Global Leader." *Forbes,* 18 December 2018. https://www.forbes.com/sites/michaelposner/2018/12/18/how-mckinsey-co-fails-as-a-global-leader/#6c060a90376d.

Rafanelli, Lucia M. "Toward an Individualist Postcolonial Cosmopolitanism." *Millennium: Journal of International Studies* (2020): 1–12, doi: 10.1177/0305829820935520.

Rawls, John. *The Law of Peoples with "The Idea of Public Reason Revisited."* Cambridge, MA: Harvard University Press, 1999.

Rawls, John. *Political Liberalism.* Expanded edition. New York: Columbia University Press, 2005.

Rawls, John. *A Theory of Justice.* Revised edition. Cambridge, MA: Belknap Press of Harvard University Press, 1999.

Raz, Joseph. *The Morality of Freedom.* Oxford: Oxford University Press, 1988.

Rosenberg, David. "BDS Is a Lot of Things, but It's Not Anti-Semitic." *Haaretz,* 21 September 2016. https://www.haaretz.com/opinion/bds-is-a-lot-of-things-but-it-s-not-anti-semitic-1.5440228.

Rosenberg, Eli. "The CIA Explored Using a 'Truth Serum' on Terrorism Detainees after 9/11, Newly Released Report Shows." *Washington Post,* 13 November 2018. https://www.washingtonpost.com/nation/2018/11/14/cia-explored-using-truth-serum-terror-detainees-after-newly-released-report-shows/.

Rubenstein, Jennifer C. *Between Samaritans and States: The Political Ethics of Humanitarian INGOs.* Oxford: Oxford University Press, 2015.

Saba, Arif, and Shahram Akbarzadeh. "The Responsibility to Protect and the Use of Force: An Assessment of the Just Cause and Last Resort Criteria in the Case of Libya." *International Peacekeeping* 25, no. 2 (2018): 242–65.

REFERENCES   253

Sherman, Mark. "Supreme Court Issues Ruling on S.B. 1070." *Huffington Post*, 25 June 2012. http://www.huffingtonpost.com/2012/06/25/supreme-court-sb1070_n_1614121. html.

Shue, Henry. *Basic Rights: Subsistence, Affluence, and U.S. Foreign Policy.* 2nd edition. Princeton, NJ: Princeton University Press, 1996.

Shue, Henry. "Limiting Sovereignty." In *Humanitarian Intervention and International Relations,* ed. Jennifer M. Welsh, 11–28. Oxford: Oxford University Press, 2004.

Simmons, A. John. "Justification and Legitimacy." *Ethics* 109, no. 4 (1999): 739–71.

Singer, Peter. *The Life You Can Save.* New York: Random House, 2009.

Sly, Liz. "Many Libyans Appear to Back Gaddafi." *Washington Post.* 24 March 2011. https:// www.washingtonpost.com/world/many-libyans-appear-to-back-gaddafi/2011/03/24/ ABHShlRB_story.html?utm_term=.43f21d4d8c07.

Smith, Harrison. "James Ketchum, Who Conducted Mind-Altering Experiments on Soldiers, Dies at 87." *Washington Post,* 4 June 2019. https://www.washingtonpost. com/local/obituaries/james-ketchum-who-conducted-mind-altering-experiments- on-soldiers-dies-at-87/2019/06/04/7b5ad322-86cc-11e9-a491-25df61c78dc4_story. html.

Speelman, Tabitha. "Tiptoeing Out of the Closet: The History and Future of LGBT Rights in China." *Atlantic,* 21 August 2013. http://www.theatlantic.com/china/archive/2013/ 08/tiptoeing-out-of-the-closet-the-history-and-future-of-lgbt-rights-in-china/ 278869/.

State of Arizona. Senate Bill 1070. Unofficial version, 2010. https://apps.azleg.gov/ BillStatus/GetDocumentPdf/192028.

Stilz, Anna. "Against Democratic Interventionism." *Ethics & International Affairs* 29, no. 3 (2015): 259–68.

Stilz, Anna. *Liberal Loyalty: Freedom, Obligation, and the State.* Princeton, NJ: Princeton University Press, 2009.

Tan, Kok-Chor. *Toleration, Diversity, and Global Justice.* University Park: Pennsylvania State University Press, 2000.

Tesón, Fernando R. *A Philosophy of International Law.* Boulder, CO: Westview Press, 1998.

Tesón, Fernando. "The Rawlsian Theory of International Law." *Ethics and International Affairs* 9 (1995): 79–99.

Tostan, "About Us," *Tostan: Dignity for All.* Accessed 10 September 2019. https://www. tostan.org/about-us/mission-history/.

Tostan, "Areas of Impact," *Tostan: Dignity for All.* Accessed 13 July 2016. http://tostan.org/ impact_areas.

Tostan, "Community Empowerment Program: Ensuring Sustainability," *Tostan: Dignity for All.* Accessed 10 September 2019. https://www.tostan.org/programs/community- empowerment-program/ensuring-sustainability/.

Tostan, "Cross-Cutting Issues: Female Genital Cutting," *Tostan: Dignity for All.* Accessed 13 July 2016. http://tostan.org/female-genital-cutting.

Tostan, "Mission & History." Accessed 9 October 2018. https://www.tostan.org/about-us/ mission-history/.

Tostan. "Today. Tomorrow. Together: Tostan Annual Report 2014." 2014. https://tostan. org/wp-content/uploads/2014_annual_report_final.pdf.

Tostan, "Where We Work," *Tostan: Dignity for All.* Accessed 10 September 2019. http:// tostan.org/where-we-work.

254 REFERENCES

United Nations Free and Equal. "Factsheet: International Human Rights Law and Sexual Orientation & Gender Identity." Accessed 23 September 2018. https://www.unfe.org/wp-content/uploads/2018/05/International-Human-Rights-Law-English.pdf.

United Nations General Assembly. Resolution Adopted by the United Nations General Assembly on 16 September 2005: 60/1, 2005 World Summit Outcome. 2005. http://www.un.org/en/development/desa/population/migration/generalassembly/docs/globalcompact/A_RES_60_1.pdf.

United Nations General Assembly. Resolution Adopted by the United Nations General Assembly: 3201 (S-VI), Declaration on the Establishment of a New International Economic Order. 1 May 1974. http://www.un-documents.net/s6r3201.htm.

United Nations General Assembly, Human Rights Council. "Report of the Independent International Fact-Finding Mission to Investigate the Implications of the Israeli Settlements on the Civil, Political, Economic, Social, and Cultural Rights of the Palestinian People throughout the Occupied Palestinian Territory, Including East Jerusalem." 7 February 2013. https://digitallibrary.un.org/record/745109?ln=en.

United Nations, Office of the High Commissioner on Human Rights. *International Covenant on Civil and Political Rights*. 1966. http://www.ohchr.org/en/professionalinterest/pages/ccpr.aspx.

Valentini, Laura. "No Global Demos, No Global Democracy? A Systematization and Critique." *Perspectives on Politics* 12, no. 4 (2014): 789–807.

Vilkomerson, Rebecca, and Richard Kuper. "As Jews, We Reject the Myth That It's Antisemitic to Call Israel Racist." *Independent,* 22 July 2018. https://www.independent.co.uk/voices/antisemitisim-jews-israel-labour-party-bds-jewish-coalition-palestine-a8458601.html.

Walzer, Michael. "Achieving Global and Local Justice." *Dissent* 58, no. 3 (2011): 42–8.

Walzer, Michael. "Beyond Humanitarian Intervention: Human Rights in Global Society." In *Thinking Politically: Essays in Political Theory*, ed. David Miller, 251–63. New Haven, CT: Yale University Press, 2007.

Walzer, Michael. *Just and Unjust Wars: A Moral Argument with Historical Illustrations*. 5th edition. New York: Basic Books, 2015.

Walzer, Michael. "The Moral Standing of States: A Response to Four Critics." *Philosophy and Public Affairs* 9, no. 3 (1980): 209–29.

Walzer, Michael. "On Promoting Democracy." *Ethics and International Affairs* 22, no. 4 (2008): 351–5.

Walzer, Michael. *On Toleration*. New Haven, CT: Yale University Press, 1997.

Walzer, Michael. *Thick and Thin: Moral Argument at Home and Abroad*. Notre Dame, IN: University of Notre Dame Press, 1994.

Watts, Clint. "Clint Watts' Testimony: Russia's Info War on the US Started in 2014." *Daily Beast*, 30 March 2017. https://www.thedailybeast.com/clint-watts-testimony-russias-info-war-on-the-us-started-in-2014.

Weiss, Thomas G. "RtoP Alive and Well after Libya." *Ethics and International Affairs* 25, no. 3 (2011): 287–92.

Weiss, Thomas G., and Rorden Wilkinson. "Change and Continuity in Global Governance." *Ethics and International Affairs* 29, no. 4 (2015): 397–406.

Wenar, Leif. "John Rawls." In *The Stanford Encyclopedia of Philosophy*, ed. Edward N. Zalta. Spring 2017 edition. https://plato.stanford.edu/archives/spr2017/entries/rawls/.

Wiens, David. "Political Ideals and the Feasibility Frontier." *Economics and Philosophy* 31 (2015): 447–77.

Williams, Holly. "Meet the Woman behind a Shortage of Execution Drugs." *CBS News,* 30 April 2014. http://www.cbsnews.com/news/meet-the-woman-behind-a-shortage-of-execution-drugs/.

Young, Iris Marion. "Responsibility and Global Justice: A Social Connection Model." *Social Philosophy and Policy* 23, no. 1 (2006): 102–30.

Zagier, Alan Scher. "Another Manufacturer Blocks Drug for Execution Use." *US News & World Report,* 27 September 2012. https://www.usnews.com/news/us/articles/2012/09/27/drug-maker-blocks-anesthetic-for-use-in-executions.

Zambakari, Christopher. "The Misguided and Mismanaged Intervention in Libya: Consequences for Peace." *African Security Review* 25, no. 1 (2016): 44–62.

Index

For the benefit of digital users, indexed terms that span two pages (e.g., 52–53) may, on occasion, appear on only one of those pages.

Figures are indicated by *f* following the page number

Abizadeh, Arash, 194
Abu-Laban, Yasmeen, 179
all-subjected principle, 187–88
all-things-considered judgments, 152, 202.
    See also collective self-determination;
    legitimacy; toleration
  amicus briefs opposing SB 1070,
    235, 239
  BDS movement, 235–37, 239
  European export ban on lethal injection
    drugs, 237–39
  Tostan, 235, 239
Alternatives to War, The (Pattison), 29
Altman, Andrew, 46–47, 148–49
amicus briefs opposing SB 1070, 38n.43,
    47–48, 191–92, 193
  all-things-considered judgments,
    235, 239
  as intra-systemic intervention, 52–53,
    127, 141–42, 152, 159–60
  overview, 38
  as persuasive intervention,
    200, 212–13
Anghie, Antony, 174–76, 177, 178n.39,
    178, 182, 186
Anscombe, G. E. M., 95n.66
anti-Semitism, BDS movement
    and, 235–37
Aristide, Jean-Bertrand, 190–91

Bakan, A., 179
basic rights
  legitimacy and, 142n.48
  moral desirability of protecting,
    101n.77, 101
  reasonable agreement about,
    101n.76, 101

recipients, 46
  urgency of intervention objectives,
    41n.49, 41–42
BDS (Boycott, Divest, Sanction)
    movement, 5, 51–52, 152–54,
    153n.70, 159–60, 179
  as extra-institutional intervention, 128
  nonstate actors and, 201
  as slightly-controlling intervention, 153
  unintended consequences of,
    216, 235–37
Beitz, Charles, 2n.3, 11n.1, 72n.31, 203n.1,
    217n.38
Bicchieri, C., 74–75
Blake, Michael, 61, 62–63, 66–67, 72, 96–
    97, 143n.49
Bouchuiguir, Soliman, 156
Boycott, Divest, Sanction movement.
    See BDS movement
boycotts, 1
  BDS movement, 5
  civil-society-led divestment
    campaigns, 5–6
  consumer boycotts, 5–6
  state-led boycotts, 5–6
Buchanan, Allen, 132, 146–48, 191

Cable, V., 50
CEDAW (Convention for the Elimination
    of All Forms of Discrimination
    Against Women) treaty body, 207–
    8n.7, 207–8, 226, 229–30, 230n.54
child marriage. *See* Tostan
China
  LGBT rights hypothetical intervention,
    76n.37, 76–77, 100–1
  Smart Cities program, 195

258 INDEX

closing off institutions, 160–61
Cohen, A. J., 64–65
Cohen, J., 165n.4
collective self-determination, 165n.2
  defining, 164–66
  degrees of control and, 39–40
  domination and, 166n.5, 166–73
  legitimacy and, 133–34
  moral standing of states and, 165n.3
  neocolonialism, 173–87, 178n.39
  obstacles to implementing standards
    of, 217–19
  overview, 163–64
  reasonable confidence
    condition, 165n.4
  responsiveness to public interest
    and, 187–96
  strengthening, 6
  toleration and, 183
colonialism, 182. *See also* neocolonialism
"Community Empowerment Program,"
    Tostan, 35–36
Convention for the Elimination of All
    Forms of Discrimination Against
    Women (CEDAW) treaty body, 207–
    8n.7, 207–8, 226, 229–30, 230n.54
cosmopolitanism, 242. *See also* toleration
counter-hegemonic interventions
  in anti-colonial sense, 179–81, 185–86
  giving political priority to, 197, 232–
    33, 244–45
  in non-domination sense, 167–68, 172
Creppell, Ingrid, 23n.9, 64

Déby Itno, Idriss, 156–57
degrees of control, reform interventions.
    See also specific types of interventions
  highly-controlling interventions, 32–33
  persuasive interventions, 35–38
  slightly-controlling interventions, 33–
    34, 39–41
  totally-controlling interventions, 31–32
de Waal, Alex, 156–57
dialogue-as learning concept, 89n.59, 89
discursive power, 198–99
disempowered, 193. *See also* amicus briefs
    opposing SB 1070; Tostan
  CEDAW and, 207–8n.7, 207–8, 226,
    229–30, 230n.54

colonialism and, 179–80
defined, 25
gender-based subordination, 4, 37, 71–
    72, 199–200
geopolitically, 136, 245
hermeneutical marginalization
    of, 244–45
stateless persons, 196
divestment campaigns, 1
domestic justice promotion, 16, 160–
    61, 241–42
domination. *See also* disempowered;
    geopolitical power
  collective self-determination and,
    166n.5, 166–73
  defined, 166
  freedom as non-domination concept,
    143n.52, 143, 146
  highly-controlling interventions
    and, 171–72
"Don't Ask, Don't Tell" policy, 71–72
duty of justice. *See* natural duty of justice

Easton, Peter, 210
Empowered Communities Network,
    Tostan, 211
equality, 23–26. *See also* basic rights;
    human rights
ethics of foreign political influence. *See*
    reform interventions
European export ban on lethal injection
    drugs. *See* lethal injection drugs,
    European export ban on
extra-institutional interventions, 53,
    128–41, 128–29n.27, 160–61. *See
    also* Tostan
  BDS movement, 51–52, 128, 216
  criteria for, 128–29n.27
  forceful, 129n.28, 129
  legitimacy and, 128–41, 150, 151,
    152, 213–14
  non-state-led, 152
  recipients' good standing in community
    and, 129–41
  state-led, 154

Fabre, Cécile, 11–12, 85–86
factual uncertainty, 40–41, 40n.48, 103–
    4, 226

INDEX 259

Falk, Richard, 20–21
Fanon, Frantz, 182
female genital cutting (FGC), 209, 210, 211. *See also* Tostan
foreign actors. *See also* reform interventions
  engaging recipients as partners, 91–92
  overview, 19–20
foreign domination, 166
Fricker, Miranda, 244–45

gender-based subordination, 3–4, 37, 71–72, 199–200. *See also* CEDAW; Tostan
geopolitical power, 134–35, 136, 167–68, 170–71, 177. *See also* counter-hegemonic interventions; domination
  BDS movement, 201
  defined, 136n.41
  foreign domination, 166
Getachew, A., 176
global duty of justice. *See* natural duty of justice
global free speech guarantee, 230–32
global governance, 222
global institutions. *See* obstacles to reform interventions
Godfrey-Smith, Peter, 60, 88–89, 97n.71
good governance standards, 174–75
Goodhart, Michael, 23n.9
good standing in community, 129–41, 131n.31
  extra-institutional interventions and, 129–41
  highly-controlling interventions and, 134–35, 138–39
  persuasive interventions and, 136, 137, 138–39
  regime change interventions and, 118–19n.16
  responsiveness to citizens' input as criterion of legitimacy, 143n.51
  slightly-controlling interventions and, 136, 137, 138–39

Hafner-Burton, Emilie, 34, 135
Haiti, US intervention in, 190–91
hermeneutical marginalization, 244–45

highly-controlling interventions
  domination and, 171–72
  recipients' good standing in community and, 134–35, 138–39
  responsiveness to public interest and, 189
  structural adjustment programs, 32–33, 84–86, 189
  toleration and, 86–87, 92
Hobson, Christopher, 156–57
human rights. *See also* amicus briefs opposing SB 1070; basic rights; Oman-US trade agreement
  CEDAW, 207–8n.7, 207–8, 226, 229–30, 230n.54
  good governance standards and, 174–75
  LGBT citizens, 71–72, 76n.37, 76–77, 100–1
  neocolonialism and, 174
  TWAIL movement, 48–49, 49n.73, 173–74
  women's rights protections, 207–8, 207–8n.7, 226, 229–30, 230n.54
Human Rights and Gender Violence (Merry), 207

ILO (International Labour Organization), 34
IMF (International Monetary Fund), 32–33, 84–86, 102, 189
immigrant's rights. *See* amicus briefs opposing SB 1070
incentivizing vs. exploiting. *See also* Oman-US trade agreement; persuasive interventions; slightly-controlling interventions
  leveraging vulnerability, 30–31
  structural adjustment programs, 85–86
  toleration, 72, 82n.44, 82, 107
INGOs (international NGOs), 11–12, 20, 35. *See also* Tostan
inordinate cost of promoting justice, 240n.71, 240
institutions. *See also* reform interventions
  absence of strong global institutions, effect on reform interventions, 203–4, 219–24
  closing off, 160–61
  self-determining, 163n.1, 163

260 INDEX

international agreements, enforcement of, 123n.18, 123–26
International Labour Organization (ILO), 34
International Monetary Fund (IMF), 32–33, 84–86, 102, 189
international NGOs (INGOs), 11–12, 20, 35. *See also* Tostan
international toleration, 59. *See also* toleration
international tribunals, 122–23
intra-systemic interventions, 125–26, 141–42n.47, *See also* Oman-US trade agreement
amicus briefs opposing SB 1070, 52–53, 127, 141–42, 152, 159–60
compatibility with recipient institutions' legitimacy, 53
legitimacy and, 141–42, 151, 214
oppositional interventions vs., 127
Israel-Palestine conflict, 236. *See also* BDS movement

Jagmohan, Desmond, 228n.53
James, Aaron, 143n.49
justice-promoting interventions, 15–17. *See also* reform intervention
just war theory, 46n.64, 46

Keck, Margaret, 228
Kerr, Benjamin, 60, 88–89, 97n.71
Koskenniemi, M., 182
Kuperman, Alan, 155–56

Lefever, Ernest, 2n.3, 11n.1
legitimacy
differing views of criteria for, 116–17n.14, 116–18
extra-institutional interventions, 128–41
freedom-as-non-domination criterion, 143n.52, 146
institutions and states, 117n.15
intra-systemic interventions, 141–42
legitimacy objection, 115
obstacles to implementing standards relating to, 213–16
oppositional interventions, 119–28, 150, 151, 213
overview, 5–6, 113–16

presumptive legitimacy, 115
recognizing legitimate institutions, 214n.34, 214–16
regime-change interventions, 118–19
responsiveness to citizens' input as criterion of, 143n.51
scalar notion of, 113, 142–50, 142n.48
toleration and, 183–84
lethal injection drugs, European export ban on, 50–51, 154n.71, 193, 197–98, 201–2
loss of profit due to, 102
as oppositional intervention, 50, 119–22, 154–55
as slightly-controlling interventions, 154
unintended consequences of, 237–39
LGBT citizens and rights
China hypothetical, 76n.37, 76–77, 100–1
in U.S., 71–72
Libya intervention, 32, 47, 49, 155–58, 223
local actors, 19–20. *See also* recipients
Lochbihler, B., 50
Luban, D., 84

Mackie, G., 74–75
manipulative interventions. *See also* totally-controlling interventions
persuasive interventions vs., 218–19
Russian involvement in 2016 US presidential election, 219, 231–32
marginalization. *See also* disempowered
geopolitical, 198–99
hermeneutical, 244–45
McKinsey & Co. consulting firm, 194–95
Merry, S. E., 207–8
Miles, Rebecca, 210
Miller, D., 32–33, 43n.57
Monkman, Karen, 210
"morally accessible" concept, 227n.49, 227
moral uncertainty, 40–41, 40n.48, 103–6, 226
moral urgency. *See* urgency of objectives
Mutua, M., 173–74
Mwangaza Action NGO, 209

NATO's intervention in Libya, 32, 47, 49, 155–58, 223

natural duty of justice, 8–9, 22–24, 26–28, 160
  global perspective, 241
  moral requirement of political actors, 110–11
  overview, 8–9
  skeptical view of, 27–28, 240–41, 243–44
neocolonialism, 173–87, 178n.39
New International Economic Order, 136–37, 175–76
Ngo, Jade, 41n.50
NGOs, 11–12, 20. *See also* Tostan
Nicholson, Peter, 66n.22
non-basic rights, 42–43
non-controlling interventions. *See* persuasive interventions
nonstate actors, 20–21, 115n.8, 131–32n.33, 222. *See also* Tostan
  BDS movement, 153, 197–98, 201, 202, 235
  extra-institutional interventions led by, 139–41, 141–42n.47
  global governance and, 221–22
non-vital interests, 33–34, 46, 169

Obama, Barack
  denouncement of Brexit campaign, 169n.20, 169
  public statement about Scotland's possible secession, 169
Oberdiek, H., 89n.57, 89n.59, 89
obstacles to reform interventions
  absence of strong global institutions, 203–4, 219–24
  collective self-determination standards, 217–19
  general discussion, 203–5
  legitimacy standards, 213–16
  toleration standards, 205–13
  unintended consequences, 204–5, 224–33
Oman-US trade agreement, 34n.27, 81n.41, 82n.43, 137n.43, 167, 191, 200n.83, 202
  collective self-determination and, 189–90
  as extra-institutional intervention, 152
  hard human rights standards, 124

international tribunal and, 127
  legitimacy and, 148–49
  motivation for, 102
  as slightly-controlling intervention, 33–35, 80–82, 200–1
oppositional interventions, 53, 128–29n.27, 148–49, 154
  attaching human rights provisions to trade agreements, 135–36
  closing off institutions and, 160–61
  enforcement of international agreements, 123n.18, 123–26
  European export ban on lethal injection drugs, 50, 119–22, 154–55
  international tribunals, 122–23
  intra-systemic interventions vs., 127
  legitimacy and, 119–28, 150, 151, 213
organized diffusion, Tostan, 36–37

pacifism, 95n.66
Palestinian BDS movement. *See* BDS movement
Pattison, James, 30–31, 99n.73, 99, 239n.70
  The Alternatives to War, 29
  moral significance of structural adjustment programs, 85–86
  "smaller and middle powers," 1n.1
persuasive interventions, 87–88, 168–69.
  See also Tostan
  amicus briefs opposing SB 1070, 200, 212–13
  CEDAW, 207–8n.7, 207–8, 226, 229–30, 230n.54
  collective self-determination and, 218–19
  equal treatment for women in India, 207–8
  global free speech guarantee, 231
  interveners engaging recipients as partners, 91–92
  manipulation vs., 218–19
  Obama's public statement about Scotland's possible secession, 169
  recipients' freedom of choice and, 190
  recipients' good standing in community and, 136, 137, 138–39
  responsiveness to public interest and, 190

262 INDEX

persuasive interventions (*cont.*)
  SB 1070, 37–38, 38n.43
  toleration, 75–80
  Tostan, 74–75, 198–200, 208–12
Petit, Phillip, 143n.52, 146, 166, 166n.10
Plessy v. Ferguson, 228
political-moral values. *See* collective self-
    determination; legitimacy; toleration
political uncertainty, 40–41, 40n.48, 48,
    103–4, 226
proportionality, principles of, 43n.59,
    43–44, 46

Qaddafi, 32, 155–58

Rawls, John, 45n.63
  good standing in community, 130–33,
    131n.31, 143n.51
  natural duty of justice, 22
  toleration, 60, 66–67, 68–69, 82
Raz, Joseph, 41n.50
Reagan, Ronald, 102
recipients. *See also specific types of*
    interventions
  basic rights, 46
  costs of reform intervention to, 46–
    49, 54f
  defined, 2n.2
  good standing in community, 129–41
  non-vital interests, 33–34, 46, 169
  relationship of existing institutions to
    reform intervention, 49–53, 54f
  representative segment, 79, 81n.41,
    83n.47, 83–84, 87
  states, 115n.8
  vital interests, 46
reform interventions. *See also*
    obstacles to reform interventions;
    specific types of interventions;
    unintended consequences of reform
    interventions
  all-subjected principle, 187–88
  boycotts, 5–6
  case selection, 55–57
  changing conditions of global politics
    and, 20–22
  cost to recipients, 46–49, 54f
  defining, 2–3, 11, 13–20
  degrees of control, 30–41, 54f

discouraging tolerant treatment among
    recipients, 98n.72, 98
  as domination, 166–73
  duty of justice and, 22–28
  foreign actors, 19–20
  general discussion, 11–13
  goals of, 225–26n.47
  local actors, 19–20
  moral permissibility of, 7–8
  as neocolonialism, 173–87
  origin of term, 2n.3, 11n.1
  relationship to recipients' existing
    institutions, 49–53, 54f
  responsiveness to public interest
    and, 187–96
  standard objections to, 2–3
  unintended consequences of, 7
  urgency of objectives, 41–46, 54f
regime-change interventions, 53, 121,
    122, 151
  legitimacy and, 118–19, 118–19n.16,
    150, 213
  NATO's intervention in Libya, 155–
    58, 223
representative segment, recipient society
  defined, 79
  interveners and, 83n.47, 83–84
  minority rights, 87
  Oman-US trade agreement, 81n.41
Responsibility to Protect (RtoP) norm,
    42n.54, 136, 203–4, 222–24
Rubenstein, Jennifer, 11–12, 185,
    198–99, 238–39

SB 1070, 37. *See also* amicus briefs
    opposing SB 1070
self-determination. *See* collective
    self-determination
self-determining institutions,
    163n.1, 163
Shue, Henry, 41n.49, 41–42
Sikkink, Kathryn, 228
Simmons, A. John, 149
skeptical view, natural duty of justice,
    27–28, 240–41, 243–44
slightly-controlling interventions, 39–41,
    87–88
  BDS movement, 152–54
  CEDAW, 230n.54

European export ban on lethal injection drugs, 154
Obama's denouncement of Brexit campaign, 169
Oman-US trade agreement, 33–35, 80–82, 200–1
recipients' good standing in community and, 136, 137, 138–39
recipients' self-determination, 189–90
responsiveness to public interest and, 189–90
risk of domination with, 170–71
toleration and, 80–83, 92
Smart Cities program (China), 195
Society of Peoples, 130–31, 131n.31
standard objections to reform intervention. *See* collective self-determination; legitimacy; toleration
states, 115n.8, *See also* legitimacy; recipients
Stilz, Anna, 72n.31, 120n.17, 124n.23, 140n.46, 180n.45
structural adjustment programs, 32–33, 84–86, 102, 189

Tan, Kok-Chor, 61, 62–63, 66–67, 72
Tesón, F., 38
    interventions, 113n.1, 128n.26
    legitimacy, 113–15
Third World Approaches to International Law (TWAIL) movement, 48–49, 49n.73, 173–74
Third World states, 174n.26, 174–76, 186
toleration
    commitment to, 107
    degrees of control and, 39
    first-order tolerant treatment, 62–63, 71–72, 76, 80
    general discussion, 59–63
    highly-controlling interventions, 83–87
    as moral ideal, 64–69, 66n.22
    moral reasons for practicing, 66
    as objection to reform intervention, 2–3, 5, 99n.74, 99–100
    obstacles to implementing standards relating to, 205–13
    persuasive interventions, 74–80, 87–88
    second-order constraint, 62–63, 70–62, 73–74, 75, 77, 79–80, 81

slightly-controlling interventions, 80–82, 87–88
thick vs. thin morality, 89–91
toleration as engagement, 88–97
toleration objection, 59, 109
totally-controlling interventions, 83–87
two-level structure, 69–74, 97n.71
urgency and cost, 97–106
urgency of intervention objectives and, 44, 45
Tostan, 3–4, 35–37, 74–75, 152, 198–200, 235
    discursive power, 198–200
    Empowered Communities Network, 211
    unintended consequences of, 209–12
totally-controlling interventions
    defined, 31–32
    domination and, 171–72
    extreme manipulation, 32
    NATO's intervention in Libya, 32, 155–58
    oversight for, 171–72
    recipients' self-determination, 83
    responsiveness to public interest and, 189
    toleration and, 83–84, 86–87, 92
    US intervention in Haiti, 190–91
transnational activism, 1
TWAIL (Third World Approaches to International Law) movement, 48–49, 49n.73, 173–74
typology of reform intervention, 28–53, 54f
    cost to recipients, 46–49
    degrees of control, 30–41
    overview, 28–30
    relationship to recipients' existing institutions, 49–53
    urgency of objectives, 41–46

uncertainty
    factual uncertainty, 40–41, 40n.48, 103–4, 226
    moral uncertainty, 40–41, 40n.48, 103–6, 226
    political uncertainty, 40–41, 40n.48, 48, 103–4, 226

264   INDEX

unintended consequences of reform
    interventions
  avoiding, 224–33
  BDS movement, 216, 235–37
  CEDAW, 208
  European export ban on lethal injection
      drugs, 237–39
  Tostan, 7, 209
urgency-cost trade-off, toleration,
    97–106
urgency of objectives, reform
    intervention, 41–46
  basic rights, 41n.49, 41–42
  non-basic rights, 42–43
  toleration and, 44, 45
US Agency for International Development
    (USAID), 209–12
US-Oman trade agreement. *See* Oman-US
    trade agreement

Valentini, L., 227n.49, 227–28
van der Vossen, Bas, 72n.31
vital interests
  defined, 32–33
  moral desirability of protecting,
      101n.77, 101

reasonable agreement about,
    101n.76, 101
recipients, 46

Walzer, Michael, 43n.57, 45n.62
  collective self-determination,
      165n.2, 165n.3
  determining recipients' preferences, 84
  legitimacy, 115, 131–32n.33
  political uncertainty and reform
      interventions, 48
  single conception of justice, 93
  Sweden-Algeria hypothetical, 32
  thick vs. thin morality, 89–91
  toleration, 59–60, 66–67, 68–69,
      82, 88–89
welfare-promoting interventions, 17
Wellman, Christopher Heath, 46–
    47, 148–49
Wiens, D., 227n.50
women's rights protections, 207–8,
    207–8n.7, 226, 229–30, 230n.54.
    See also Tostan
workers' rights. *See* Oman-US trade
    agreement
World Bank, 32–33, 84–86, 102, 189